Black Magnolia
An Unequivocal Southern Belle

Sherry Denise Henderson

Black Magnolia: An Unequivocal Southern Belle
Copyright © 2023 by Sherry Denise Henderson

All rights reserved by the author/publisher. No part of this publication may be reproduced or transmitted in any form or by any means, electronic or mechanical, including photocopy, recording, or any information storage and retrieval system, without the prior written permission of the author or publisher except by a reviewer, who may quote brief passages in critical articles or reviews.

Any web addresses or links contained in this book may have changed since publication and may no longer be valid due to the changing nature of the internet.

ISBN: 979-8-9851885-8-5
Published by: I Write Writing Academy, LLC.
Location: Denver, Colorado

Edited by Naomi Books, LLC
Printed in the United States of America

DEDICATIONS

I dedicate this book to the memory of my great-grandmother, Martha Magdalene Adam Henderson. You were the lady who breathed life into me during the early years of my life. Each day, I would gladly and deeply inhale those breaths as I learned to survive and thrive. The breaths were like extra oxygen that made me feel invincible, fearless, and free. Though you were a woman of very few words, your presence personified the essence of your beliefs and values. You didn't talk too much about the walk; you walked the walk every step of the way, every day of your life.

I thank you for influencing my journey as a role model in motion. You always "made a way out of no way." Because of you, I am filled with wisdom, strength, compassion, and a no quit attitude that helps me face the world each day with the pride of being your number one great-granddaughter.

~~~~~~~~

In memory of you, Mrs. Bettye Lue Brown, my mother. You were never short on words. You always spoke and lived your truth. There was a time I thought you were all about words without meanings. Boy, did I learn that you were wiser and smarter than I will ever be. Looking back, I now realize that your vision always saw what I could not see or comprehend. I had knowledge (formal education), but you were a master of common sense. Believe me, learning the value of common sense from you made my life a little less challenging.

I believed you when you told your friends and every member of our community how proud you were of me. You kept every card and newspaper clipping. I tried to take advantage of all the opportunities you never had. I also believe that when I hit home runs in the game of life, you would have hit grand slams, under different circumstances, in a different time. My stance to shout my truth from the mountaintops came from watching you blaze the trail before me. If I never told you, I want the world to know that I am prouder of you than you were of me. It was obvious we learned the art of making something out of nothing from the best, your grandmother, my great-grandmother, Martha Magdalene Adams Henderson.

~~~~~~~~

In memory of my mentor, life coach, and lifetime friend Vernell Rhodes, I write this book with both joy and tears. Joy that you made a seat for yourself on my life's journey. You saw something buried inside of this very shy wallflower. I am forever thankful that you literally pulled me off the wall and kept me on a path to discover my worth, value, staying power/stamina, never-quit spirit, and how to fish to feed my dreams and ambitions. Your guidance helped me discover myself—a fire lily, always rising from the ashes. You lit a fire under my wings to help me find my assertive voice as I blossomed into an advocate for myself and for many others who crossed my path. I continue to hold every piece of advice you gave me very dear and close to my heart. I am most proud of the moments I was able to give your advice back to you. It was great to tell you that if the advice was good for me; it was also good enough for me to pass back to you. Words cannot express how your value-added presence touched my soul.

In the connection between life and death, the memory of your words helps me to calm the storms or ride the rocky waves of my adventurous life. I miss you so much. Rest in peace. Your voice is still one of my beacons of light that continue to motivate and guide me.

ACKNOWLEDGMENTS

My Best Friend Forever, Betty Story-Wiley

When your mother introduced me to you as "Shedby," little did we know there would come a time when we would weather many storms, climb mountain peaks, and wade murky waters together. Whenever I am down with the world, I call you and we face whatever the problem is, hand in hand. We laugh about the happy times; we cry when sadness shows up, and it reminds me that our emotions are plentiful and help to color all the chapters of our lives. Thank you for being my "ride or die" and showing me the true meaning of best friends forever (BFF). I asked God for a flower; He gave me a bouquet. I asked for a friend; He gave me you. I will always be there for you. Love you now and all the way to eternity and back.

~~~~~~~

My Once Best Friends Forever

You know who you are. Everyone who has traveled my path of life knows who you are. They know you simply because I talked about the love, admiration, and hope between the three of us to everyone I met. Best friends are ones who will go the extra mile—stay the course no matter what. They share the good, the ugly, the bad, and all the gray between these colors of their lives. The closeness of their sisterhood is the cornerstone for them to always find a path to forgiveness, through love and commitment, to the safety and welfare of each other. I once thought we had all of that, but only God knows where we lost our way and what His well-designed plans for the future hold. All I know is that I am ready to follow His divine plan. I love you now and always.

~~~~~~~~

My High School Classmate and Boyfriend

I have no regrets that my dream of us being forever lovers in a house with a white picket fence, two children, and a dog did not materialize. Our love was thornier than any beautiful red rose. But I must acknowledge your positive influence in my life. There were many paths I could have taken. The core values that your mother taught you (even though you chose not to apply them to our romantic relationship) showed themselves to be important in my life. We dreamed outside of the box, watched Star Wars to enhance our imagination, read thought-provoking literature, and constantly explored the world as we looked for answers to all our Why questions. These are just a few of our together experiences that nurtured my innate ability to dream and lean into the Why questions with such passion. Your presence in my life brought out the possibilities of dreaming of a life outside of Mississippi and helped me to realize that I could never be an extension of anyone—not even you. I was destined to be my own unique self. My first major clue that we were destined for together should have been when you couldn't see any beauty in the old raggedy shack where I was born. That shack represented my ability to learn to not only survive, but to thrive. It also represented my ability to rise from the ashes. Perhaps that is why you never saw the real me.

Because we never stop talking about reaching for the moon just to make sure that we would land among the stars, I am becoming the best version of myself. For your influence with that, I thank you.

~~~~~~~~

My Family: My DNA Family and Extended Family

Thank you for all your support. I have stood on the shoulders of those family members who came before me. I sincerely extend my shoulders for each of you to stand on because it is your love and support that makes my shoulders so strong.

~~~~~~~~

My Aunt Jannie

Life offers few precious gems. You are one of the precious gifts I have been given. Your young spirit keeps me young as I see you as a mirror to my future. We have our shattered, spirited moments, but each moment causes me to pause and ask myself, "What would life be like without her?" Because I don't want to know the answer to that question, I just come back, ask for forgiveness, and apologize so we can show the world what it is like to love each other through life's many growing pains.

~~~~~~~~

Table of Contents

Foreword 1

Introduction - Synergy Of Equality — A Bouquet Of Flowers 5

Chapter One - African Violet: A Flower Of Pain And Struggle 14

Chapter Two – Sunflowers: Free-Spirited Joy And Endless Energy 27

Chapter Three - Maui King Protea: God's Watchful Eyes 42

Chapter Four - Dancing Honeysuckles, Vines, And Hummingbirds 53

Chapter Five - Four O'clocks: Flower Of Reliability And Strength 69

Chapter Six - Petunia: A Flower Of A Mixed Presentation 85

Chapter Seven - Candytuft: A Flower Of Indifference, Even In Death 102

Chapter Eight - Verbena: Flower For Protection

From Harm And Evil 120

Chapter Nine - Red Rose: A Flower Of Love And Pain 133

Chapter Ten - Daffodils: Unrequited Love 151

Chapter Eleven - Snapdragon: Underestimated Underdog 163

Chapter Twelve - Black Roses: Death And Mourning "Gone Too Soon" 187

Chapter Thirteen - Gladiolus: Strength And Fragility Of Friendship 206

Chapter Fourteen - Cotton Thistle: Pain And Aggression 225

Chapter Fifteen - Lotus: Surviving And Thriving Through Violence 241

Chapter Sixteen - Purple Lilac: Flower Of Growth And Change 260

Chapter Seventeen - Jasmine: Sexual Eroticism .. 267

Chapter Eighteen - Purple Orchid: Lasting Love And Reverence 278

Chapter Nineteen - Forget-Me-Nots: Remembrance 301

Chapter Twenty - Fire Lily: Flaming Fire 330

Conclusion	344
References	351
About The Author	356

FOREWORD

When my mother introduced her to me as "Shedby," I didn't give it much thought. Sherry and her mother, Bettye (who shares my name), were just another couple of people to whom my mother was happy to introduce me. At the time, nothing special stood out about her. Sherry was quiet and appeared unassuming. Then, we were two teenagers with very little in common. Fast forward to today… I still call her *Shedby* as a term of endearment. Sherry stands now as passionate, fearless, fiery, and fierce. I now call her my friend.

Since what appeared to be a meaningless day of introduction, we have shared many cherished family moments. We sang in the church choir together, and Sherry would encourage me to sing lead as she stood way in the back cheering me on. We have shared family events, which include Thanksgiving and Christmas dinner at my oldest sister's dinner table; reminiscing about childhood dreams while vacationing together; laughter as well as tears; and sadness during weddings and funerals.

She was the firstborn, and I was the last born. We compared many experiences to our family birth positions.

How we were treated according to our birth positions may have been different, but the clear connection was our belief that as strong Black women, with our life experiences always front and center, we were born to champion diversity, equality, and inclusion. Sherry seemed to always feel comfortable and ready to walk up to the table and have a seat to discuss these issues. I would say, "Hold on, let's think about this for a moment." Whereas Sherry would say, "There will be time for thinking on my way to the table. I just know I have to *be* at the table." It was as if fear, doubt, and disappointment didn't weigh into her decision to champion these *steppingstones* as she called them. She would always say, "We are not going to waste our energy fighting these mountains head on. We are going to outsmart the opposition; when they look for us, we will be two steps ahead of them. Plus, they will not be worth the energy to look back for them in our rearview mirrors. We will just keep looking forward to the future."

Fast forward to the future… Sherry has found her strong and assertive voice. You might not see her name on marquees or hear her voice on huge stages, but when I am in the company of Sherry, her friends, and associates, it is obvious there is a shared impact they have on each other. When you listen to her family speak of her, it is crystal clear that they have been listening and watching as they are following in her footsteps. Her footprints will be heard and seen through her family's and friends' achievements for generations to come. As a Nurse Practitioner, she medically advocates for mankind as she attempts to save lives, one person at a time. Through this book, Sherry's voice will touch both the young and the seasoned as she confirms that mistakes are learning opportunities only if you recognize them and are open to learn from them. She often speaks to her belief that it is the measure of where you are, in relation to where you came from, that is the depth of your success. Coming from mismatched spoons and forks without privileges to a full set of gold-plated silverware with privileges well-fought for is a lot more of an achievement than going from one silver spoon with privileges to a bigger silver spoon with more privileges. Now, all I know is *This Girl is on Fire*, and I am incredibly inspired and proud to call her my friend.

She took the time to follow her vision to dream as she speaks power to her truth and forges her fearless path. Sherry invites us to glimpse what it is like to come from very little to having everything needed to live a fruitful and prosperous life. She takes us along as if we were there living this journey with her. You will laugh (and most likely, you will cry) as Sherry shares her deepest heartaches and mountaintop triumphs. This book is for anyone who is seen as the underdog by everyone except themselves.

As I write the foreword for her book, I am touched by her fearless spirit to tell her truth and empower others to do the same, especially women who were once battered and broken. She reminds us that *battered* and *broken* serves a purpose in our lives, but they are *not* our lives.

It is my pleasure to introduce the world to my friend, confidante, my "ride or die." Pull up a chair. I ask you to sit back and enjoy a journey of resilient truth and passionate human growth. Her truth is laced with a dash and pinch of humor and a pound of naivety and honesty.

I thoroughly enjoyed reading her refreshingly honest and uplifting story. I am confident that you will as well.

Thank you,

Betty Wiley,

Besties Forever

INTRODUCTION

Synergy of Equality — A Bouquet of Flowers

As a retired Nurse Practitioner, my thoughts and days had become less fulfilled than before. The joy (yes, I mean *joy*), of the hustle and bustle of my career had come to moments of much less excitement. In those less than exciting moments, dreams of traveling the world as my next adventure had been crushed by COVID-19. Traveling the world with friends and family had suddenly become a delayed (if ever), reality. *So, what would I do while COVID-19 controlled my path?* As I began to search for my deeper purpose in life and my secondary dreams, I decided to go back to deep thoughts about my legacy. These thoughts were energized by the images of black and white angels on my refrigerator. They had become a constant reminder that I was living my truth of seeking equality for everyone, especially the underprivileged and the *underdogs* of the world.

I was practicing what my great-grandmother had preached and modeled to my young soul. Every child should be raised by their own precious mother and father. That is the order of nature. I have always wondered if kids who were raised by their grandparents and great-grandparents benefited from the older generation's wisdom, endurance, and gratitude. From those thoughts emerged a dream I have held dear in my heart for such a long time. It is a dream of telling my story of surviving and thriving, from a position of undiscovered love and power, to discovering my hidden strengths and determination built on a foundation of deep family love, strength, and power.

I had always wanted to tell the story of a child who was born and raised in the backwoods of Mississippi on a modern-day plantation ("cotton-cultivated land," as her friends prefer she calls it). I say *modern-day* in the sense that my family was no longer enslaved. They were one step removed, though, as a single-parent household led by a female sharecropper with her five grandchildren as supporting laborers.

The first thought that comes to my mind now is how mesmerized I was by the wild and well-manicured flowers I saw while roaming the open plains of my birthplace. Reflecting on the memories of those beautiful flowers that engulfed my mind, provided me with vivid images and compelled me to take pen to paper and tell my story, using flowers as threads of symbolism. Those threads enabled me to share how beautiful, individual flowers, when combined, can create an even more magnificent bouquet and how this concept could reflect the chapters of my life.

As I give thought to the environment where I was born and raised (Route 1, Box 204 between Sherard, Mississippi, and Farrell, Mississippi). I realize I had known the flowers were wildflowers because we never planted a single flower seed. Nor could we afford to buy anything to enhance the natural beauty we woke up to each morning. At our house, if it was not free, it did not exist. I was born in an old raggedy, unpainted, nature-worn house that was leaning toward waiting for a demolition crew. The only curb appeal it had were the colorful wildflowers. It most definitely had to be the power and beauty of nature that soothed our souls. I vividly recall wildflowers such as sunflowers, honeysuckles, red roses, forget-me-knots, and four o'clocks in the wild section of the plantation where my family lived. On the other side of the plantation, at the landowner's house, I saw well-manicured gardens of orchids, snapdragons, fire lilies, petunias, gladiolus, and what looked like woodlands of magnolia trees. The magnificent white blooms of the magnolia trees constantly caught my attention. The magnolia trees encased a beautiful, nicely painted, white house that had a lawn consisting of carpet-like grass.

The contrast of wildflowers running wild on my side of the plantation and the manicured garden of flowers on the landowner's side was crystal clear. The flowers were equally beautiful, but the families and their lives were quite different. Interesting enough, my curiosity kept me searching for what the flowers and the families had in common. Looking back, I can see the similarities of the flowers' equally eye-catching beauty, despite the stark contrast of the families' existence. Heightening my curiosity was the thought: *imagine what beauty would be bestowed upon all the humans on this plantation if their family histories and these flowers could be combined to create a synergistic bouquet of flowers* representing *the unity of mankind*. Please note that I didn't say one bouquet of flowers or family history was greater or less than the other. This would speak to superiority and inferiority, and let me be clear, that is not the intent of this story. I hold steadfast to the fact that equality for all is found while traveling the high roads of life, while the practices of both superiority and inferiority are frequently found in the crowded traffic of traveling the low roads. Once I discovered peace and quiet on the high roads of life, I vowed to make a conscious effort to stay on those roads. Whenever I take a detour, I hit the brakes and make a conscious effort to navigate my way back to the less-traveled and less-crowded high roads.

Although I remember these flowers existing in different scenes on the winding country plantation roads, it was obvious the flowers didn't abandon their beauty as the scenery changed. But I was still stuck with another curious question: "Would the magnolia tree blooms be just as beautiful if the blooms were black instead of white?" I visualized one of many black blooms representing the little Black girl (me) who lived in the old raggedy shack in the middle of a panoramic view of cow pasture and cotton field with the woody forest in the distant background. Amid this scenery, believe it or not, I could still see the beauty of nature and the freedom to soak it all in every day.

Now, I must pause and look back to a period of time in my family before I was born. The questions that arise are:

- *What if my great-grandfather had not died from a massive heart attack at age forty?*

- *Would we have had more opportunities, such as education, which could have possibly led to having educators and landowners in our family much earlier?*

- *How dare I dream that we may have had nurses, doctors, and lawyers in our family way back then?*

- *Would we have skipped the period when my family was seen as less than human, as they held their heads up high and maintained their dignity while living in the middle of a cow pasture and a cotton field?*

- *Would I have been born with matching silverware to eat with? (Instead, I was raised with practically no silverware at all being lifted to my mouth. The sparse silverware we had was as mismatched as you could find).*

Yet, I learned to see myself as a *Cinderella* princess who experienced richness as I humbly and proudly traveled out in the world in my very raggedy, yet clean, clothes. I was poor with rags, but I was rich with love and humility, and I had the wisdom to "see the forest for the trees." At an early age, I was seeing myself as a young girl with a passion for equality for young girls all over the world. Like most of the people living on the plantation, I was physically trapped by my environment; therefore, I am sure no one saw me as being so wise beyond my years.

At eleven and a half, I lost the only person who provided me with shelter, food, and, most of all, love and wisdom. She was my great-grandmother. She was a lady of few words, but when she repeated something, it was in my best interest to listen. She made it her legacy to impress upon me the importance of equality. She instilled in me the belief that no one was superior to me, nor was I superior to anyone else. The example that "brought this home" was when she told me, "No beautiful Caucasian girl or beautiful Black girl is more important than you. Yet, you must understand and embrace the fact that you are not any more important than *they* are." That was not a hard pill to swallow, because at an early age she had planted the seed that we are all equal, and she nurtured it all throughout my young adolescent life.

As I reflect, I realize I was oblivious to the fact that I was born Black and born into poverty. It was society that made this known to me, and it could have been a major issue in my life if I had let it. I never remembered being hungry for food, without shelter, confined to limited thoughts, or most of all, ever without love. As I roamed the open country range, I remember always feeling like a free spirit. I felt like the world was just as wide open to me as anyone else. I strongly believed that nothing could hold this rich (in love and freedom) *Sistah* down. It was obvious, even at an early age, life offered me more questions than answers. Fortunately, because of so much time alone, I contemplated deep *Why* and *What's the reason for that* type of questions. These questions lured me into continuing my travels on the road of curiosity. My family called me "L7" (Square). What they didn't know was that while they were happy doing things (getting into trouble) that didn't have any thought-provoking *Why* questions associated with them, I was shooting for the moon as my curiosity would stumble upon another *Why* question. I was Curious Sherry long before there was a Curious George. My brother calls me, "Junior Oprah." He starts our conversations with, "You can ask me only two questions." After that, he says, "I am done; that is too many damn questions."

My great-grandmother's presence in my life sustained me on my quest for answers. My curiosity was fueled by my obsession and yearning for mankind to champion equality. I must admit, I did not have a clue about how difficult a task that would prove to be. I could only clearly see the expression of beauty via the white blooms of the magnolia trees. However, my curiosity and imagination dared me to step outside the box and envision a magnolia tree with black blooms having an equally eye-catching and admired impact on the sceneries of the world.

Now, I tell my story. I want to touch the minds and the hearts of my readers, to share with them how confident I am using this book as a vessel to pass on my great-grandmother's **wisdom and advice**, not only to my creative inner circle, but to people all over the world. Her lifelong wisdom helps me find the perfect voice for the depth and structure of my words as they flow from my soul to the pen and paper. I just want to make sure that my words are dynamic and come to life, making the reader feel and breathe each word as they read them.

Yes, I was a child beyond my years. But this is what began my journey—living a life that would make people take note that a little Black girl could also be viewed as *An Unequivocal Southern Belle*. I couldn't think of a better way to tell the story of such a curious little Black girl (me) than to tell it through the beauty of a collection of symbolic flowers being seen as a synergetic bouquet that could illuminate any scenery on any occasion. The beauty of the bouquet will symbolize how the chapters of my journey have led to a beautiful and colorful mosaic of life.

Chapter One

AFRICAN VIOLET:
A FLOWER OF PAIN AND STRUGGLE

The African Violet is chosen to begin my story because, to me, it symbolizes the beauty and growth of life's struggles. We often miss the beauty in our life struggles because the pain that comes with them clouds the beauty hidden deeply within our hurtful experiences. Sometimes it might be our own selfishness that keeps us from seeing the beauty. We don't usually take the time to weather the clouds of the storms, which would enable us to take an introspective look at ourselves and see the silver linings. If we were strong enough to do this, we would gain fuller knowledge and expression of ourselves.

This flower also symbolizes the strength, courage, and staying power that has been passed on from one generation to another and how these traits connect our past to our future. We look up and before we know it… we see a family member a bit too proud (as if their staying power was mustered up by their own present accomplishments). It's as if they stand alone on their own merits as they march through their life journeys. We must not forget the sacrifices of our forefathers who came before us, because (most likely) it was their sacrifices that shaped us into who we are today. This reminds us of how our past impacts the present and the future. Just think, the courage to dream may have been lying just beneath the surface for several generations; and then someone steps out and brings the family's dreams into fruition.

But not for the beauty of the struggles of my ancestors would I be the strong, fearless, and courageous person I am today. I have grown up to become an unequivocal African American Southern Belle, *in spite of* or maybe *because of*, the painful struggles of my ancestors. The fact that they somehow found strength in themselves, their surroundings, the universe, and God to climb the highest mountain peaks, cross the deepest valleys, and travel into the future so the world could bear witness to their genes remaining strong and unwavering—is nothing short of amazing. I would never feel whole in my heart if I denied any part of my ancestral past. This includes my Native American kinship, because this heritage, along with enslaved Africans, is a part of the legacy to which I lay claim.

Being introspective about oneself, one's heritage, or one's life can be very therapeutic. It keeps us busy enough, so we don't have time to *fix* other people, because we are so busy working on ourselves. We must buy into this concept to see the beauty in the struggles of our ancestors as well as our own. This is a very ironic symbolism of the African Violet because it is known to be one of the most sensitive and delicate plants on earth. It must be watered in a particular way and raised with great care, attention, and exposure to sunlight. The irony is that what gives it life can also kill it if we are not mindful of its strengths and weaknesses. Being in tune with this makes us aware of the importance of a critical balance to survive and, even more so, to thrive. I learned that African Violets can survive up to fifty years with proper care. To me, this symbolizes how a family's lineage can survive generation after generation, if emphasis is placed on how the past generation is a steppingstone for future generations.

My great-grandmother was my generational steppingstone. Her love and respect for her ancestors helped me to understand the significance of building on their past contributions. She was my North Star. As I write, my ears remain sensitive to hear her words of wisdom. I use my imagination to visualize her relying on wisdom that was passed from her forefathers to help her overcome one struggle after another. This points back to the staying power of the African Violet and helps bring out the spirit of the layered meaning of all the flowers in a bouquet.

The mastery and staying power of my great-grandmother defies my ability to give a great description of her heroic struggles. Sometimes, the essence of a great person or a significant thing is too difficult to describe—it takes intuition and inspiration. But perhaps it is the nostalgic symbolism of the African Violet that inspired me to travel back in time and try to paint a colorful backdrop of what life for the Henderson family was like before I was born.

My great-grandmother was tall in stature. It had to be the luck of the DNA draw because most of her nine brothers and sisters stood on the short side, especially her brothers. As the family stories are told, it has been etched into our memories that her mother was short, leaving me to believe that her father must have been tall. Unfortunately, my ancestry search only revealed that her father, John Adams, was married to Jannie McNair, and to that union were ten live births. There were five boys and five girls. The story continues with pride that Jannie McNair Adams was the midwife for all the plantations in the area. She delivered nearly every baby (Black and White) as far as her horse, buggy, and midwifery bag would take her. Family history has it that she also trained her successor well, who went on to deliver the next two generations of babies, which included me.

My great-grandmother had natural beauty and stunning Native American features. She didn't need to wear makeup because her high cheekbones, dark eyes, and silky, golden skin tone were enough to make her face look as if someone had painted beauty on a glowing canvas. Her thin, yet shapely body gave an inviting contour to the plain dresses she wore to give thanks to God Almighty every first Sunday of the month. She matched the dresses with dainty costume pearl earrings and inexpensive, but classy shoes. Let me not forget the one black, shiny patent leather "church pocketbook" she laid across her long, skinny legs during each service.

Her signature hair style was a low maintenance take down of her two long braids (plaits), letting her *bluing*-tinted hair flow freely. No rollers, pins or curling iron were necessary. Tightly rolled, brown paper bag strips, secured with bobby pins, were used to get the fancy hairstyle on very special occasions. Her presentation in these inexpensive clothes and effortless hairstyles were plenty of competition for the few well-dressed ladies who could afford more expensive clothes from well-known department stores such as JCPenney, Sears and Roebuck, and the famous F.W. Woolworth. On weekdays, she moved about with the same grace of a woman of innate sophistication as she wore her shift-like dresses covered with well-worn aprons.

She was seen as polished on Sunday, but in the privacy of our home, you could see the pain in her eyes. She longed for the dream that had been forever interrupted by the sudden death of her beloved husband. She had been loved, protected, and treated like a queen, and now she had become the only protector of five grandchildren and one great-grandchild. She had no formal education; therefore, she had to rely on pure instinct and faith to help her as she rose each morning to do the best she could. Her ongoing surviving ritual was to start this journey again the next day. She raised those five grandchildren with the strength and grace of God Almighty. They all grew into respectable citizens, and they raised their own families.

Before my great-grandfather's death (at forty), he had been successful in leasing/tenant sharecropping in Sherard, Mississippi. This was considered two steps up from being a human being who was worthless to the landowners after slavery ended. The first step up was a person who worked daily as a hired hand and got paid at the end of the week. They got paid what the landowner determined was the value of their time and service. This was during the time when the service of African Americans was viewed as a hot financial commodity for the landowner and less than rotten soil otherwise. Making an honest living was hard in the backdrop of no bookkeeping nor accountability that favored African American's attempts at making a reasonable living.

My great-grandfather's livelihood consisted of the second step up. As a leasing/tenant sharecropper, he rented the land and equipment from the landowner to farm the land. He had significant autonomy to farm the land as a *business* he managed for the landowner. Within the limits set by the landowner, he planted the crops that would produce a profit to keep his family comfortable in a big, well-built house surrounded by plenty of rented land for his grandchildren to roam and play. Typically, at the end of each year, his success had secured them with sufficient farm animals and equipment, plenty to eat, and the freedom for their five grandchildren to dream of further education as they attended public school daily. His only child, a son, was very little help to him. He rebelled against the idea that he would be a common day laborer, even if it meant assisting his father. As the story is told, it appeared that his son was a moonshine entrepreneur in his own rights. My great-grandmother, who was a good soul, managed her family's *big* house and the household duties that came with her role. No, she didn't have to work at the "Big House" for the White landowner.

My great-grandfather had good business sense and kept financial records of his business and sat down at a formal business meeting at the end of the year to settle intelligently with the landowner. This agreement came with limited voice and power, but as far as my family was concerned, it was progress on the way to a better future. There was no talk about the size of the settlements he received at the end of the years, but it appeared his livelihood afforded him the opportunity to invest in the education of his son and his five grandchildren. It was not clear if his son took advantage of the opportunities that my great-grandfather's hard work offered the family.

If I understand the story correctly, my great-grandfather was the head of a happy family. It was a family that played together, sang together, loved together, and most of all—prayed together. My great-grandmother was also blessed and enjoyed her responsibility of raising their five grandchildren. As one of the five grandchildren, my aunt recalls her and her siblings roaming the acres of land that their grandfather farmed as happy and healthy kids—just being kids.

My good-looking grandfather (who was considered "GQ") lost his wife and the mother of their five children at twenty-seven. She was known to be very sickly; she had given birth to five children. In addition to the five living children, she had another single birth and a set of twins who didn't survive beyond birth. Do the math; that was eight children by the age of twenty-seven. It is not conclusive, but it is believed that she died of cervical cancer. She would go north to Chicago and Saint Louis to receive adequate medical treatment, but she wanted to be home in Mississippi with her husband and children. Each time she returned home, it would not be long before she would have a setback. Healthcare in Mississippi, for the most part, was denied to her because of the mere fact that she was a Black woman. On the rare occasions that healthcare was offered to Blacks, it was so subpar that it was not uncommon for them to live their last days with death prematurely circling their bedside. Most of the time, death won the battle and family members were gone too soon.

After the death of their mother, the five grandchildren lived happily in the Henderson household with their loving and responsible grandparents. For most children back then, after the loss of their mother, they would be placed with their mother's family. The family of their deceased mother stepped up to the plate with an offer to take the children, but acceptance came with personal cost to the five siblings. They would be split up here and there. My great-grandmother was not having any part of that—not even for one moment. She countered their offer and decided to raise all five of her son's children together. I don't want to think for one moment what their lives would have been like if they didn't have each other. The same unconditional love that my great-grandmother gave me was the glue that held her five grandchildren together until only death came and claimed three of them one by one.

Just imagine—one day, my great-grandmother was suddenly left with five grandchildren and nowhere to live. My great-grandfather (the landowner's cash cow) was dead at the age of forty from a massive heart attack. She had no formal skills for their current landowner to invest in. Therefore, she was told to pack up their things and vacate the house and the land as soon as possible. She had to leave a life of comfort and take her belongings and her five precious grandchildren elsewhere. My great-grandmother headed approximately fifteen miles up the road to Mr. Randle's cotton-cultivated land to join her family, who had settled there many years before.

There were no tenant sharecropping agreements that mirrored the business-like concept my great-grandfather had conducted in Sherard, Mississippi. First, my great-grandmother didn't have the skill to tenant sharecrop, even if the opportunity *had* been available. Therefore, she decided to follow in the footsteps of her family members, who were living on this land at the time. The model of plain hardcore sharecropping on Mr. Randle's land was such that she and her five grandchildren were forced to trade a decent past life for a future in which they were assigned cotton fields to manage. She didn't have the opportunity to rent the land or the equipment to manage the cotton crops. My great-grandmother found herself entering a "business contract" with the landowner to sharecrop a certain number of acres of land without any skills to do so. She had only known this business from a distance as she watched her husband financially provide for the family. She and her laborers (her five grandchildren) were clueless.

Year after year, she was visited by the landowner, only to be told time after time that she had come up in the RED, owing one too many dollars she didn't have. Because she was a Black female, she didn't even get the courtesy to sit at the landowner's formal business table. It was obvious that the agreed upon "business contract" was a disaster. My great-grandmother had no other choice but to take a step *down* and watch herself and her five precious grandchildren all become mere subordinated hired hands for the landowner while she made a measly, seven dollars per month. This appeared to be a *lose-lose* proposition from the very start. She, being a female head of the household, gave the landowner permission to pay her and her hired laborers the lowest amount of money possible.

Her five grandchildren missed so much school that their dreams of decent education were halted as they labored in the cotton fields, day after day, while the family became more and more broke. They had to work the land to put food on the old, raggedy table in their old, raggedy house. My aunt told me they spent at least 75 percent of their waking hours working the cotton-cultivated land that only offered them merely a life of survival—one step slightly above starving. She also told me that when they were able to go to school, their clothes were raggedy, but clean. Their shoes had so many holes that they were close to what we now call *flipflops*. There were no such things as Sunday clothes or dress shoes for them.

Still today, my aunt will look me in the eye and tell me the story of how my great-grandmother kept a Chester trunk of beautiful clothes that she had from the time when life was better. She talks about how she and her siblings would take these clothes out of the trunk without permission. They would smell them and wrap themselves in them as they dreamed of how things used to be and hoped that things would be *good* again. But the miracles that existed during all these challenges was that they had love, survival skills, and most of all—they had each other.

My great-grandmother's innate grit, her ability to make something out of nothing, her sheer determination, and her faith in God were the anchors to her soul that kept her and her family above ground. I am sure there were times when death seemed to be an easy way out, but she was not about *easy*. She was all about her commitment to give her grandchildren everything they needed and hold on to everything she had. Materially, that wasn't much at all. But the love, determination, wisdom, and instinct to survive were PRICELESS.

Chapter Two

SUNFLOWERS:
FREE-SPIRITED JOY AND ENDLESS ENERGY

Sunflowers are known to stand tall as they sway freely in the wind. As the tall stalks sway, it appears they never lose their stunning, broad, sun-like shape. They are so spirit-lifting with their cheery, warm and inviting petals stretching toward the sweet sunlight.

The sunflower is a unique species that blooms during the summer months and its meaning can differ between cultures. Whilst some cultures believe that it is a sign of positivity and strength, others believe that it is a sign of loyalty and admiration. (Adam, 2021).

The strong, yet beautiful sunflowers remind me of the strength and beauty of my great-grandmother. As the sunflower droops and faces downward in the absence of the sun, she had many such moments in her life before and after my birth. Before my birth, she and her five grandchildren had done their best to make a decent life on Mr. Randle's modern-day plantation, despite all the family struggles. Then came *me*. On one hand, I was a bundle of joy, but on the other hand, I was another baby born into the family's financially strained environment. I was told that I was born on a typical day on this modern plantation. I can only imagination that on the morning of my birth, the sunflowers stood true to form and were swaying in the wind. Their petals were uplifted and bright as they faced the shining sun.

My mother was a strikingly beautiful sixteen-year-old teenager. As she often did with other families, the midwife came to deliver our family's first great-grandchild. Congratulations were in order for my mother and great-grandmother for another miracle, blessed by God. But if the truth be known, there must have been some thoughts of sorrow, pain and regret... another mouth to feed for an already struggling family. Yet, God's miracle was accepted, and the family looked forward to whatever He would send their way.

My father was a vibrant, sexually mature twenty-year-old, who traveled the country plantation in a dust-raising 1955 Chevy. Having a car was leverage for almost anything: money to take someone into town or an exciting joy ride just to disturb the dust on the dirt roads, especially at a high speed on the adrenaline-provoking curves. Cars were also like inexpensive hotels and unspoken invitations to negotiate sex with the girls.

I grew up thinking that he had raped my mother. He was never around. No one mentioned his name; *mum* was the word. What else could have happened for a beautiful, smart, tenacious sixteen-year-old girl to have a child without a happy man waiting outside to hear the baby cry for the first time? In my mind, his absence had to be associated with something nefarious. He had to be just another buried secret that my family would do anything to keep from seeing the light of day. Of course, this perspective was through the eyes of a child.

The house where I was born was in the middle of a large fenced-off cow pasture and a cotton field. I later learned that at one time, the house had not been fenced off. The cows once coexisted with my family. Wow! I guess the cows must have felt like humans, too, because I don't recall my family members ever saying that the less than humane environment caused them to lower their heads or their sense of dignity and integrity. If the landowner thought it would, he misjudged the character of my family.

Each day, my family members gathered their strength, held their heads high, and marched on to make the best of the circumstances that were out of their control. Imagine waking up to mooing cows, chewing and gazing back at you through broken and filmy windowpanes. They must have taken deep breaths, hoping the cows would not make one more crack in the windowpanes. Forget about what the smell outside had to be like. Another crack in the broken window would increase the space for the smell to come into the house. But it would also increase the space for the heat to escape and the cold to enter and cause more pain and suffering. It was beyond sad that another human being thought it was appropriate to subject humans to such a dehumanizing environment.

If our house would have still been in the middle of the cow pasture, I can imagine that my first sight of the world could have been of cows peeking thru the windows to witness the miracle of the year. Even though the cows were fenced off into the pasture by then, the crop-duster planes were out as usual, spraying pesticide on the cotton to save it from destructive insects. Ironically, because my family was one with the cotton field, when they were outside, they, too, were sprayed with the same pesticide. It was obvious that our lives were worth less than the cash-producing cotton crops. I am sure I received my "welcome to the world" spray of poison pesticide shortly after I was born.

In stark contrast, the landowner had his classic plantation home encapsulated on about five acres of land. His yard had at least three operational vehicles and kids' toys to die for scattered throughout the yard. I describe it as a *home* instead of a house. It was a big, picturesque, white home with a garden of flowers and a forest of magnolia trees with dark-green, glossy leaves that bloomed the most breathtaking, beautiful, white blossoms. This was nothing short of portraits that can be seen today in *Southern Living* magazine. The white blooms of the magnolia trees were off the chart, refreshing my soul with beauty, giving me hope that I would find beauty in the ashes embedded in my life. Yet, I always wondered if the trees would be just as pretty if the blooms were black... Black like me.

As the beautiful magnolia blooms helped to showcase the landowner's home, a newborn baby was the excitement in the house on the other side of the plantation. I don't remember anyone telling me that people came from near and far to see the new baby. Although babies were still miracles, it was not uncommon for teenage mothers to give birth without a father in sight. My mother says I was a good child—sleeping, eating, and crying as any normal child—a first-time mother's dream. However, as she matured into a more beautiful young woman, by the age of seventeen, she gave birth to my brother.

It was obvious that the guilt of bringing one more mouth to feed, along with the fact that she wanted to venture into a world outside of those limited spaces, was a frequent lingering thought for her. What young woman would not want to see the world without the baggage of two young children? This is especially true because she knew I would be left in the hands of someone with great wisdom, knowledge, love, and determination. I can imagine she was happy and wanted to jump for joy (if only in her mind) when my great-grandmother stood her ground and stated, "You can leave and see the world, but you will not take this child with you." Two sunflowers (my mother and my brother) lifted their roots and swayed the essence of their petals toward the bright, shining sun to the nearest town—Clarksdale, Mississippi.

As a young child, I found myself often spreading my arms and running through the sunflowers, basking in the warming glow of the sunlight. All I knew was that I felt the gifts of free-spirited joy and endless energy. Limitless freedom and my great-grandmother were what I had—and all I needed at that point in my life. As I grew older, I was left with deeper questions about why she left me behind.

After my mother and brother left the open country plains, my household consisted of my great-grandmother, my uncle, and myself. My uncle (who was described as having a "chip on his shoulder") had become the only hired laborer in our household. He once told the story of passing the landowner on his way to work one day. The landowner told him that he had heard he was leaving and asked where he was going. My uncle reminded the landowner that his existence on the plantation had always only been temporary. The landowner informed him that if he left the plantation, he would be more of a loser than he thought and would definitely starve to death. Therefore, we were not surprised that the landowner never upgraded our cow pasture/cotton field living quarters. The *upgraded* shacks (those with less broken windows and less creaky and worn floorboards) were incentives for the committed residents; the ones who were loyal and showed no sign of disagreement or evidence of leaving. Those committed residents were too busy surviving to notice the swaying sunflower or spend time thinking of how they were absorbing energy from the sun.

With an exit plan in mind, it was clear my uncle was not committed to a dream not worth dreaming. True to his word, he packed an old suitcase, bought a ticket on a scenic

Greyhound bus bound for a three-day ride to Denver, Colorado. He couldn't have had much in that big suitcase because he didn't have much. He was wearing the one bright-red, plaid sweater he wore so often that I thought it was painted on him. When he was not driving the red pesticide-spraying tractor, that sweater was attached to his body.

Once my uncle left, the only male figure in my family was my grandfather. He was raised as an only child, and even as an adult, he was SELFISH. I never saw him come to our home to initiate one single repair. He was never observed cutting wood or priming the water pump. He declared himself a carpenter and always presented himself with a pencil behind his ear and an 1/8-inch leeway (a carpenter principle) in his conversation. Yet, I never saw him hammer one nail. I would see him go to his boss' "big house" (a different landowner) intending to work. The two would start out sitting on the back porch, only to still be in the same place at the end of the day. The day always ended with them both being drunk from too many beers and rotgut moonshine. But guess what? He still got paid. The beer and moonshine were perks of his job. He was, no doubt in my mind, a classic good-looking alcoholic who didn't take a break from drinking when he visited us. He *did* occasionally come by to see that we had not been in a thunderstorm and blown to Kansas with Dorothy and Toto.

My grandfather drove a standard truck and would make it do a dance as he drove it down the winding dirt roads. One thing I noticed about him was the fact that he would slow down on the curves. I am sure this was because by the time I was born; he had torn up too many cars and landed in too many muddy, snake-filled ditches. He was also known to never turn down a fight. He once fought this guy and pushed him into a ditch. He could not just take the win and leave, though. He lunged as if he was going to jump down in the ditch with his opponent. The man asked him to think twice about jumping and told him not to do it. My grandfather didn't take the advice, and he jumped. Just before he landed, he met a sharp switchblade that cut off two of the fingers on his left hand.

Despite all that, my love for my grandfather ran deep then and will continue to do so. I loved both my grandfather and my uncle, but it was not hard to see that I had more respect for my uncle, who had great work ethics and made his dream come true. He escaped the cow pastures and the cotton fields. I am sure the cows missed the red plaid sweater as he traveled those country roads of Mississippi (as a hired laborer) for the last time.

The absence of my uncle forced me and my great-grandmother to become closer—if that was even possible.

We didn't have a man around to protect us. We had to rely, more than ever, on her faith in God. She seemed to believe that without Him; we didn't stand a chance of surviving. Watching her work miracles through her faith, amid her hardships, made *me* believe that GOD *had* to be real. I could not find any other explanation for our survival.

I was baptized in the Mississippi River when I was eight years old. If that was not faith, what was? The fish, snakes, and turtles (*yes*, turtles bite) were all looking for food. It had to be the power and grace of God that kept them at bay. I entered the water as a sinner and emerged as a child of the Almighty God. I attended Zion Traveler's Missionary Baptist Church every first Sunday of the month. The church was a common small, white building with a steeple. The pews were worn, but still provided moderate comfort. There were no stained-glass windows to keep the kids from being distracted. The look on the elderly faces would make any kid aware of the consequences of not being still or not looking like they were paying attention. If that was not enough, the church was so remote and isolated that there was no outside scenery to captivate anyone's attention. We had a couple of *mothers* and approximately five reliable choir members. I couldn't help them sing, because even with a prayer, my singing was on the level of a chorus growl. We had a few deacons, along with a congregation of approximately twenty never-dying faithful members. They were faithful to sing, shout, pray, and praise the Lord all over the place! If you passed by during the church service, you would have thought the church consisted of at least twice as many members.

The first lady would sit quietly unless she was moved by the yelling voice of her deeply spiritual husband, the pastor. He would start the sermon in Genesis (at the beginning), leap forward to Matthew, zigzag to Psalms, and rewind at Revelations. An hour later, his white shirt would be washed down in sweat, as it held the evidence of his vigorous, wordy sermon. There were no air conditioners; sometimes it felt like the intent was for the heat to sweat the sins out of the church folks.

During the sermons, the *Why* questions about religion and spirituality overwhelmed me. They were beyond confusing and complex, especially for a *Why*-searching young girl like me. It was not uncommon for me to struggle to follow the spiritual take-home messages of the sermons. At the end of the day, all I got was, "Jesus died for our sins, and now we should thank Him by living out the Ten Commandments and hope to see Him on Judgement Day." Because I had these questions, the ushers didn't have to keep me quiet by waving the fans in an ominous motion. I was too busy listening and hoping I would not miss any answers to my many burning questions. I faithfully gave my nickels in the church offering and my fifty cents for tithes once I became a member of the church. I would not let "cheating God out of his monetary sacrifice" keep me from getting the answers to my questions.

Just a few feet from the church doors was the graveyard, mostly covered with overgrown grass. Because of the closeness of the graveyard to the church, after each service, I would go to the gravesites and share moments of deep family history with family members who had passed on and hopefully gone to heaven. I would have private conversations with them, but in these conversations, *I* asked and answered all the questions. After these experiences, I would feel closer to them because I had spent some quiet time with them. My transportation to church and everywhere else I went on the plantation was my two feet: "Tom" and "Jerry." Yes, they took me on a five-mile journey to and from church (a total of ten miles) every first Sunday. This included ten o'clock Sunday school and the eleven o'clock morning service. My church visits became daily trips for vacation Bible school and for the weeks spent on the morning/moaning/mourning bench during church revivals. Still, to this day, I don't know the official name of the bench. I just know it was where I sat and prayed for God's salvation. At the age of eight, I took the leap and surrendered to my faith. I remember my quiet lady of few words, my great-grandmother, standing and shouting her way to me when I stood up and took the walk of faith to God.

Thank God, my great-grandmother was a faithful member, but not the first lady or a mother of the church. That would have added a deeper need for me to understand and interpret what was happening in the church environment. By her not preaching religion at home, I could somewhat compartmentalize my feeling about church. I could make my deep feeling about God a priority on Sunday and just be a child on most other days. I believe if she would have been a first lady or a mother of the church, religion would have chased my soul twenty-four seven. Also, her not having those roles meant we never had to entertain the minister at our raggedy kitchen, devoid of gourmet food and matching silverware. That made me happy. Our delicious finger-licking, *everyday* food and mismatched silverware were good enough for us on any given day. That included Sundays, and being without the snobs made everything even more delicious.

My great-grandmother would *shout* every now and then, but she was not the church's shouting queen. She was also not the church member with the big flamboyant hats or the flared dresses and fancy high-heeled shoes. But she was the queen who sat there with natural regality, beauty, and pure grace, with her perfect "one and only" Sunday pocketbook draped across her long, skinny legs. Even as a child, going to church also appeared to be a social outing, and most of the time it felt like we could be at church forever and a day. My *Why* question was, *If God is everywhere, couldn't we just do some of this stuff at home, or at least in other places?* I was thinking, the more places we went, the more I would be grateful to God for introducing me to other people and other places.

As a child, every time someone fainted, I was afraid they had died and might not come back to life. I just knew I was watching the magical power of God when the usher would take off his or her shoes and wave it over the person's face. The person would come back to life every time. I was sure that God had instilled in ushers the power to make the odor from a well-worn, old, sweaty shoe save them.

After becoming a nurse, I realized that the old, sweaty shoes had produced *free* ammonia (smelling salts). *Free* in the sense that they didn't have to buy ammonia. Because she was not a shouting queen, I had no reason to think that I needed to keep my shoes ready to save my great-grandmother every time I went to church. It was hard enough just to focus my attention on not missing answers to my *Why* questions. To have to share those church moments with the idea that I could lose my great-grandmother at any given moment was more than I would have been able to handle.

Dehydration can also make the sweat smell like ammonia. This is because the body needs water to get rid of ammonia through sweat. If there is not enough water to dilute the ammonia as it is released by the body, the smell of ammonia may be stronger. ("Sweat Smells like Ammonia: Causes and Treatment," 2021).

Chapter Three

MAUI KING PROTEA: GOD'S WATCHFUL EYES

Let me be crystal clear: I didn't see this popular tropical flower on any path of my life's journey. I don't even recall seeing this bold and colorful focal piece in any bouquet or arrangement I had ever received. It was only when I wanted a flower that would symbolize the literal life of my family from the burning ashes of Mississippi that I did the research and discovered its existence. My research revealed that the Maui King Protea is not only a beautiful tropical bouquet staple, but it is the national flower of South Africa.

[Maui] King proteas grow along the coast on the Cape of Good Hope in South Africa… They have thick stems which extend deep underground; a survival mechanism for wildfires, since these stems can sprout subterranean buds that will then grow into new plants after a fire. ("All About King Protea," 2020).

It is ironic that I would discover this unique flower to express how I felt that the eyes of God had to be watching over me and my family. Our surroundings destined us for death and destruction, but God had other plans. He destined us for greatness. No, thus far you will not see our name on the biggest and brightest marquees in the world, but we have taken our burning ashes and sprinkled them around the world. From the burning ashes, we have rooted many successful American citizens. This, within itself, was one of God's greatest miracles, but my family is destined to be blessed with many more. Keep your ears and eyes open to hear and see great things attached to the Henderson name in the future.

In relation to my family, this is symbolic of the fact that while the flower itself is a rare native to South Africa, horticulturists around the world pay special attention to it, and its beauty has traveled worldwide. For me, this confirms that when my family was in a dark place and thought they had been buried under, they had actually been planted where God wanted them to be and were waiting to be nurtured so they could become like the beautiful flowers that now bloomed brightly around the world.

I have learned that throughout my life, God placed us in hard and tough environments for a reason. The evolving reality is that somewhere along the way, we will come to understand the logic behind what sometimes seems to be *madness*. As we grow in our spiritual journey, He will reveal, as He promised, that we will understand "by and by." The pieces of life's puzzle will come together and let us know He was actually grooming my family for the cold, harsh world. For a long time, my family appeared to be floundering in the darkness and then, it seemed we were *suddenly* able to see the light. The truth of the matter is *nothing* was sudden. It was just that in *that* moment, our eyes gained the ability to see the light that had been there all the time. The light revealed that God had been carrying us all the way during the darkness. When He felt we were ready, He lifted the darkness.

I still believe that while in the world's darkness, my family was weeping, and yet God was still speaking to us through flower petals and blooms. When we wept, we watered the earth with all our sorrows, but we came to understand that *tomorrow,* although it felt too late, God came. I think sometimes He came through beautiful flower bouquets with audacious flowers that revealed their tenderness and mercy. This reminded us that through the beauty of the flowers, we have an opportunity to find a way to slow down our minds and our hearts and recognize what we have to be grateful for—all the miracles that He has bestowed upon us.

This brings me to the chapter in my life when I was growing up, and it appeared my family was bound for their share of more dark days. Then, along comes a little girl who never *saw* the darkness, therefore, she never *felt* that with darkness came life-changing limitations. Looking back, I always believed that God's watchful eyes were watching over me and my family, every step of the way, through those hard times. Just like He created the features of the Maui King Protea flower, he prepared us with resiliency, perseverance, fortitude, and the ability to adapt to less-than-optimal conditions over the years for us to survive. His intentionality in all our trials and tribulations taught us how to move from surviving to thriving. It began with my great-grandmother teaching us to make *somethings* out of a lot of *nothings*. We learned to bloom where we were planted. Then, one day someone or something inspired us to pick ourselves up, like flowers in the faraway fields. We spread our beauty all around the world.

I learned how to use my environment to see the open plains as gateways to the power of limitless thinking while I lived in the backwoods of Mississippi until the age of eleven and a half. During that time, our shelter was a four-room damp and chilly shack. The shack had rags in multiple cracks in the unstable and broken windowpanes. The front door had cotton sacks to keep the wet, chilled-to-the-bone cold at bay during the winter and added a cool breeze at night in the summertime. The wallpaper was mostly peeled away, leaving frays of paper hanging as if it was intentionally and authentically done. The kitchen had a big, black woodburning stove and the living room/bedroom had a potbelly woodburning heater. The red fire sparks from the burning wood were our nightly entertainment. The house was so raggedy that I would go outside and look up to the sky and pray that a spark from the heater or stove would not burn down the house before daybreak the next morning. This nightly thought would immediately take away the entertaining value of the fire sparks and haunt me with a fear of being burned to death or becoming homeless, at the least. The mattresses for the two beds in the living room/bedroom consisted of homemade cotton tics (made of dried cotton pieces). I learn to ripple and rump the tics so well until the bed would look like a mattress from Sears and Roebuck during the day. At bedtime, once we sat on the beds or dashed into them for a good night's sleep, it wouldn't take long before reality would set in. Thank God, after the sudden deflation, we would still be left with enough cushion to have a soft landing. The top covers for the mattresses were homemade quilts made of many scraps and raggedy pieces of old clothes that we could spare. The house had a tin top roof with many raised edges. This brought a new meaning to sleeping in the rain.

Only two of the four rooms had lights. One room was always dark because of non-working electricity and no windows to bring in the sunlight during the day. This room also had a large hole in the creaking floor that was covered with a large brown barrel. Despite the coverage of the barrel, in the summer I would see where snakes had shed their slithering skin after taking shelter in the house during the winter. Snake hides were often seen behind the black, kitchen stove after very cold falls and winters. Well, I guess snakes like to lie by the cozy, country fireplace and keep warm just as much as we did. I am glad that I never saw a live snake in the house; I was told to stay away from them because snakebites could be dangerous. We would often see green snakes when we moved old logs and stray tin that covered the tall, grassy backyard. Dangerous or not, seeing a live snake in the house would have been a "pee in my pants" moment to never forget.

The room with the big hole and no lights housed artificial flowers from dead family members' funeral services. *Who would keep such things in a dark room?* To make things just a little bit scarier, the room was occupied by a life-sized doll with one good eye and one cracked, damaged eye. For pastime fun, my uncle would lure and trap me in this room and then he would shout, "See them? They are looking at you. They are standing next to you!" I would scream to get out of the sight of the one-good-eyed doll and stop my imagination from making me think the dead people to whom the flowers belonged would reach out and grab me at any moment. Still, this cruel pastime never caused me to be afraid of the dark. It did, however, set the tone for me to never have any appreciation for horror movies. It may have been because horror movie scenes caused me to have flashbacks regarding those very scary moments.

There was no running water in the house; therefore, in the winter, I had to boil water on the woodburning stove to prime the pump for water that came from a distant well in an unknown location. Priming the pump in the summer was time consuming and bad enough, but pouring boiled water to thaw the pump during winter days was a test of survival skills and developing an art to keep from scalding yourself. One of the silver linings was that the well water was so soft, and it made our clothes feel soft and look pure white.

My great-grandmother's friends and distant neighbors would go to the *forest* and chop wood before the winter, but when we ran out of chopped wood, I had to learn to chop logs for the rest of the winter. Somehow, we had to keep pushing wood into the burning, fascinating, and mesmerizing fire of the woodburning stove and heater. We didn't have a television, just a white radio that only seemed to blast when the Chicago Cubs and White Sox were playing.

We didn't have a refrigerator, washer, dryer, or food pantry. Meat was preserved in a barrel with salt. We had powdered milk, buttermilk, and cheese that (under these circumstances) didn't reach a point that was too spoiled to consume. Our eggs were freshly laid by chickens daily. There was no feeling sorry for the chickens when it came time to whirl them high in the air without blinking or without feelings. We would ring their necks until they reached death, as evidenced by blood squirting everywhere and feathers scattering. We were unmoved by the scent and act of death while seeking food to satisfy our hunger. We would throw them in a black pot of boiling water and pluck the feathers, cut them up, and fry them for dinner. This was certainly the definition of a timely and fresh meal.

I could cook a full-course meal at eight years old, but the limited list of food items helped to determine my cooking skills. We couldn't afford most meats or an icebox/refrigerator, therefore meat was not a major part of our diet. We had hoecakes (whole cakes) for bread instead of rolls and croissants. We got our first icebox two months before leaving the plantation, when I was eleven and a half.

It had been our first housewarming present when we moved to our home in town.

From time to time, we had what was considered food for survival back then, but today is considered a delicacy, such as fresh rabbit, squirrel, perch, and bass fish. Some people were known to eat raccoons and possum. Not me—even at a young and adventurous age. I just didn't get *that* hungry. But the gravy my great-grandmother made from these delicacies would make you eat almost anything and lick your fingers afterward. She didn't measure ingredients. She cooked with dashes of this and pinches of that. Most of our food consisted of fresh chicken and fresh vegetables from the small garden adjacent to our front yard. Tomatoes and watermelons were my favorite garden foods. I was allergic to tomatoes, but with salt and pepper, I ate myself right out of that annoying allergy. I would sit in the watermelon patch and partake until I felt like my stomach was going to burst.

Meals frequently consisted of unforgettable hot water spaghetti (seasoned well with the perfect amount of salt and pepper, diluted tomato sauce with no meat), homemade buttermilk biscuits, and fresh eggs. Hot water cornbread was a specialty all by itself. This was an example of how food made with the bare basics could taste so good. I ate so many eggs—boiled, fried, scrambled—I ate them every way. Today, I am very *iffy* about eggs. I will only eat them occasionally, fried very hard or boiled. Desserts were bread pudding, Rex jelly cakes, tea cakes, peanut butter and sugar sandwiches (too poor for jelly or jam). Fish (the head, eyes, and eggs) completed a lot of our meals. I can't say we were eating caviar, but I can say I liked the fish eggs and brains prepared by the common people much more than I liked the fish eggs (caviar and pâté) of the rich and famous. We were consuming extra-high levels of Vitamin A, Omega-3 fatty acids, iron, zinc, and calcium. Little did we know then, we had some of the top-of-the-line healthy, nutritional foods and delicacies—right in the hands of us poor folks.

I will never forget the grace of embracing the outside toilet, which was at least twenty-five feet from our back door. The outside toilet gave the cotton field, the comic section of a very old newspaper, and brown paper bags new purposes. Not having an indoor bathroom led to baths (washups) in a number five, tin tub of water. The first person in the tub had the advantage of clean water. As others followed, they would encounter water with the oil-filled dirt of everyone who came before them. This was not the most efficient and relaxing way to keep our bodies clean, but we were always presentable with a fresh smell of cleanliness.

I washed long lines of clothes with an old, snaggy wash board and steamy, hot water in a big, black pot with homemade lye soap because we couldn't afford real soap.

With that soft well water and natural rainwater, the clothes would be white as snow as they blew through the unblocked wind on the clotheslines in the backyard. The laundering of clothes was done by hanging them on the front porch and letting the wind blow out the musk. These tasks for everyday living came easily because other options were limited or nonexistent.

I know not everyone believes in God. For those of us who do, however, we must give His watchful eyes credit for keeping us safe, healthy, and well-fed. For me and my great-grandmother, He kept us with only fifty dollars per month. For those of you who don't believe in Him, you must admit that the universe's alignment had to be consistently leaning in our favor. When I speak of GOD in this book, it is from a deep spiritual belief in a higher being. It is not in the name of religiosity.

Chapter Four

DANCING HONEYSUCKLES, VINES, AND HUMMINGBIRDS

Honeysuckle trumpet vines encased the frame of the front porch of the house where I was born and raised. They were also plentiful outside the raggedy, front yard fence. The honeysuckle stems trailed and climbed over all the other vegetation in the yard and on the fence. Their succulent blossoms added the only color and beauty to our worn and run-down, gray house. The house didn't have one ounce of paint on it. Inside the honeysuckle blossoms nested an abundance of sweet nectar that attracted the enchanting hummingbirds.

> Hummingbird mating rituals are unique natural events unlike any other. Every year, male hummingbirds put on an elaborate aerial show in their quest to attract females. The hummingbird mating process is a short but dramatic affair... it always involves some sort of display from the male hummingbird in order to impress the female... The male makes a series of impressive deep arcing swoops to catch her attention. Male hummingbirds, which can reach a speed of 60 miles per hour according to Encyclopedia Britannica, dash through the air, soaring high and speeding back down within inches of the female before repeating this U-shaped display of aerial acrobatics... Once the female has accepted a mate and the courtship ritual is over, the mating process is short, only lasting a few seconds. Then, the two go their separate ways. Males may reproduce with multiple females over the course of a year, and a mating pair doesn't raise young together... Once a female hummingbird lays eggs, she will care for the nest all on her own... The actual act of sex takes

only a few seconds in which the male puts his posterior opening (cloaca) against the female's. After that's done, the male moves on to find another female mate and start the process over again. (Swanson, 2022).

After reading about the hummingbirds, I was fascinated to learn that they remember migration routes and every flower they've ever visited. Another interesting fact is that "[m]ost of these birds DO return to the same feeders or gardens to breed year after year. What's more, they often stop at the same spots along the way *and* arrive on the same date!" ("How Do They Find Their Way Back?" n.d.) I had always wondered if the same hummingbirds ever came back to the same vines or if each honeysuckle vine was just a hit-and-miss pit stop on their traveling path.

As kids, we would pick the blooms from the vine and suck the nectar for a sweet treat. So, we understood why the hummingbirds loved the vines and appeared to be intoxicated from the sweet nectar. It is also fitting for me to choose the mating dance of the honeysuckle vine and the hummingbird to tell the story of my conception.

I can only imagine that on the night of my conception, the hummingbird and honeysuckle vine ritual occurred between my mother and father. I can imagine my father's debonair presentation and salty, sexy voice enticing my mother to accept his invitation to dance. I can see him with a pipe in the corner of mouth. The smoke in the pipe would be making circles in the air. He would ease up to this young, innocent girl as the hummingbird flocked to the inviting, lusty, honeysuckle blossoms waving in the wind. He had to be drunk and disoriented from the sweet, hypnotizing, and intoxicating scent of her venerable body. So captivated with her, he didn't recognize the disguising beauty of the smooth, clean, sweet scent that circulated in the windy, rain-filled, fresh air. He proceeded to persuade her to let him into her life to take the ultimate short-term landing. His deep, smooth, and convincing voice (and an offer she could not refuse) was his secret weapon to entice her to accept an invitation to dance. I would guess it didn't take long for their relationship to resemble the honeysuckle bloom that had been hard kissed by the dashing hummingbird. It would not have been a life-shadowing surprise if my father got my mother pregnant and flew away at the speed of lightning like the hummingbirds take flight after they pollinate the honeysuckle flower. It is also not surprising that he only performed this captivating ritual once before he disappeared into the land of those who are not spoken of. He became the family's buried secret.

The hard landing of the hummingbird was my retrospective interpretation. Later, in his own defense, he told me *his* side of the story; he held his head high, and proudly said that for a moment in time they had a strong bond of love and devotion. In my opinion, it was too bad the length of time and perception of a loved-filled relationship can be defined differently by all parties involved. He expanded on his story to swear that once he discovered my mother was pregnant, he asked for her hand in marriage, but she declined it. My mother would say "HE DID NOT RAPE ME. We were a couple of young people who should have been doing something else." She never voiced what that *something* else could have been. She was just always quick to tell me, "Let's just put a period behind the conversation."

Like she asked, I would put a period behind the conversation. But if given a choice as to whom to believe, I would believe my mother. I still think that undue pressure from a more experienced man had to be involved in that life-changing decision. I would be willing to bet that my father was humming, "Give it up if you want a ride to town where you will find the real action that you are seeking." According to my mother, the only action she was seeking was getting a ride to town so she could go out and have fun with her sister and other friends.

Regardless of my mother asking me to end the conversation, left with my own interpretation, I feel compelled to make my sentiments clear. It was clear that she was a young and innocent fifteen-year-old, and he was a very mature and experienced nineteen-year-old. If I checked the laws (then and now), the legal language would clearly read that, at the least, it was STATUTORY RAPE. I don't say this with malice. I say it with the understanding that facts do not lie. Only the two of them know if the facts included a deal being made. Nevertheless, their actions on that night certainly resulted in a well-kept secret. Perhaps she initially thought it would be a secret kept only between the two of them. Little did she know that this night would ultimately result in a lifelong reminder of a life-changing decision—a decision that she wished she could forget even if she could not take it back. Of course, I was not there and don't know what really happened, but I am entitled to fill in the gaps on the pages as I see fit.

One thing is true, it didn't take long before he was off to pollinate another honeysuckle blossom. He did not fly very far. He flew back to the honeysuckle vine he had pollinated before that moment in time with my mother. They lived on the same plantation where everyone knew each other. The fact was that he had one child with his *true* girlfriend and my second half sister was born two months after I was born. I would think this is how he explained away his guilt for following his true girlfriend to Santa Barbara, California. He later married her and started a respectable family. I really think this was the most honorable decision for him to make. It was clear that he should have been committed to her before the brief relationship occurred between him and my mother.

Their brief relationship remained a buried secret. Fast forward—life kept moving. Because our household was managed so well by a strong female, I never asked why the males were absent from our lives. For the most part, things seemed to get done without them. There were whispers and loose talk that I was related to this person and that person. No one dared to say how my father was associated with this or that person I was supposed to be related to. I did not care to take the time to explore the talk. My great-grandmother was all I needed because she was my everything. Who would care about the missing pieces of the puzzle that I didn't emotionally know were missing? I was so happy being raised by my great-grandmother. I didn't give a first or second thought about who my father was. These *Why* questions didn't even pique the curiosity of Curious Sherry. As far as I was concerned, we didn't need to fix a problem that no one acknowledged existed. The problem that was not acknowledged among my family must have been a known (but unspoken) fact. I felt this way because no one ever approached me to let me in on the family secret. They did not speak of my father. He was part of a truth that was buried, only to stay buried if you understood the family's unwritten and unspoken codes. Those codes regarding my father remained just that… unwritten and unspoken.

Even so, it was strange when two ladies would come from Santa Barbara, California, for yearly visits. They presented as my great-grandmother's well-known friends, who had once lived on the same plantation. They had escaped the plantation, only to come each year to stay connected with the unfortunate people who had not found a way to escape or didn't have the desire to do so. They would laugh loudly and chat about how things remained the same on the plantation. They didn't do much, if any, talking about the advantage of living in California. I guess that was a dream too big for those who remained on the stagnated plantation. Their loud chatting and laughter would eventually come to an end. Before they would leave, they would ease over and kiss and hug me tightly. They would both also give me some warm clothes and a couple of dollars for my pocket.

I took their money and the clothes, but because they were not staying to help me with my many chores, I was not interested in who they were. I was satisfied that they made my great-grandmother happy. I was not even interested in what a wonderful life they had in the distant universe. California was like a distant planet in the universe to me and my great-grandmother. We had only traveled that scenic Greyhound bus to St. Louis, Missouri, and Chicago, Illinois. We had never heard the Greyhound bus driver mention California, so we had to assume we had never been close to the California state line. Later, I would learn that these two ladies were my paternal grandmother and great-grandmother. They had been delivering gifts on behalf of the genetic lineage on my father's side of the family.

The visits and gifts from these two ladies continued, and I continued *not* to ask questions or give my connection to them the time of day. In 1972, the older of those two ladies (my paternal great-grandmother) passed away. She had planned her own funeral. For the Black culture, especially back then, this was rare. For me, it was both fascinating and scary. This meant that she had envisioned her death in great detail. In my mind, *who would be brave enough to think about death while they were living*? Even scarier was the thought: *who would want to write about it?* As expected, all the people she and my great-grandmother knew in common and those related to her showed up to express their respects and say their goodbyes. (Remember, I still didn't know that this lady was my paternal great-grandmother at the time of her death.) But what happened a couple of days after I found out about her death had to be one of the biggest bombshells of my life.

Not knowing if it was a tradition for the hummingbirds to return to the honeysuckle vines was a distant thought. But even if they returned, it was never known if the same hummingbird came back to the same vine on the return trip or if another one would be just taking his turn to taste the honeysuckle flower's sweet nectar as he traveled the path that was once traveled by another. Well, the hummingbird (my father) *did* make his return. He was not seeking sweet nectar from the honeysuckle flower (my mother). He had yet another mission. His mission was to claim the fruit that had bloomed from the union of that brief, long ago, and regretful moment in time.

Unaware I was the fruit to be claimed, I was standing in the kitchen of our four-room home when the telephone rang. As usual, I answered. A man on the other end, with a smooth, deep voice, said his name was Cleveland Lee ("Redd") and that he was my father. I told him he had to be mistaken because *my* father was L.A. B. (my mother's husband). I knew that the man I had given credit for being my father was actually my stepfather, but he certainly had more of a right to be my father than a stranger calling to deliver such foolishness. Before he could finish his fantastic wishful thinking, I hung up on him. I didn't even rush to find my mother since I thought nothing could be further from the truth. As I kept washing dishes, I thought for a moment, *no one has the right to spread such lies. How dare he?* But I was willing to forgive him because he had a right to find his daughter. My next thought was that he had just dialed the wrong number. He would review the number and dial it correctly. Once he reached the correct number, he would reach his daughter, who would be happy to hear from him.

Putting the mistakenly dialed number in the back of my mind, I finished the rest of my chores. When my mother came back into the house and found me in the kitchen, I calmly told her what had happened. She casually and very quietly held my hand, took me to the kitchen table, and asked me to pull out a chair and have a seat so we could talk. That conversation answered a lot of questions that had been bothering everyone except me. I had no desire to know who my father was. I was no dummy; I was very intelligent (if I have to say so myself). I knew about the "birds and the bees." For me, a father was just a part of the concept to explain the analogy of the birds and the bees. I was not happy or sad about having this conversation. She was very matter of fact and straight to the point. She didn't bother to explain how this had come to be. And guess what? I did not bother to ask for an explanation. I just didn't have the energy nor the desire to assign a value to something or someone who had not contributed positively or negatively to my life. *(At this time, my beloved maternal great-grandmother had gone to glory, so if they were not talking about her coming back, I didn't give a freaking care about a stranger who was confirmed to be my father.)*

Whether I cared or not, there was no way I could put the genie back into the bottle. The originator of the secret had unearthed it and broken all the unspoken and unwritten codes. I finally gave this matter some quick thought and begin to ask myself questions. *How could I trust him?* I had heard whispers of who could be my father. I had previously experienced an incident that made all whispers look like a back-page newspaper story. This incident could have been a front-page headline.

In my mind, I had seen this movie before. One day a strange man (Willie) came from who knows where to see his child. Of course, he was a man who my mother had a past relationship with, but just like my father, no one had ever mentioned *him* either. I was not sure if he knew enough to know if his child was a boy or a girl. If this strange man didn't know before that day whether *I* was a boy or a girl, he would never know because I heard someone come to the back door and shout, "Run, Sherry, run!" Without asking any questions, I took off running like *Forrest Gump*. I think I just went to the nearest grocery store and waited for someone to come find me and let me know the coast was clear. When I returned home, my cousin informed me what all the drama had been about. Having experienced such an incident before, it was only my mother's confession that locked me into the reality that I *had* a father, and he was now boldly attempting to make up for lost time.

It was difficult for my newly discovered father to make up for lost time because I did everything to avoid him. I *had* to have seen him at my paternal great-grandmother's funeral, but our eventual interaction didn't make an unforgettable impression either. When we *did* manage to get together, the relationship between us kicked off with him offering me the dream of opening the Sears and Roebuck catalog and choosing two hundred dollars' worth of clothes. This was exciting because this was a better use for the catalog than what we use it for in the country outhouse. I was like a kid in a candy store as I flipped the pages in the catalog and picked out my own wardrobe for the first time in my life. What sixteen-year-old girl would be able to see the forest for the trees in this situation? I was too busy picking out clothes! In the eyes of a teenager, for a short period, he was finally well on his way to making up for all the empty father spaces in my life. But the reality of the significance of such a gesture soon came blasting through.

For a while, the empty father spaces were filled with glitz and glamour. The newly purchased clothes didn't get or keep my full attention, but they *did* move the needle ever so slightly in his direction. He then upped the ante and enticed me with an offer to travel to Santa Barbara, California, the place that existed in the distant universe. By now I understood this could be a dream of a lifetime. It didn't take much convincing because I was now of the age and maturity that any place outside of Mississippi, St. Louis, and Chicago was a far, faraway dream. What young person wouldn't be intrigued by the opportunity to leave the Mississippi state line to see the wild, wild west?

Crossing the Mississippi state line, headed for Santa Barbara, captured the classic bright-eyed and bushy-tailed sixteen-year-old blitz. The reality started to set in when the three-day scenic trip became quite the surprise. The open plains reminded me of my everyday views on the country plantation. It seemed as if the Greyhound bus stopped at every stop sign between Clarksdale, Mississippi, and Santa Barbara. Honestly, I remember the bus driver stopping at a house to pick up a cake. Along the way, an elderly lady walked out of her house and handed the bus driver a cake in a fancy portable cake carrier. It was surprising and disappointing that I was not the least bit impressed with such stops. My anticipation was clearly too much for such slow travel.

When I arrived in California, I was shocked again. The condition and location of the houses in my paternal grandmother's neighborhood made me feel like I was still in Mississippi. I didn't immediately see mansions on the hill. I was not making fun of their lovely home. It was just that as a sixteen-year-old teenager; I was looking for what I had seen advertised on the television. I didn't understand at that time, but for anyone to be out of Mississippi and not living in a mansion was one hundred percent better than living in a mansion *in* Mississippi. The teenager in me was disappointed that instead of movie stars and the Hollywood Walk of Fame, my eyes stared upon chickens in the backyard and no mansions in sight. It was also interesting that Santa Barbara didn't seem to have any Magnolia trees. I am not sure their presence would have lifted my disappointment. The return of the hummingbird turned out to be less than glitter and luster for an adventurous sixteen-year-old. The honeysuckle dance between him and my mother had long been over. My mother had never given any indication that she had wished for his return. Now, I was sure his return would not be the catalyst that would change my life for the better or the worse. His impact on my life would keep him in the neutral zone of my life.

My feelings about my father remained neutral. My mother didn't speak of that brief moment in time shared between them until we later spent ten years together in my home in Denver. I used to guess that she told her sisters, but now, I no longer have to wonder. Recently, my aunt told me that my mother had always told her and her older, twin-like sister that she *was* raped, and she swore them to secrecy. That confirmed my teenage speculation. Perhaps she wanted to spare my feelings because she never wanted me to feel I was not loved. After the passing of my great-grandmother, I occasionally felt that way, but after therapy and graceful maturity, I came to understand the situation. Sad to say, she was not the first (nor the last) fifteen-year-old young girl who would find herself in that situation. My hope is that mothers teach their young daughters that the pressures of compromising situations can change the trajectory of their lives forever, and secrecy can add to the bandwidth of the emotional trauma.

I dealt with my emotional trauma with healthy therapy. I also embraced the fact that the "moment in time" between my mother and father impacted my life. But it certainly did not define me. Once the secret of my conception became common knowledge, I used to make my mother laugh about it. I told her they could have been somewhere picking up daisies when I was conceived. I always wanted her to feel that I understood her decision to make a *deal* with my father was nothing she should have been ashamed of. I also wanted her to know that I didn't love her any less and didn't feel that she loved me any less. She didn't have to be ashamed because I was not conceived in everlasting love. Despite all the drama, I was happy and focusing on how to appreciate my current life instead of dwelling on how my life began. I was content we could genially laugh about such a serious matter. Just like water is the universal solvent, love is the universal connector.

Sometimes bad and painful decisions come with a silver lining that turns into precious joy. Now, I am mature enough to put a period behind the dance of the hummingbird (my father) and the honeysuckle vine (my mother).

Chapter Five

FOUR O'CLOCKS:
FLOWER OF RELIABILITY AND STRENGTH

Inside the front yard of our raggedy shack, flanked numerous four o'clock flowers. They, too, are wildflowers. If I ever needed a flower to paint a portrait of my maternal great-grandmother, the four o'clock flowers flood my memory. Like her, the flower reminds me of ongoing hope for another poor family's adventurous day.

The flowers usually open from late afternoon or at dusk (namely between 4 and 8 o'clock), giving rise to one of its common names. Flowers then produce a strong, sweet-smelling fragrance throughout the night, then close in the morning. New flowers open the following day. (Wikipedia, 2023).

Each spring morning, I continued to walk among fresh-looking blooms that seem to appear like magic. When the blooms fully open up late afternoon or early evening, I enjoyed the strong, sweet-smelling fragrance, only to look forward to this ritual again the following day. My research revealed that once the blooms wither and fall to the ground, the seeds are known to die back in the ground and root after the first frost or as the weather starts to cool down (especially after it fully matures and finishes self-seeding). They return late the following spring. This reminds me of the fact that my great-grandmother worked hard to get me to bloom as a healthy, beautiful, Black woman and to plant my dreams, so I could reap the fruit of her strength and wisdom year after year.

This memorable flower also reminds me of her reliability and stamina (staying power). She matched the flower's reliability by being a person who you could "tell the time of day by." You could count on her to keep you safe and hopeful that your dreams could come true someday. Her multi-tasking ability was as plentiful as the multiple-colored blooms of this special flower. The way the flowers opened up around the same time each day was quite helpful because I don't recall any clocks hanging on the walls in our house. Needless to say, a watch was nowhere to be found, especially not a Sunday watch.

No matter the time of day, I saw my great-grandmother exhibiting constant, unwavering faith and unconditional love for me and all those who crossed her path. I remember being first on her list to experience her adoration and love each morning. She constantly reminded me that she felt a radiant glow as she looked at me and held me like a bundle of joy. She was a warrior and the master of making something out of nothing with the *magic* of fifty dollars per month and a small, well-producing garden. Although she was a lady of few words, her presence was powerful as a ray of sunshine. She quietly radiated internal peace, positive energy, good vibes, and pure, quiet joy. Instead of being bitter that her most personal dreams and aspirations had been extinguished, she lived a life of playing the cards she was dealt. She made me feel that a bright future was out there for me and anyone who envisioned it and worked hard for it. Her success of making something out of nothing gave me ongoing encouragement and cheer.

To this day, it is hard for me to throw anything away because I was taught to find a use for everything. Now, I must embrace the thought of making my nothings into someone else's treasures by passing things on to others.

As a young child, I recognized that she stood her ground. She was very intelligent and resourceful. I saw her presence as a perfect reflection of a quiet, warm, and fresh summer day. We had an unyielding bond like no other that stretched on for miles, with no end ever seen in the distance. She lit up my world and did everything to steer me in the right direction toward a bright and energized future.

A great deal of the guidance for my conscience came from my great-grandmother's consistent discipline. Yes, I was *whipped* with thin peach tree limbs. Yes, sometimes they were braided together. But the constant thing was her being true to her word. She stated, "If you do ABC, I am going to do DEF." Believe me, she kept her word every time. I learned to measure the value of my fun against the pain I knew I would experience for disobeying her. I couldn't visit any of my school friends since they lived miles and miles away from me. Most of my pain came from disobeying her by extending my stay while playing with my friends who lived about three miles from us. As I watched the sun go down, I would clearly remember her saying, "You must be home before sundown, or else." Well, there were times that the fun was just so good, and I choose to stay longer than I should have. Just as promised and advertised, she would whip me. It was never a "beat down." It was punishment, as she knew it, and as she promised. But I could most definitely feel the tearing and burning from the thin, braided switch from the peach tree.

One of our small playgrounds was in old, junked cars in the yard of our neighbors, about three quarters of a mile away. We would sit in these old cars and pretend to be driving. We happily played games inside the cars, and they were frequently used as great hiding places for hide-and-seek. As you can see, our imagination made our limited resources fun and exciting.

It was not uncommon for grandparents to raise their grandchildren, nor was it common for great-grandparents to *commit* to this daunting task, especially if they had other options. My great-grandmother was over sixty-three years of age when I was born. She had raised her son. He was not a totally disappointing failure, but he was clearly not the outcome she had prayed for. She had also raised his five children (her grandchildren). During her golden years, she took on the responsibility of raising her first great-grandchild. Boy, that was bravery captured in a bottle!

I sometimes wondered why I didn't live with my mother, like my brothers did. During those times, I felt abandoned; but I was enjoying my freedom, roaming the plains and open fields, being a freethinker, and being loved so much by my great-grandmother. So, as frequently as that feeling came, it left. I did not entertain the thought very long. Unfortunately, those thoughts would intensely haunt me later in life. Once I matured, I sought professional help for the complex issues of my life. I never told my mother because I didn't want to hurt her feelings, but I feel I got the greatest bargain out of this complicated, yet loving and courageous decision made by my great-grandmother. Living with the blessing of her wisdom was a priceless gift. I would never suggest defying the natural order of parenting, but I strongly suggest we purposely look for the silver lining or bright side when these hidden blessings rain down into our lives.

Oh, I remember the times my great-grandmother would "let her hair down" and relax. A few of her friends would come over and they would all take a nip of whiskey. When this happened, it would not be long before her friends would leave, and she would fall asleep earlier than usual. I guess that is where I get my intolerance for alcohol today. I can't drink much because the next thing I will need is a pillow. If I drift off to sleep, that only meant I would miss all the fun and action. So, I choose to drink a lot of soda and a very little wine. That way, I can remember who did what to whom while we were out on the town.

More important than the friends she would occasionally take a nip of whiskey with, my great-grandmother had other friends within walking distance of our home (about a quarter mile away). Outside of school, her friends were my friends, too. Being around all these seasoned, wonderful friends, I learned things well beyond my years because I was listening and fully engaged. Just like they did, I put together many large jigsaw puzzles, watched a lot of old cowboy movies, listened to them talk about their youthful days of fun, nonsensible years, and predictions about my future. They predicted I would be tall and heavy (fat) since I had big knees. I was fascinated by their wisdom, resiliency, and ability to live their lives without bitter regrets. I didn't feel the least bit shy with them, making my world thought-provoking and wondrous. I was like a sponge, soaking up the wisdom their actions and conversation provided.

If only I could have engaged just as easily at school—there, I didn't have many friends. I'm sure that being extremely shy and introverted contributed to my limited circle of friends. I remember being bused fifteen miles from our home to the county school. I saw the school, including the students and teachers, as limitations on my autonomy and ability to run wild. I couldn't wait to get home to run wild with the sunflowers as they were swaying in the wind.

My teachers gave their best efforts to get me past my shyness. Overnights with the teachers in town, comments on my studiousness, and arranged socializing groups didn't help much. I remained a wallflower at school, but boy, when I got home… I would roam until I was exhausted!

Sometimes, my brothers and first cousins would come to visit at the same time. We would play with the kids who lived a quarter mile down the road. Their mother would leave them with their grand aunts for their summer vacations. When we all were together, we were several handfuls, and I don't know how those elderly ladies handled all of us. But it was extra special when just my brothers, Michael and Ronnie, would come to visit me on the weekends. I called them the "city boys." In reality, they lived in a small town, but *city* boys sounded much better than *town* boys. It was obvious they were green to the country life and would never master it. Michael was born in the country, but left with my mother when she traded the darkness of country life for the bright lights of life in the small town.

My brothers and I would go fishing, and I had to teach them to how to come home with a small tin tub of fish. Instead of using a fishing pole, we would find a pond that was drying up and grab the fish with our bare hands—an alternative form of fishing. Turtles were watching and enjoying the action of fearless or clueless kids handpicking the fish from the snake-filled waters that were only half a knee deep. None of us ever entertained the thought that the snakes were quietly eyeing us as easy prey. We would step over the gar fish that looked like a snake with skin like an alligator.

We would pick blackberries by inserting our hands into the thick, dark, thorny vines. Gloves weren't a part of our outdoor exploring tools. The thoughts of the delicious mouth-watering juice from the berries and an award-winning homemade blackberry pie made by my great-grandmother were more important to clueless kids than remembering that snakes and wild animals also loved berries as well as the tender flesh of young fools. It must be true that God protects fools and young children.

One of our favorite "theme park" experiences was climbing on top of the tin roof and sliding down into the front yard. The tin top roof had edges that could cut our bottoms into strips. Most of the time, we were masters at navigating these edges; but we still managed to get badges of honor (scars for life). These were the only "sliding boards" on the plains, and the radiant, hot sun beamed down on us as we slid. We would swing from tree limb to tree limb and thrashed through the pecan trees. You would have thought we were monkey-like humans. We had watched too many Tarzan movies. We didn't have sophisticated toys, like bikes, wagons, kites, or Ken and Barbie dolls; the paper cutout dolls were just too boring. My brothers wouldn't play with dolls, but they shared their marbles and jumped hopscotch and rope with me. We were greatly entertained by playing croquet and running and jumping around the Mayflower pole.

Once, one of my brothers was so bored that he peed on the electric wires that were a deterrence to keep the cows in the pasture. That was a jolting mistake! The charge of the liquid and electricity collision gave him a technical knockout (TKO). He recovered and found that the electricity had interrupted his perfect aim. As a result, he was soaking wet with urine. Interesting enough, he didn't complain about the jolt. His feelings were hurt because we would not play with him; he had been doused with an uncontrollable flow of pee from his waist to his toes. Only happy children would not understand the danger of an electrical shock.

When it came to sibling rivalry and fighting, it took both of my brothers to even consider calling the fighting moments a tie. Those city boys didn't stand a chance with their "skinny, but country-strong" sister.

My brothers and I ran our pet chicken, Dino, so hard until his tongue hung out and he fell dead. Dino was the most beautiful chicken we had ever seen. That is why he had earned the title of *pet*. Because food was limited, animals had to be very special to be considered pets. We just wanted to share our endless energy with him; we didn't know God had planned for us to be the cause of his last heartbeat. My great-grandmother saw what happened and waved her hand to call us home for a lesson that we never forgot. The lesson was: if you cause death to anything or anybody, there will be consequences to pay. Our sore behinds were clear reminders not to do that again.

One day when I was eleven years old, the freedom and fun on the country plains came to, what seem to me as a child, an abrupt end. My mother came and informed my great-grandmother that she had found us a house in town. She told me, "You and Mama are moving to town in a couple of weeks." It was in the winter and in the middle of the school year. I can only imagine what my great-grandmother was experiencing. She had to face the fact that she had reached a point in her life when she had to give up her freedom to walk the countryside, visit, and complete challenging puzzles with her long-time elderly friends. She had a lifetime of memories to package in her mind and come to grips with the fact that her life would no longer be filled with long, quiet and peaceful walks in the country. I could see her pain; but *I* was also having a hard time thinking of the adjustment I would have to make. I had lived the contrast between small town life and country life. I didn't ever want to let go of my world of roaming the plains and limitless frontier, but I had no choice.

We moved to town with the sounds of traffic all night long, and houses so close together that you could reach out and hold your neighbors' hand. There weren't any quiet places to roam and embrace your thoughts, let alone thinking of walking another open plain. We still had four rooms. But one was a bathroom, even though it was on the back porch and pretty much exposed to the winter elements. It was better than the country outhouse in the distance. Thank God for that.

My great-grandmother's brother was a surprise part of the move. I later discovered that his wife had kicked him out, and he didn't have anywhere to go. So, the next best thing was for him to move in with us as our protector. His wife might not have wanted him, but we loved him and were very glad to have someone protect us from strangers and bright lights. We both missed the familiar darkness and the thought of never meeting a stranger. My great-grandmother and my mother must have known that we were vulnerable—alone in the country. Crime and violence were getting closer and closer to us. It would have been only a matter of time before danger would have come, bringing overwhelming challenges to our doorsteps. The sad truth was that we would have been defenseless. I later learned that my mother and great-grandmother had discussed that the dangerous country environment was no match for a vulnerable elderly woman in her mid-seventies and a defenseless eleven-year-old child who lived alone in the abyss of the backwoods' darkness. Waging a war with broken windowpanes, locks on the doors (only for show), and a house that could surrender to a few sparks from the firewood or a match thrown by a stranger at any given moment, were odds that we would eventually have lost.

We moved into our house in town by the middle of January 1970. My great-grandmother was dead by March. Not only was it March, but her death was on Friday, the 13th. One day, I got home from school and was told that she went to the hospital because she was having heart problems. I remembered her frequently going to the doctor's office where the "for colored only" signs were front and center over the water fountains. The waiting rooms were separate with an even bigger "for colored only" sign inside. I never asked my great-grandmother about the meaning of those signs. I just remembered how she marched to the "for colored only" water fountains and waiting rooms with her head held high, very interested in soaking in all the information the doctor gave her to take care of herself. She never held her head low or portrayed herself as a lesser human being. So, as far as I could tell, those signs were a waste of time if they were meant to strip her of her dignity. I never felt that she was just content with society's defined place for her. It was just the opposite; she gave me the impression that society could label her, but she had a choice to accept or decline the label. She was living with an internal spirit that defied that label with every breath she took.

I could only imagine that the hospital in this new town had the same signs. I could not have imagined, however, that I would be told I could not see her because I was only eleven and a half years old, not twelve. If only my mother would have thought of telling the hospital staff that I was twelve. Maybe there was a valid reason for why she didn't tell them; maybe she felt the need to protect me and wondered, *how would this eleven-year-old girl handle this life-changing experience?* Well, I will never know. What I know for sure is that on the day of her funeral, I accidently fell onto a heater and branded myself for life. This constant reminder of that day could not have been any worse than saying goodbye at the hospital, even if I wouldn't understand the meaning of the loss until much later in my life.

The loss of my great-grandmother was bad enough, but when my mother looked into my eyes before the blood was cold in her body and said, "You have nowhere to go, so I am taking you home with me," it got even worse. I still cry when I remember that moment. That same night of her death, I moved in with my two brothers, my mother, and my stepfather. It was another house with four rooms. Again, the bathroom was on the back porch, but my stepfather would enclose the bathroom in hard plastic during the winter. I slept on a fold-out couch in the front room with my brothers, who slept together in a queen-sized bed. This room was both a bedroom and the living room.

During the day, we sat on the couch (my bed) and watched the one television we had. At night, we turned off the TV and eased into a quiet resting mode in the same one-room space.

The shining beacon of light in my life had gone out. I found myself in a state of pitch-black darkness. I remembered the character of the four o'clocks, dying into the ground, only to return year after year. This memory strengthened and sustained me, as I looked for my great-grandmother throughout the years. It still brings me comfort to have four o'clock blooms in my front yard every spring and summer and to have the seeds implant themselves in the soil and germinate, so they will return each year. It was interesting that when I bought my first home, four o'clock flowers came up that first summer, but never to be seen again. I took this as a spiritual message that my great-grandmother was saying, "I will follow you to the ends of the earth until we see each other again."

Many years later, I found a home that was supposed to be "handicapped equipped" to accommodate my mother's disabilities. In actuality, the house only had handicap *bars* in her bathroom, but I was so happy to see four o'clocks bloom that spring and summer and every year after we moved in. It comforts me to know that the four o'clocks came without me planting one seed. I am not willing to guess they appeared out of nowhere. I am happy to think I picked the right house to keep her memory alive. I admire them, yearly, with the comforting memory of my beloved great-grandmother, my North Star.

Chapter Six

PETUNIA:
A FLOWER OF A MIXED PRESENTATION

My North Star was gone. Being told that she would "live in my heart" was not good enough for me. My emotions began to spiral. Being wise beyond my years didn't offer me much help. I found myself processing my feelings about her death as a lost child. I chose the petunia to represent what I was experiencing.

> The symbolism of the petunia flower today dates back to the Victorian era. The blossoms were a symbol of Queen Victoria's abrupt outbursts of anger and irritation… Petunias symbolize anger and resentment probably because of how delicate and sensitive its flowers are to the cold weather and to the touch! The flowers symbolize two very important reminders. The first is a reminder that you should never give in to despair or sulking and the second is to always remember to keep your promise! (Cruz, 2021).

The more I read, the more this flower appeared to have mixed messages that fostered mixed feelings. Understanding exactly what it symbolizes became quite confusing. Coming from a medical background, I would say, "The petunia has a schizophrenic presentation."

This description of the petunia's history describes all the emotions I felt after the death of my great-grandmother: motherless, loveless, and an altered state of perception. In addition to those emotions, I was immobilized with uncertainty, resentment, and anger.

People tried to comfort me with soothing and calming thoughts and words. Though their acts of kindness and good intentions didn't go unnoticed, the effects were short-lived. The more they consoled me, the more I cried tears of anger. My anger stemmed from a feeling that my relationship with my great-grandmother had fostered the false hope that I would always be able to sink into her lap as my safe haven—my security blanket. Each morning when I woke up, I resented that the unspoken silent promise that she would never leave me was overcome by the truth and reality that she was gone. I would never be able to look into her eyes again to see my value or my worth. I began to question whether those qualities had left with her.

Questioning my value and worth was just the tip of the iceberg. I was so used to letting my thoughts have free range when it came to joy and happiness. I never dreamed of the challenge of having to deal with emotions of deep pain, sorrow, and finality. I quickly discovered that both joy and pain were on the highest and lowest ends of the spectrum, yet they were equal in many ways. I was angry with everyone in my life, but the biggest conflict was that I was angry with God. My great-grandmother had trusted Him, so I trusted Him. He became the main target for my *Why* questions. *How could He have allowed me to live such a fantasy and a lie?* Although the lie (in my head) was of my own making, it was no less real to me as an innocent child.

I believed that God would *never* take her from me. I believed that she had the power to stop Him.

With this thinking, I initially felt I could no longer trust my great-grandmother because she left me when I needed her the most. We were just getting acclimated to our new home and environment. Moving was tough, but we had each other, and we had a long history of getting through hell and high water together. She had made me feel that she would never do such an awful thing as leave me to fend for myself in the world. Once she was gone, I didn't see the need to trust God anymore. I certainly did not trust my new family. They were familiar people, but the trust ended there. *If I couldn't trust either God or my great-grandmother, who could I trust?*

The answer was no one.

I became more isolated and distrustful. I reverted to relying on my own knowledge and understanding. At age eleven, I had such a limited knowledge about life and less knowledge about death. I urge all parents and grandparents, for God's sake, please consider introducing your children, at an early age, to facts about death and dying. Preferably, teach them between the ages of three and five. I don't have children, but even *I* know these are the most precious years for their molding and learning. Yes, I saw the pet chicken die (I was even a part of his sudden death), and I saw my dogs die. I mourned them all, but *they* never promised me or made me feel they would never leave me. If the reward for living a God-spirited life is death, then we must learn to embrace the process of letting go at the time of death as naturally as we embrace the process of giving birth. Moving on with life without my great-grandmother was difficult for me.

I began my attendance at Myrtle Hall Elementary School when we moved to town. When I got there, my sixth-grade teacher had the smart idea of giving me the lead female role in the school play. She thought this would decrease my shyness and increase my engagement with my new classmates. She accomplished her goal of decreasing my shyness, but neither she nor I realized the unforeseen, long-lasting consequences. It was bad enough that my mother had found a way to dress me like a princess. I wore shiny, sweaty, toe-blistering, black patent leather shoes that were too small and matching skirts, blouses, vests and sweaters. I remember one day being dressed in all purple and looking like "royalty sitting on my throne" at my desk. This was not the era when you told your parents that your shoes hurt your feet. One reason was that as a kid, I thought if she took my shoes away, I would not get another pair. Going barefoot was a common theme, and definitely a theme I didn't want to bet against. My mother was now able to shop at the high-end boutiques in our hometown, nothing but the best for her little princess.

Desperate for my great-grandmother's love, I began having thoughts that I really didn't have a clue regarding whether these expensive clothes came with love or not. I started guessing that they were supposed to "bridge the gap" and replace my mother's love for me. In my mind, I was still a living memory of her unforgettable life-changing moment with my father. Dressing me as a princess had to be easier than showing deep love as she dealt with her deep pain of my existence. *Living together had to make me a constant reminder of her painful past.* There was no way of avoiding each other. We had to interact with each other practically every waking hour that I was not in school.

How could she afford such clothes? Even at that age, I thought love would have been cheaper. At the end of the day, it appeared she had learned to make something out of nothing like my great-grandmother. She would put expensive clothes on layaway and pay on them *forever*. My mother may have dressed me like royalty, but it didn't take my classmates long to start treating me like I was the poster child from the country and green behind the ears. In Mississippi, the name for someone like me was a "country bumpkin." So not only was I dressed like a princess, daily, but now I was the new girl who was given the lead role in the school play. This lead role landed me "smack dab" in the middle of childhood trouble. It was clear that I *could* benefit from a shy-busting opportunity; but *what had I done to earn the role?* Yes, I was studious and intelligent. So were so many other girls who had worked hard and waited a long time for the role. Now, I show up, and it was so obvious that I had done very little to earn the role. Many students wouldn't have given this opportunity a second thought; they would have accepted the role and moved on. At eleven, I was struggling with getting the lead role in the school play since I had done *nothing* to earn it.

An example of how I couldn't even speak up for myself was when I was asked to *clap* the notes in my music class. I did not have a clue. I was too afraid to tell the instructor I had never been in a music class. Therefore, I kept my mouth shut and took the paddling as if I should have known how to complete such tasks.

I was eleven, not eighteen. I eventually stop overthinking the situation. I settled down and accepted the role the teacher decided was perfect for me. Surprisingly, many of my fellow students thought I was a success in the play! But it was not so much the lead role that helped me with my shyness, it was learning to make friends that saved my ass. I became the "hated, but well-dressed princess" overnight. I managed to save myself from most of my overnight enemies, but a couple of them became lifelong enemies. I remember one girl and I ending up at the same college. She still resented me. It didn't help that I was friends with her boyfriend and knew he was going steady with someone else. This goes to show that good intentions, even when they come from smart adults, can also come with unintentional consequences.

Life just kept moving. My great-grandmother had been gone for three months. I had starred in the school play at my new school. Winter and spring had opened up to summer. I was getting more familiar with my now-permanent, new "family in tow." By then, I was twelve and still missing my great-grandmother profoundly. I was having frequent crying spells and distancing myself from the rest of my family. Not only had the joy of feeling free not returned, but I also wasn't sleeping or eating well either. Perhaps, it was the guilt of not telling me that my great-grandmother would leave me someday or not letting me say goodbye to her that prompted key members of my family to come up with the idea that I should spend the summer with my Aunt Jannie in faraway Denver, Colorado. I really didn't know what life outside of Mississippi, St. Louis, Missouri, or Chicago, Illinois, had to offer. Therefore, I found myself being just a bit skeptical about their idea.

The skepticism of the idea of spending the summer in Denver, Colorado, went away when I arrived. I immediately saw the beautiful skyline. There were no chickens in the backyard or dark rooms in the house. There were open fields to roam in short distances, along with beaming bright city lights. This was a big city with an open country feel. I had arrived in heaven outside of the Mississippi state lines. Amazingly, I got the strange feeling that this was where I wanted to live when I grew up.

The feeling that I would like to live in Denver when I grew up fueled my excitement at looking forward to coming back almost every summer. It was there that I had my first job outside of school. My cousins and I worked at the Dolly Madison Ice Cream shop. We ate so much ice cream that we felt like we were carrying around the weight of Dolly Madison herself.

One summer, I got an upgraded job working in a GI Clinic at Fitzsimmons Hospital. Watching GI procedures such as colonoscopies, sigmoidoscopies, etc., was not enough for me—I volunteered to see an autopsy being performed. The doctor made a vertical cut mid chest, then a horizontal cut in the middle of the person's stomach. When he pulled the skin back, I fainted. I just knew, if medicine was going to be a part of my future career path, I would have to work on staying upright instead of passing out at the site of blood and guts. I had thoughts (even then) that I could have saved my great-grandmother if I had been a nurse or a doctor. *Thank God, I didn't have to wait for the odor from my shoes to wake me up.* Boy, I had come a long way. I was working in a big city, and they were using *real* ammonia to wake fainting victims up.

My grief and loss were still deep, but I had found a place to roam as a free spirit and prosper. I no longer had to swing from tree limbs to tree limbs or slide on the roof of tin-top houses. I was riding roller coasters and rock climbing at Elitch Gardens Theme & Water Park, a Six Flags amusement park. During my vacations, the rides at the amusement park were great, and I was inching… somewhat moving out of my shell of shyness. I continued to have problems fitting in and engaging with people, even with my family members.

One day, I got mad about something and started pouting. I decided to hide out in an old washing machine. The agitator had been removed. It looked as if the machine was waiting to be taken to the trash, but I crawled into it, anyway. It helped that I was very thin, and therefore, could easily get into it. My plan was to stay in the washing machine until I was missed long enough for someone to come looking for me. Well, I closed my eyes and waited and waited. Approximately one hour passed. No one came. I finally struggled to get out of the washing machine. It was a lot easier to get into it than it was to get out of it. It was at that moment of my struggling that I realized I had to learn to "get in where I fit in." I also learned that shyness and not speaking up for what I believed in was not helping me to express my deep passions, communicate with, or help other people.

My interpretation of that learning moment was that I had an obligation to navigate my path within my family. It was not their fault if I missed the fun because I made a conscious decision to "leave the party." What a lesson for a twelve-year-old to learn! But that moment of a lesson learned stayed with me for the rest of my life. I felt as if my life was taking on an alternate perception. In reality, I was being introduced to the emotional extensions of life.

I found hope for another way of life outside of Mississippi in Denver, Colorado. It was the big city with small-town country hospitality and generosity. When I returned home, my next milestone was to continue my public education at Clarksdale Junior High. I had started adjusting fairly well to my new family environment, but I was still shy in the company of strangers.

Junior high school had many valuable lessons that were also aligned with good intentions and unintentional consequences. It was our first year of school desegregation and integration. The parents of the Caucasian students worked three jobs, if they needed to, to put their kids in private school and keep them from going to school with African American children. My most disappointing memory about inequality during this time was that with all the effort from the federal government to integrate the schools, my school ended up with only two Caucasian students. As I write, my computer just reminded me that the word

Caucasian automatically capitalized itself. What a statement of superiority, even by Webster's definition. We must thank Mr. Webster for that. *Sorry for the deviation from my story; but I found that to be very important as I write this chapter.*

Getting back to the story... CF and PP were the two Caucasians students. PP was once thought to be the forgotten cousin of Elvis Presley. I remember thinking it was obviously a mistake or blind justice for the two Caucasian students. It made me feel that justice needed to remove the blindfolds and see through the lens of humanity to right this wrong. The thought of them going to school in an environment that was so unbalanced with racial or ethnic representation was so unfair. They had to attend a public, predominately African American school because they were too poor to attend the private school (we only had one). We had "being poor" in common. I felt we must have some other things in common, too. Looking for those things prompted me to befriend both students. I wanted to welcome them and let them know that some of us saw them as equal human beings. I valued their walk of life, their opinions, and their freedom to live their truth among so many minority students. Instead of having a mindset of superiority because we outnumbered them, I lived on the high road of equality, as I had been taught. Now, thinking back on this phase of my life, I guess I was beginning to yearn to do my part to correct injustice, no matter how small my contributions would seem.

To this day, when I see CF working at our local, hometown convenience store, I take the time to say, "Hello." I still take pride in the fact that I wanted to do my part (if only so small) to shelter them from acts of racial injustices. I wanted them to have the opportunity to focus on pursuing an education instead of having to be bombarded with fear and harassment. For sure, the opportunities were less than those they would have had if they had been able to attend the private school. But they both were equally appreciated and respected by *me* in that environment. I went on to keep "shooting for the stars" of equality at school and at home. I also went on to star in other school plays, but mostly, I remained in my shy shell. It would be a long time before the end of my shyness would come to pass.

Initially, as I wrote this chapter, I was beginning to see that I had a footprint to make; I had to find a way to make a difference in the lives of others, especially the underserved and those impacted by gross injustice. I wished I would have asked them how they felt about their school experience. I thought it would have been great to share their perspective of their personal experiences with you, as readers of my book. As mentioned, I had crossed paths with CF, but I had no idea what happened to PP.

My commitment to shooting for the stars continued as another *What if* or *Why* question came to me. *What if I would stop guessing what happened to my endeared classmates? What if I reached out to CF and PP and asked them to share their memories of their experience at school?* This would also create an opportunity to ask if they would mind sharing their perspective with my readers. I had to turn over a few rocks and lift a few stones to find them. The turning and lifting paid off—I found both of them. When I asked to speak to CF, I heard the person who answered the telephone say, "Okay, let me get him." My heart started beating faster. What if she comes back and says that she was mistaken, and he is actually not there?

When he said, "Hello," I immediately recognized his quiet, somewhat high-pitched voice. I then had to frame my reason for calling him. I told him about my writing a book which included the theme of equality. I set the stage about how I felt about integration during that era. I gave him permission to tell me that he didn't want to talk to me at all or that he just wanted to forget about those days. He graciously said he was comfortable talking to me. So, I just proceeded to ask him questions:

What was your experience like during those times?

Were you ever afraid?

Were you bullied?

What was your reason for attending Clarksdale Junior High (CJH)?

His responses were somewhat surprising, yet they were also uplifting. He stated that he had no choice but to play the hand that he was dealt. That meant that he *had* to attend CJH. He confirmed that his parents were poor and couldn't afford to send him to the private school. I tried to level the playing field and informed him that my parents were also too poor for me to attend the private school. We *did* come to an agreement that I would not have been able to attend the private school even if my parents *would* have been able to afford it. First, he said that his strategy was to try to get along with everyone, hoping that he would never have a problem. He went on to say that he was never afraid while attending CJH. As the conversation continued, he stated that a fellow student got smart with him one day (bullied him). The teachers got word of it. They stepped up and disciplined the student. It was encouraging to hear him say that after the student was properly disciplined, he never experienced another bullying episode.

We went on to briefly discuss how these (current) days, minority students are now attending what was still our one and only private school. Many of the parents, grandparents, and students who were denied the opportunity to attend the private school are now taking advantage of attending events at the school to see what they missed and what it feels like to walk on the sidewalks and get into the doors you were once forbidden to walk through. I am looking forward to the day when I can seize this opportunity and have that experience.

Today, we both are retired and happy that race relations have inched forward to this point. We both agreed that Mississippi still has a way to go to be the champion of race relations. I was especially inspired by the fact that the teachers of CJH rose to the occasion and protected PP and CF. Even though I was shy back then, I was bold enough to stand up for others and model how to treat those who were different and didn't look like you with dignity and respect.

The persistent and determined person I am didn't stop there. I got on Facebook and found PP. She remembered me. She went as far as to call me, "the quiet and smart one." She also agreed to have lunch with me if we were ever in our hometown at the same time. Unfortunately, when I asked to interview her about her feelings related to the beginning of desegregation, she gracefully, yet firmly, declined. With the utmost respect, I accepted her decision to decline.

Although my struggle to survive the death of my great-grandmother was tough, the more I matured, the more I learned to process my *schizophrenic-like* emotions. I learned that many of them were normal for my age. I also learned that I was still thinking beyond my years. Most of all, it dawned on me that my great-grandmother was not preparing the road for me; she was preparing *me* for the road. Her plan may have been well thought out or carefully designed. It was, most likely, by default that it had been crafted by her and our ancestors before her own struggle to survive with only a few, yet harsh, options. Elementary and junior high school helped me progress toward coming out of my shell to make friends and start my discovery of fighting injustice. It had taken a long time for me to emerge from my shell. These days, I have a very hard time convincing those around me that I was once shy.

Now, I am working on how I view the role that God played in the timely death (according to Him) of my great-grandmother. The depth of the pain I felt after the loss of my great-grandmother is only a testimony of how deep she touched my heart and soul. I must admit, I am so grateful for the time she was in my life. Her presence shaped the solid foundation of my life. It also makes me the luckiest great-granddaughter in the world.

Chapter Seven

CANDYTUFT:
A FLOWER OF INDIFFERENCE, EVEN IN DEATH

Thus far, my life had withstood the crossroads of facing the reality of my conception, the discovery of my biological father, and coming to grips with the baffling trauma of the death of my great-grandmother. By now, I had also cocooned my way through elementary school and the desegregation of my junior high school. The next phase of my life dealt with how I really felt about my father. From my point of view, he had burst into my life with the intent of making up for lost time. Or maybe he just needed a chance to tell his side of the story. From where I was standing, it didn't matter what he wanted. Although I was still a child, I believed I should have been asked how I viewed his self-imposed role in my life. No one bothered to asked for my input.

I have chosen the Candytuft flower to represent my feeling concerning this blindsiding period of my life.

A Candytuft flower has nothing to do with candy, nor does it symbolize beauty or lack of it, love or hate, not even sweetness or bitterness.

In the language of flowers, candytufts carry the symbolic meaning of vitality and a zest for life which are thought to originate plant's Iberian roots. Some plant enthusiasts associate the flower with beauty, joy, and sweetness. Conversely, the candytuft (iberis) can signify indifference. (Petal Republic Team, 2022).

As a teenager, my life didn't skip a beat. I kept doing all the things that young adults do. Later in life, I found myself numb to my feelings concerning my father. I realized that in order to become healthy, the numbness I felt for my father had to be processed sooner or later. Since this was not a common emotion, I didn't understand it at the age of sixteen. Back then, my term for it was *nonchalant;* I just didn't have time to worry about it. Today, as a mature adult, I describe those feelings as *indifference*. This is the perfect word to describe what I felt then and what I feel today. This emotion evolved to play a significant purpose in shaping my future connection with my father.

I had to learn that contrary to what most of us believe, indifference did not mean that I was cold and calculated. Just the opposite, it meant I had to go deep into my inner self and find a warm way to identify the true meaning and value of this emotion as it related to making me whole. Most important, I had to step outside of my comfort zone and let myself own the feelings that came with this confusing and heavy challenge. I stood steadfast and made a conscious effort to process my emotions as I felt them as they flooded my thoughts. This meant I had to embrace instead of avoid the uncertainty and make peace with my true feelings. I didn't know then, but facing this unpopular emotion would yield a healthier *me* for years to come.

As I contemplated this confusing and serious stage of my life, this became the hardest chapter for me to write so far. It is difficult enough to find an equally valued thread of life in the myriad feelings of love, hate, joy, and pain. Then the question became, "What do I do when the less identified emotion of indifference enters the equation?" I had to process this emotion based on the values I had applied to the experiences of my life. I came to realize that I had to live a "true to myself" life and shape my deepest truths as I matured. Dealing with such insightful emotions while young was both a blessing and a curse. I was forced to adapt to a wider range of emotions and face more intense realities than the average child. Most children my age were dealing with issues such as getting homework done, making friends, etc.

I don't know how I survived those emotionally tough years. Being very young perhaps made the situation easier in a way. I didn't understand exactly what was happening to me, as I dealt with a wide range of emotions; I just knew these emotions existed. To feel and express what I felt and not fake a minute of it was rewarding for me. Understanding the positive meaning of the emotion *indifference* brought me a sense of peace.

The peace that came with my owning my feelings of indifference regarding my father served me well during my visit to Santa Barbara, California. Once I arrived, I began to explore the Mississippi-looking homes. Let me make myself clear: these homes were lovely and housed great, loving family members. Through the lens of an adventurous sixteen-year-old girl, though, they just didn't fit the cover image of the *Southern Living* magazine.

It wasn't long before my uncle and I began to venture out. He was not twenty-one yet, so he couldn't hang with his older brothers as they lived the exciting nightlife. This made him the chosen one to show me the wonders of California. We started traveling to many places along the California coastline. I was so excited because I noticed things I had never seen before. My eyes were in awe of the beaches, rolling hills, houses on mountain foothills, multiple lane highways, and the Hollywood Sign off in the distance. I enjoyed being at my paternal grandmother's house. She was very attentive, just as I had remembered her being during her Mississippi visits. The food and the company were great, but it was not enough to keep me from longing for my great-grandmother, who had raised me.

The love from my paternal grandmother was no less precious; it was just different. The Santa Barbara home was not only restricted in roaming space just because they lived in a metropolitan city, but the home environment fit right in with the rule for a child to be *seen* in controlled spaces and not be *heard* for their opinion in any place. My love and respect for my paternal grandmother's home was genuine, but I felt like my feelings and what I thought didn't matter much since I was a child. This culture was not unique to her home; it was mostly universal for the Southern culture. After a few days there, it was time for me to continue to soak in the wonders of Southern California, but in the place that was the actual reason for my visit.

I had come to California, committed to the dream of spending the summer with my father and his happy family. That happy family included his gracious wife and five happy children. Off I went to live with my extended family in San Luis Obispo. When I arrived, everyone was cordial, but only one of my half-siblings jumped at the opportunity to welcome me with arms wide open. I got the feeling that no one had asked them how they felt about a stranger joining their household. I remember my two half-brothers and one of my half-sisters moving on to do their own thing without a second thought that I existed. Saying, "Hello" was the end of the line for getting to know me. It appeared that saying, "Goodbye" could not come fast enough for them.

The one humane moment came when the half-sister, who was two months younger than me, embraced me and told me that she had been waiting a long time to meet me. Soon after unpacking my clothes, she told me that she and our father were very close. He had told her, a long time ago, that I existed. Listening to her echo the stories he had told *me* confirmed that she was not in the dark about my existence. I hated to break the news to her that the only part of his version I believed was that I existed in the flesh. But I couldn't help but drop the bomb that I had long thought our father had raped my mother. Remember, I was a sixteen-year-old teenager, and I didn't have any evidence of this bold accusation. I just could not see my fifteen-year-old mother seeking to be in the company of a mature man with a pregnant wife and child under normal circumstances. I repeat, my mother *had* to have felt pressured. I was sure that my father was out of my mother's league for a suitable lifetime companion for those aforementioned reasons. Because I was so convincing, I don't remember my half-sister attempting to debate my lackluster and unproven position.

My father and his wife would make it a point for me to see them happily go to bed, only for me to wake up in the middle of the night and observe my father on the couch alone. He would be so sound asleep that my observations remained an unshared secret. Even a sixteen-year-old could smell a dirty rat (one plus one was not adding up to be a happy twosome). Surprisingly, my half-sister continued to work on being an engaged friend to me. Her friendship was appreciated, but it was not enough to make me comfortable in what I perceived to be a deceptive home. I was fascinated with the lemon, peach, and orange trees in his backyard in San Luis Obispo, California. But that was not enough to keep me from feeling lost and out of place. There was no way to sugarcoat the situation. Sadly, *this* arrangement was not working for me either. It seemed I was on a roll, looking for a place to spend the summer in the majestic sunsets of California.

I stepped up to my father and his wife and requested to go back to my paternal grandmother's house. Remember, I had just left there less than a week ago because I didn't feel at ease there, but back I went. When I returned to my paternal grandmother's house, I had to break the news to them that I was not comfortable living at my father's house, and I wanted to go home to my mother. My step-grandfather weighed in on my request, and the fireworks started flying like those long ago, red-hot wooden sparks back in the old raggedy house that I lived in! I was up against an adult in a household where children didn't have any rights, surely not the right to declare what they wanted. My mother's brother happened to be there at the house and began to look nervous as he witnessed this one-sided discussion. My argument was that I was not happy, and I wanted to go home as soon as possible. Although my uncle didn't have the DNA test to prove that my father was authentic, the one thing he knew for sure was that I had my *mother's* genes. He knew that even though I was the underdog in this child-adult debate; it was not a good idea to bet against me. My uncle quietly pulled my father aside and asked him for a meeting in the next room.

When they returned from the decision-making chambers, it was clear that my uncle had convinced my father that things could possibly go from bad to worse if they didn't grant my request and get me out of their town ASAP. The expression on the face of my step-grandfather appeared to me that he didn't take the defeat kindly. It wasn't so much that I was getting my request to go home. I am sure he couldn't wait for me to be gone *bye-bye*. It was the idea that a teenager had stood up and firmly voiced her opinion. I had been heard and my request was being granted. In this household, he ruled with an iron fist, and no visiting teenager was going to control his kingdom.

I added more fuel and sparks to the fire when I boldly stated, "And I am *not* going back on that three-day Greyhound bus." I was taught not to disrespect my elders; therefore, to disrespect my step-grandfather or his home was not my intention. But no matter how good their efforts at hospitality were, I felt restricted and caged like a wild animal. I don't think it was anyone's fault. It was just that I was not used to being unable to roam and respectfully speak freely. Well, needless to say, I was on my first airplane trip out of LAX the next morning. My monopoly analogy for this was, "Go past everything. Get out of jail, and go straight home." No one wanted to deal with my mother's personality, even though she was almost two thousand miles away. Although young, I showed confirmation that I was my mother's daughter and a tiny force to be respectably reckoned with. Now, even my father's family knew there was an intentional, yet respectable voice underneath my shy and quiet exterior. I am sure that me no longer being in my step-grandfather's home was enough for him. I am also sure that with genuine love for me, he was still able to say, "good riddance," and wished me well. Looking back, I can't blame him. What else could I expect when two generations of values and cultures have different points of view?

After my experience in California, I can remember speaking to my father on only a couple of occasions. If I spoke to him more, I guess the conversations just were not memorable. I remember him telling me that while he was living in San Luis Valley, Colorado; he drove to my house, and I would not open the door to let him in. I could not, for the sake of saving my soul, convince him that I had been out of town. I think I would have answered the door if I would have been there. I was never afraid of him or closed-minded about what he had to say. It was clear for the most part, I never understood what he was saying and how it related to me. We both had our ways of expressing ourselves and those ways appeared to be on the opposite end of the spectrum—perhaps they were just different spectrums.

Speaking of different spectrums, I also remember, when I was in my first year of nursing school, he called with a "granddaddy of them all" idea. He flat out informed me that he wanted to adopt me. While listening to him, there seemed to be no room for discussion. Mind you, by this time, I was a young adult in my early twenties. I asked him to repeat his request, just to make sure my Mississippi, country-girl ears heard him correctly. Once I confirmed his repeated words were the same, I emphatically, with no room for discussion, told him, "Thanks, but NO thanks." My explanation consisted of the fact that giving up the Henderson name would be disrespectful to the lady who had been my mother, father, and everything in between. I had lived with an illegitimate name long enough that I *now* knew it was the only damn legitimate name I would ever claim. I recall thinking, *If I get married, I will hyphenate my name no matter how long of a name I would have to live with.*

I didn't know his motivation for wanting to adopt me and change my name. I really did not care. Perhaps he was trying to deal with the guilt of not being around for my childhood years. The other thought was that maybe he thought one day I might make something of my life, and he wanted to share the credit. Whatever the reason, Henderson is my name and no one, especially a lost and self-proclaimed *found* father, will ever take it away from me. I was not angry with him for thinking that legitimacy was more powerful than the heritage of the greatest love I had ever known. *How could I have anger for someone whose highest level of emotion in my life was indifference—sometimes known as neutrality?* I just wanted to use the energy of the emotions in my life on people who had invested and left their footprints on my remarkable growth and development. That concept was a no-brainer seared into the fabric of my being. He was just *not* one of those people.

He had done the honorable thing and married the mother of his five children. What a bad place to be—where you had to choose between two families. If I had to choose, I would vote for ruining the life of *one* outside child instead of the lives of *five* children who would have the chance to become close friends and emotional support each other. Please don't forget, my mother aided his decision by completely taking herself out of the equation for the possibility of marriage. In this case, I couldn't speak for my half-brothers and half-sisters, but I felt that I greatly benefited from my mother and father separately making the decision many years ago to move forward and not look back for each other.

The goodbyes between my father and mother helped them to move forward and embark upon their futures. Sometimes, goodbyes are temporary, as if to say, "Goodbye for now." As for me, on those occasions, I would rather say, "I will see you later." But with my father, I was comfortable saying, "Goodbye," when I left Santa Barbara, California. I felt that if I saw him again, I would deal with it. If I never saw him again, I would not carry the burden of guilt. No one has a blueprint to navigate their family dynamics, but surely a teenager should not have to deal with such heavily emotional adult tasks. It was the steadfast wisdom from my maternal great-grandmother from which I had learned to cope with skills that made me wise beyond my years.

Being wise beyond my years held me together later, when I had to deal with other issues related to my father. In 1995, I was informed that he was sick and was being taken care of by my half-sister in Tucson, Arizona. Approximately two weeks later, I was at a conference in Washington, DC. When I came back to my hotel room from all-day meetings, my roommate was very distraught as she approached me. She told me that she had some bad news, and she stated that she had received a call from my paternal grandmother. She continued by saying, "I'm sorry to have to tell you that your father has died."

With a straight face, I thanked her for the message. I didn't show any emotion as I sat down. Sitting turned out to be the best vantage point for me to see the television show I proceeded to watch. I was still on a neutral playing field when it came to my feelings regarding him. I had long ago promised myself that I would not lie to myself by faking my feelings. The question at hand for me became, *are you going to the funeral to pay your last respects?* After an honest internal discussion with myself, I decided to go, not so much to pay respects to him, but to be in the mix of my paternal family. I thought I could benefit from being around the family memories to see if I would regret that I had not made more of an effort to forge a meaningful relationship beyond the level of neutrality or indifference.

After his death, it was discovered that he had a fifty-thousand-dollar life insurance policy. I was told he had held a decent job at Hughes Aircraft Company. That landed on my conscious as a note of respect. My grandmother called to ask me if I received my share of the fifty thousand. I informed her that I had not. I respectfully told her that if he had wanted me to have a share of it, my name would have been on the policy. If I didn't already know how my half-brothers and half-sisters felt about me, it was clear when money arrived on the scene. Legally, the fifty thousand dollars was split five ways instead of six. Once again, that was confirmation enough that I was truly a victim of mother's *baby* and daddy's *maybe*. To say the least, my mother was angry and wanted to come to my defense. But I was not angry—not in the least little bit. I didn't feel like I should make a big deal about money from a person who chose to leave me out of the money-splitting equation and for whom I was so indifferent toward regarding the amount of energy I wanted to give him while he was alive. I had nothing more or nothing less to give after his death. I knew the value of eight thousand, three hundred thirty-three dollars and thirty-three cents. It was not enough for me to fight over.

Perhaps there was another reason, though. There was talk that he had two other sons who were seen as another reason for him to spread his wings, proudly, as the male peacocks ritually did. Needless to say, they had been left out of the fifty-thousand-dollar windfall as well. That would have made the monetary windfall take a dive to six thousand, two hundred and fifty dollars. When it comes to money, people, in general (especially Black people), do not seem to have anything to do with a fair and equal kind of logic. Anyhow, I was blessed. I was taught that doing the right thing would often be trampled over by the power and evil of doing the *not-so-right* thing. I say not so right because who am I to judge what would have been the right thing to do in this situation? I just hold stronger and stronger to my belief that God blesses the child that has his or her own.

I went to his funeral; I was taken aback because I had only known cremation to mean that one's body had already been burned into ashes and placed in an urn. Therefore, I was not expecting to see him lying in a casket. (I didn't realize cremation would occur after the funeral.) Needless to say, when I saw him lying there, I was not prepared. I didn't think I had to have any words prepared to speak to an urn, but I found myself searching for final words to speak or internally contemplate about speaking to a dead man lying in a casket. My mental search didn't uncover any additional words to say or thoughts to consider. My bonding with him was profoundly a done deal. Sadly, I *did* benefit from learning that one of his sons did not attend the funeral.

As my half-brothers and half-sisters spoke, it resonated with me that he was a complex and complicated man. He had left them confused about him and about the road they had to travel—built on the relationships they had shared with him. Some things they said appeared to be very raw and not so kind. For example, one stated that he was not the best father, and they were not sure if they would miss him. It was obvious they were struggling with very painful and raw emotions. These emotions appeared to be dangerous lines between love and hate. My heart went out to them, but it appeared I was finding more comfort and peace in the neutral/indifference zone than they were finding in the love and hate relationships they seemed to have with him. Their regrets of the finality of this moment came front and center as they spoke their truth. Some would have found this shocking, but I saw it as their story and their truth.

I didn't take any happiness or pleasure from what I observed. I just felt, once again, how lucky I was to have grown up far, far, away from those witnessed cries for peace caused by so much internal conflict. Being among my paternal family members also increased my knowledge of the fact that my father had suffered from an untreated mental illness known as, "bipolar disease," mostly with depressive episodes. Based on my history in healthcare, that diagnosis explained a great deal. In African American communities, treatment for medical problems was a hard topic to discuss and treatment for mental illness (most of the time) was totally ignored, and therefore, not discussed. The stigma of mental health during his lifetime was one thing, but the money to afford treatment was another issue and perhaps not an option for him. Suddenly, I understood much of his behavior.

I didn't regret not knowing his mental health status sooner. *What would I have done with that information?* I didn't feel we had the type of relationship that a presentation on mental health treatment would have changed, either the dynamics or the outcome of his life. I am at peace with my limited relationship with my father. I don't think it was meant for our relationship to begin or end on a different trajectory. Sometimes, indifference or neutrality is all the reality you get. You have to take reality as a fact— sometimes things are what they are and not what you wish or want them to be. God bless his soul and may his soul rest in peace.

I am most definitely at peace with my feelings about the tapestry threads of this period of my life. I learned that the Candytuft flower also symbolizes having a voice to stand tall and speak your truth, even while understanding that there is no hope of reconciliation after death.

Chapter Eight

VERBENA:
FLOWER FOR PROTECTION FROM HARM AND EVIL

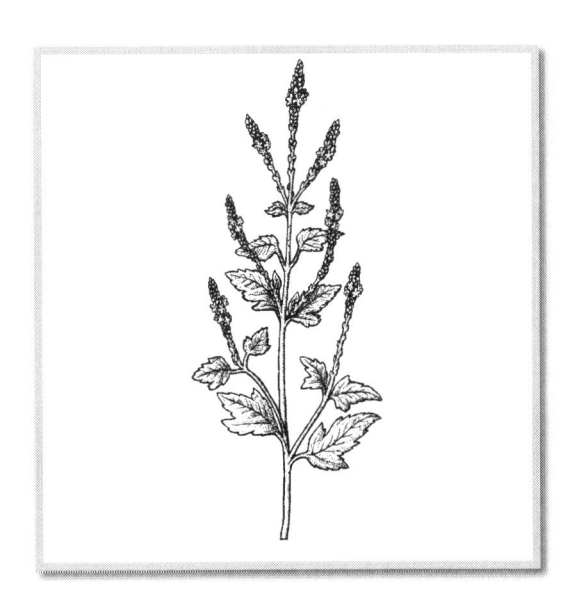

I have come to believe that innocence is a virtue owed to a child. When someone violates a child's innocence, I view it as a cardinal sin. The Verbena is a plentiful southern flower known for keeping people safe from danger and wickedness and expelling evil spirits.

> They [Verbena] are also said to provide protection from danger and evil... A verbena flower meaning is tied to safety, healing, creativity, and joy... The verbena flower tells us that no matter what life throws at us, we have the capability to heal from them on our own. (Forbes, 2022).

It would make sense that this flower represents the part of my journey when I needed protection against harm and evil.

This flower is known to be plentiful in the South. Yet, I do not recall any obvious presence of this flowering plant on the open plains I roamed. I find this very ironic because if there were ever a time that a flower that symbolized protection was needed, it would have been as I navigated my path of innocence. Being surrounded by this flower would have been especially helpful for me (a helpless, defenseless, and innocent young girl). Perhaps the thought that the absence of this flower symbolized the rationalization that some adults used to violate innocent, young children is a bit far-fetched, but if the power of this flower holds true, one cannot help but cling to any hope of protection for the young and defenseless. I was no exception; I needed to be protected.

Some would say I was lucky because I was only molested. Well, who really knows the difference in the emotional scars left by molestation versus those of penetrated rape? In many cases, they are emotionally viewed as the same. I was sexually assaulted and touched in my private areas, but I was never penetrated. Both traumatic acts of sexual violence will send you to a psychiatrist if you are lucky or brave enough to believe in their value. These heinous acts usually leave the victims wondering what *they* did to cause this to happen to them, while the perpetrators are protected with another cardinal sin (silence). These sickening behaviors also lead to social judgments and difficult family discussions (*if* you have a supportive family), or the absence of family discussions if the lines of communication are unopened or broken.

I don't know many African American families who are open-minded enough for young girls to feel comfortable enough to call their mothers into a private conversation about sex, let alone put this particular issue front and center on the kitchen table. If you feel that you "got this" (pertaining to this type of emotional trauma), I beg you to reconsider and reach out for professional help. It can save your life by offering you emotional healing, as well as a greater chance for healthier relationships in the future. Yes, you have to do the work. Yes, the work is hard. But, girls, it is so worth it.

The first time I experienced such behavior was at the age of six. My grandfather was a drinking-most-of-the-time alcoholic. When he was sober, he was very kind and respectful. However, he was not exempt from outrageous behavior while under the influence of alcohol. One day, he came to our house. I could see him moving slowly and erratically in the car as the car came to a stop. It was taking him longer than usual to get out of the car. So, being the little six-year-old that I was, I rushed to his car. Without hesitation, I opened the door and jumped into the back seat. He spoke what I now know to be *alcoholic* talk, and I spoke *six-year-old* talk. Needless to say, we did not understand each other. I remember him slipping his hand under my little baby doll dress. Even though we didn't understand our incompatible conversation, what I suddenly understood was that something was wrong. *What was wrong?* I did not know, but just as fast as I ran to get into the back seat of the car with him, I ran even faster to get away from him. Although I was only six years old, I can remember my emotions being off the chart! How was a six-year-old supposed to handle such ambivalent feelings? I wanted to reach out to him for love and run away from him for safety… all at the same moment.

Of course, I didn't share those dreadful moments with a soul. I wanted the memory of them to go away forever. What a heavy burden for a six-year-old! I did, however, address this later in psychotherapy. I was also able to share it with my aunt (his daughter) many years later. She didn't express how she felt, but I felt free of guilt that I had somehow done one single thing to cause or facilitate his actions. In therapy, I also learned the lesson of loving him, but hating his alcoholic behavior. He and I never spoke of this, not even as adults. What would have been the point? Many alcoholics don't remember what happened when they are not drinking. It would have been foolish for me to expect him to remember how he behaved while he was under the influence of alcohol.

At the age of six, I was clueless about sexual behavior. I surely didn't understand downright sexual abuse. Again, at the age of nine, I fell victim to another adult who crossed the line. My great-grandmother remarried once. I believe it was only to have someone help her take care of her five grandchildren. A few days after she got married, her new husband assumed his innate rights and immediately attempted to take over the household. Boy, that did not go well. It went so badly that she sent him packing, never used his last name, and did not acknowledge their marriage personally or publicly.

The person she married was still living on the same plantation where we lived. He was in the circle of elderly people who I talked to in order to fill the gaps of boredom. One day, I was bored and wanted to help someone. I had the great idea to go over to Mr. Miles' house (my great-grandmother's ex-husband) and help him clean up. I didn't understand the clutter in his home. Our house was raggedy, but it was clean—spic and span. The front porch was frequently scrubbed and bleached with Clorox. We did not have roaches or other bugs like I would see at a lot of other homes I visited. These critters were very common in houses with children and folks having no clear focus on keeping the kitchen clean. Flies didn't come through our back screen door, even though it had plenty of holes for easy access. It was obvious they did not like the smell of bleach.

I felt that Mr. Miles could use some help. Everyone could see he had physical challenges, especially difficulty with the flexibility of his hands; they were afflicted with rheumatoid arthritis. Because his environment was very different from the house I lived in and he was disabled, I thought I was just the one to help him. With my little red plastic water bucket in hand, I cheerfully headed to his house. I happily whistled in the wind as I skipped along the way. He gladly accepted my bright Good Samaritan idea and welcomed me as he had done many times before. However, this time was different because I didn't usually enter his home. Before that day, I would sit on his front porch or on the steps to the house. We would sit there and talk, mostly about the weather, what I was learning in school, and about how life was for him in his good old days. Strangely enough, he never mentioned his union with my great-grandmother. That day, I innocently entered the front room. Like most houses in the area, his bedroom and living room shared the same space. When I began to clean, he grabbed me around my waist from behind. No one had warned me of finding myself in such a situation. Who would have thought that a nine-year-old reaching out to help someone out of the goodness of her heart would be met with such horror?

When he touched me, internal alarm bells of horror went off. The signs of danger were flashing in my head. Thank God, he had rheumatoid arthritis, which left him with deformed, partially closed fingers that prohibited him from getting a firm grip. As he grabbed me, I went under his arms and ran for my life like a wild jackrabbit. I was running as fast as the one I had remembered chasing while roaming the open plains. Like I had no chance of catching the white cottontail jackrabbit, he had no chance of catching me. It did help, of course, that he was in his seventies, and I was nine.

After running like a jackrabbit, I was panting and totally out of breath with my tongue hanging out when I got home. I didn't truly understand the essence of what had just taken place. But all the red danger flags were still waving in my head. I kept thinking; *I was just trying to help him. What could he have been thinking?* I just knew his touch felt wrong, and I did not want any part of his firm grip. Again, I never told anyone, not even my great-grandmother.

I didn't tell my great-grandmother because this incident had to be my secret. If she had found out, I was sure this would have been the time she used her old, rusty pistol. For heaven's sake, it was for the purpose of protecting us. I could only imagine that the bullet would go straight forward with her perfect aim. I could also imagine that the kickback would have been so hard that she would have stumbled backward and perhaps landed on the floor. I was okay with the thought that the pistol would come in handy for burglars, wild animals, and strangers. It was out of my realm of thinking, and never did it cross my young mind, that it could have possibly been used to defend me from my elderly (former) friend. It was much later in life when I realized in that moment; I had escaped my second sexual abuse experience. Nothing or no one protected me from this horrible danger. *Why did this happen to me or why does it happen to any child?* These were just some *Why* questions that ran through the brain of a nine-year-old. Remember, I was wise for my years, but I was no match for a sexual predator.

Later, I would learn that even at the age of seventeen, I was *still* no match for sexual predators. My mother went to Chicago to attend her best friend's birthday party. She hugged me and my brothers and said that she would return very soon. Unbeknownst to me and my brothers, she or my stepfather had arranged for my stepfather's brother to stay with us. His responsibility was to keep us safe until my stepfather returned. My stepfather worked out of town during the week and would be coming home on the weekends to make sure that we were okay. Technically, at the ages of seventeen, sixteen and fourteen, we could take care of ourselves until our mother returned.

One weeknight, I heard my stepfather's brother's voice after he opened the front door and entered the house. I expected him to take the right turn to his temporary bedroom at the back of the house. I didn't feel the need to worry that he would come toward my mother's bedroom. Everyone knew that her bedroom was off limits unless you had a personal invitation from her. She had given me clear instructions to sleep in her room while she was gone. Because they shared separate rooms, it appeared that this rule included my stepfather. So, the thought of my stepuncle taking a left turn and entering her bedroom never crossed my mind until he was standing there in the doorway. As he stood at the door, I could feel the fear growing inside of me. I felt my blood turn into cold despair, traveling through my entire body as I shivered. I was in shock.

Holding my breath and shivering made me feel as if I was starring in a slow-motion movie. I felt him crawling into the bed with me. As he got closer, I could see the devious and seductive smile on his face, showing the white of all his teeth. We always call his type of smile a "Cheshire Cat" grin. He proceeded to touch me in my private area. I immediately felt violated. I was still a virgin and would barely let my boyfriend touch my exposed body parts, and certainly not my most private areas. When his touch landed, I jumped straight up and sprinted out of the bed. I did not care if he slept there, but it would definitely *not* be with me!

The question now became, *who was supposed to protect me from the man who had been given the responsibility of protecting us?* It was clear that the fox had taken advantage of his invitation to watch the henhouse. I was so devastated that I had to tell someone. I was shaking like a tree leaf with fear. I cried quietly because I didn't want to wake my brothers in the next room. While shaking and crying, I managed to walk to the room where my two brothers were in a deep sleep. One was snoring so hard that a freight train coming through would not have disturbed his sleep.

I went into deep thought when I got past my brothers without waking them up. Don't ask me why I didn't scream and yell, "Help! Fire!" *Something!* After all these years, I still do not know the answer to that question. Perhaps I went into a semi-catatonic state. I was shocked to think that my mother never thought this could happen, or she just didn't care if it happened. I did not dare call her and spoil her visit with her birthday friend or risk facing the fact that she didn't care and would not come home. So, I called my cousin and told her what happened. I begged her to keep this incident a secret between the two of us. Well, she immediately picked up the phone, called my mother, and told her everything I wanted to keep as our secret.

I am not sure she told the secret for my mother to come home and protect me. She just might not have been able to resist the drama. She was a drama queen, and this situation was certainly prime to be followed by fireworks and drama. My mother took the next train and came home to see about her horrified daughter. Her support did not last long. I thought she would be mad that she had to cut her trip short. However, I never dreamed that my stepfather would be able to convince her that I was lying. Wow, *that* went over like a lump of burning coal on my skin. I assume that my stepfather's brother had convinced him that he would never have done such a thing. Who would believe a seventeen-year-old girl when the accused was a churchgoing adult? I am sure he would have sworn to God on a stack of Bibles if he would have been asked to do so. He must have convinced my stepfather that he was not capable of such behavior. I didn't attempt to put the incident up for discussion at the family kitchen table. If my mother didn't believe me, I had already lost before I could defend myself. I took the approach that I had no reason to lie. I knew, and he knew, what he had done.

I was once again defenseless and learned quickly that I had to fight such battles on my own. I was taught to be cautious of the strange men in the streets, but no one bothered to talk about the predators who would visit every weekend, just waiting for an opportunity to pounce on an innocent child. What a responsibility for a young teenager to be faced with! It was one thing to find myself vulnerable to sexual abuse again, but it was a more sensitive situation for my mother to find herself in. I was seventeen, and I would be going to college in a few months. My mother had to provide a home for my brothers to continue to live in. What a tough decision for a mother to have to consider.

The sad solution I resorted to was to avoid being alone with my stepfather's brother for the rest of my life. When he came over to visit, I always went in the opposite direction. I made it clear to him that if he attempted such behavior in the future, I would leave irrefutable evidence that no one would question. I would use my fingernails to leave undeniable, scarring evidence. I would attempt to kick out the functioning ability of his private parts if I found myself in such a position with him again. I did not know if my warning would work, but using my voice to stand up to him appeared to work.

Standing up to him was my way of taking control of the situation. Yet, I was afraid that because he was so comfortable approaching me and getting my family to distrust me, that this was not his first attempt to violate a young girl. Physically, I had dodged another sexual bullet, but I wondered *how many young girls had not been so lucky*. Emotionally, I learned the lesson that no young girl should have to learn. You can be violated in what you consider one of the safest places on earth—in your home and in your mother's bedroom—which was known to be off limits. The other sad lesson and the worst of all was that you could find yourself without the support from those you expect to at least believe you. I was not protected, but I learned to protect myself. Again, what a heavy responsibility for a teenager.

My stepfather's brother would attempt to hold a conversation with me from time to time. I always walked away from him. Even at my mother's funeral, I could not stand in his presence and hear his condolences. The nerve of him for thinking we would ever have a causal relationship, let alone a friendly relationship. Thanks to successful psychotherapy, I was not mad at him. I just didn't care to stand in the circle of his negative energy.

We should plant verbena flowers in every flower garden to protect the young and innocent from all harm and evil. If only it were that simple.

Chapter Nine

RED ROSE:
A FLOWER OF LOVE AND PAIN

By now, I had become good at protecting myself from sexual predators. I was learning to ease from the path of puppy love toward true love and affection.

> One of the most universal symbols of love is the red rose. This incredibly beautiful flower is known to represent true love and affection. In fact, in the 18th century, a special rose language evolved as a means of communication between lovers who were forced to keep their relationship a secret from society. The red rose... remains to be an inspiration to lovers across numerous cultures... [R]oses are a great symbol of love in new relationship and budding romances... [they] often symbolize a message of commitment and everlasting love. (Larson, 2017).

If you have ever been given roses or bought some for yourself, as you admired the mood-lifting aroma, you may have felt pain from the sharp thorns. At that moment, you experienced the entanglement of joy and pain. A person's love life is always a book within itself. I plan to just hit the highs and lows of my first true love affair.

In high school, I found myself sitting two seats in front of the person who became the first true love of my life. Only one student was between us in our row in Ms. Williams' literature class. It would be Shakespeare's Romeo and Juliet that brought our eyes together. I was so in love and thought he was just as much in love with me, so I didn't grasp that the Romeo and Juliet romance ended in ultimate tragedy. I was still in that shy and giddy mode. I did not dare entertain the thought of looking back and letting him catch me staring at him. I just sent verbal love messages through the person who sat between us. Fortunately, unlike Romeo and Juliet, I did not drink any poison, but our love was nothing less than toxic. He was a tennis player who reminded me of a light, satin-skinned Arthur Ashe. He was not athletic enough to play basketball or football, but his White-boy shaped legs and muscular arms owned the tennis court. We were nerds, so the lack of great athleticism was not a deal breaker.

I will never forget his eagerness to help me enact our literature assignments. The assignment for the poem, *The Rime of the Ancient Mariner*, by Samuel Taylor Coleridge was our favorite. I remember the line, "Water, water, every where, Nor any drop to drink."

He was every bit a tall glass of milk—chocolate milk. It is ironic that chocolate milk had always been my weakness. I loved it so much that I would drink it, even though it would bring me to my knees with bent-over stomach cramps and sickness. When asked, I skeptically agreed to be his girlfriend. I soon found out that I was not his only girlfriend. I was the nerd and studious bookworm. He was the nerd and playboy. At one time, I would watch him ride his little blue bike out of my front yard, straight into the yard of his other girlfriend's house a block away on the same street. His story was that the other girlfriends were only sex objects. He explained that he was young and needed the sexual experiences to confirm his maturity and manhood. Today, if I only had a dime for every time I was told that and a nickel for every time I believed what he said, my piggy bank would be full. I was from the country in the backwoods, green behind the ears, and believed what he said. I believed in trusting until there was a reason not to trust. I was clueless that his behavior was the definition of a womanizer—a *player*.

There was also the voice in my head reminding me that my mother would kill me (not make me wish I was dead), if I would not have held true to the values I had been taught. So, I cannot personally take credit for religiously refusing his sexual advances. At the same time, I made it clear I would love to have a future with him if he would stick around until he was ready to settle down with one woman. I was so committed to having a monogamous relationship that I had him take me home after our senior prom. I was dressed for the occasion in my long, black, low-cut A-line ball gown with a flair skirt. The dress was fitting enough to accent my thin hips and long skinny legs. He was dashing in his dazzling light blue tuxedo trimmed in black. If I have to say so myself, we looked like a giddy, future power couple. I enjoyed the prom theme, "Climbing the Stairway to Heaven," as we held each other ever so close. We were holding each other like we were the only people in the world as we danced to the beat of the theme's slow song by the O'Jays. The room was decorated with an illusion of stars and the moon in the midnight scenery also included a staircase leading to the sky to complete our dream imagination. It felt like a small piece of bliss. But when the clock struck midnight, reality came back into view. I had to remind myself that I wanted to make sure I was not the talk of the school the next day. I did not want to be a part of the conversations about who discovered the real stairway to sexual heaven. If my name would have been mentioned amid such conversation the next day, at least *I* knew it would have been a lie.

The prom was awesome. I kept true to my values. My mother did not have to kill me. So, life moved on. My boyfriend and I both graduated from Clarksdale High School in the top five of our class of sixty-eight students. He had a decent, above-average SAT college entrance exam score. This score offered him good scholarships to many universities, both in and out of the state of Mississippi. He chose a scholarship to the University of Mississippi (Ole Miss). What his scholarship would not take care of, his mother, who was a teacher in the community (which was considered a decent job), took care of the rest. My mother was a domestic engineer, earning an allowance of twenty dollars a week from my stepfather. She may have lucked upon another couple of dollars, from time to time, when she found loose change in the washer from the pockets of my stepfather's work clothes. Although I tried, I was unable to raise my SAT score high enough to obtain a feasible scholarship for an initial entrance into the University of Mississippi. Therefore, the full scholarship offers I received were limited to Historically Black Colleges and Universities (HBCUs).

I didn't have anything against HBCUs, I simply did not understand their connection to the African American culture. I was not familiar with their heritage and missions. In the back country where I was raised, college was a long shot, and I did not know the difference between one college or university or another. I was so green behind the ears that when Delta Sigma Theta awarded me a scholarship, I wore the loudest hot pink and green pantsuit *ever* to accept my award. I was totally unaware that these were the colors of a different sorority. It was not my intent, but the Delta Sigma Theta sorority got disrespected by a scholarship recipient that night. The Alpha Kappa Alpha Sorority thought it was one of the funniest things they had ever seen. Sadly, the laughter was at my expense because neither sorority saw this as a teaching moment to educate this little country girl. Thank God, I did not understand what the laughter was all about. In the long run, though, it didn't really matter because I was born without any shame in my game, and I kept moving forward.

Ignorance of the different sorority colors was not my only "not ready for elite society" moment. I was not invited to the debutante experience or recruited to join a sorority. My family was not even at the level of an afterthought for this upper-class status that was bestowed upon young women who were making their first appearance into fashionable and elite society. That twenty dollars per week allowance would not have helped my mother get a bird's eye view through the peephole of a door in that world.

My family didn't move in the elite society circles of our community. Well, thank God for the Federal Pell Grant. I lied about not having a father, so I could fill in zero dollars in the required blanks. It really wasn't a big lie that I didn't have a father, but I knew they were looking for our household income. The truth would have revealed that my stepfather made just a few dollars over the required limit. He also seemed paranoid about having his name and income associated with the federal government. He would rather I didn't get an education at all than to have the federal government breathing down his neck. Despite the lies and all, the Federal Pell Grant was enough for me to go to the local community college and have a few dollars left over. I would live at home instead of in the dormitory.

My boyfriend was still frequently coming home from the university. Our relationship remained on the same toxic terms. He appeared happy as a pre-law student. The girls on campus did not disappoint. They were still helping him with his sexual maturity and manhood. I was still determined to hold firm that I would rather we break up than face the wrath of my mother. I honestly believed if I made the life-altering mistake of getting pregnant and becoming another teen statistic, my mother would kill me. He kept the magical words that I was his number one girl smoothly blowing in my ears. I was filled with more than enough naivety to keep believing him. As long as I was not sleeping with him, the fact that he had other girlfriends didn't strike me as the ultimate relationship deal breaker.

Community college was like an extension of high school for me. I excelled with ease. I had the opportunity of a lifetime to attend Howard University. While there, I took physics under the leadership of one of the world's renown physicists, Dr. Eagleton. There, I experienced my queen bee moments as one of only two females in the class. The guys were falling all over themselves to help us understand physics. Unlike me, the other female student was brilliant. I give her credit, but I was pretty smart myself. I was a long way from being a dummy. I really did not learn enough physics to pursue a career that operationalized or used the principle of physics. I was very appreciative to walk away being able to hold my own in a light principle of physics conversation. I also walked away from the physics class, believing that men like to teach their craft if we let them know we are interested.

The excitement of my Howard experience remains with me even to this day. When I returned, I continued to excel at the community college. My grades there earned me salutatorian status. Because of such status, I had the honor of giving the Class of 1978 motivational speech. I remember speaking to the theme, "Moving on up as you dare to dream." My family was beaming with pride as they proudly sat in the audience. They were witnessing the first family member to graduate from high school, standing tall on a college stage, motivating her class to make their higher institution educational dreams come true. Of course, this made me the first family member to graduate from any college as well. With these educational accolades, my scholarship to Ole Miss became big enough that I could manage the tuition with the scholarships, a job, and seven of those twenty dollars my mother earned each week.

My job turned out to be valuable and comical. I worked as a waitress at Danver's Restaurant to supplement income for my tuition. It was nothing less than interesting to watch me in action. My long skinny legs in a short skirt, my tennis shoes and a funny-looking hat didn't bring many tips or admiring whistles. My looks did not even entice corny pickup lines. I was too thin, not just in the hips and thighs, but I looked like a picture of a starving child that the wind might blow off the front porch. I just did not have what most men were interested in. Most of them wanted to see meat on a woman's bones. I *did* have a little more than an ironing board (flatter than a pancake) butt; but I didn't have enough meat on my bones to hold the appreciative eyes of big-tipping customers.

More important, I was smart and plenty of men didn't like smart women whose heads were always in a book. At that time, the average man didn't seem to like women who talked back and asked questions. I was always walking side by side with the men in my life. Oh no, I never found my place to be in the background. Well, needless to say, I was able to work at the restaurant without being distracted. That should have been my first clue that the days of really being viewed as a pretty woman were hopefully yet to come. The hope was that my body would mature one day, and I was just simply destined to be a late bloomer. I didn't appreciate my delayed physical maturity back then, but now I am so grateful. This was one of my rationalizations as to why I stayed with my boyfriend, waited for him to reach mature manhood, and hoped that by then I would have reached womanhood.

Delayed maturity and womanhood were the least of my problems. My introduction to university life was a "stop and take a deep breath" experience. I felt like a fish out of water. I was floundering around from place to place, trying to catch my breath. It did not help that I knew my so-called *boyfriend* was still sowing his wild oats because he kept me up to date on his escapades. I know the question on the table is, "Why did I stay in this relationship?" I guess I just wanted to trust that he would make himself worthy one day. The parade of women immediately made their presence clear. This indicated that these seductive and mature women knew about me and our one-sided open relationship. As crazy as it was, there was some consolation in the fact that he *did* respect me as his main girlfriend. Under the unusual circumstances, that was enough for me. Thank God, I never had any of them confront me or roll up on me. That would not have been a good idea because this *tomboy* would have made them regret that decision. I continued to rationalize that because I was not sleeping with him, I could hold on a little longer.

Momentarily, my relationship with my boyfriend had to take a back seat to the real reason I was at the university. The next step was to focus on my major. I made an appointment with my career adviser. He reviewed my grades and asked me why I was pursuing nursing school instead of medical school. My grades were his confirmation that I had graduated salutatorian. I realized at that time my choice was based on the fact that I felt perhaps I could have saved my great-grandmother's life if I had been a nurse. The thought of being a doctor was just a little more than my brain could concede. I had made a vow that I may not have saved her life, but I was going to save many lives through a nursing career. I was going to approach each patient as if I was taking care of my great-grandmother.

My career adviser appeared pleased with my answer to his question. When he finished his educational interview, he slowly opened the drawer of his beautiful wooden desk and pulled out an impressive picture of the Ku Klux Klan (KKK). They were dressed in full gear. They were wearing their famous white robes, conical hoods, intimidating masks, and all holding blood dripping, burning crosses for the finishing touch. He unassumingly and shamelessly asked me what I thought about the picture. His facial expression showed that he was intensely and inquisitively waiting for my response. He approached me as if this was just another legitimate and necessary part of the interview. I was so ignorant regarding the connotation or meaning of such a presentation that I calmly, in my clueless *Sherry-go-lucky* mood, said to him, "If they don't bother me, I will not bother them." I didn't have the knowledge or wit to be afraid or question his intent. Just as smoothly as he pulled the picture out of his desk drawer, he put the picture back into the drawer. The conversation ended as if nothing strange or unusual had just taken place.

Despite that conversation, as I continued pursuing my education, I realized something life-altering had happened.

I was supposed to recognize what life on this university campus would look like, accept the warning, and run home to my mother and tell her I was not going to school in such an intimidating and condescending environment. I was so green behind the ears that this is one time ignorance was bliss. Who knows what decision I would have made if I had been aware of the actual intent? I often wonder how many students recognized the warning signs and decided to decline the opportunity to attend this university or any other predominately White university. This was a moment that my inner spirit guided me to see myself as a Black (African American) magnolia blossom who was declaring the same equality that the White magnolia blossoms had claimed privilege to from the beginning of time. I later learned this was a common practice at many universities in the South. Who would have guessed? Anyone, except a country bumpkin like me.

Now, it was time for me to continue to move forward, after I had placed my stake in the ground, survived my career adviser's deliberate intimidation, and decided to stay. I do not remember my boyfriend being around to welcome me to my dormitory. Perhaps he was too busy working on his manhood and maturity. Crazy me. I was still rationalizing that his behavior would benefit the future of our relationship. My mother and stepfather drove me to my dormitory. When I stepped through the doorway, the

Dorm Aide was making an announcement without a bullhorn, but just as loud. She announced, "Your roommate is White; you can see the proper authorities on Monday morning if you have a problem with it. In the meantime, deal with it." To this date, I don't think I asked my roommate if she got the announcement that I was African American. My roommate and I lived together for one year, despite the fear and hatred shown by our friends. Most of our friends were going equally crazy about the arrangement. Her parents called every night to make sure she was alive and doing well. My parents were less afraid. They knew I understood the consequences of bringing harm to such a representative of so-called *pure* beauty (a Caucasian woman). We didn't have visitors. We visited our friends at their residences, and we never had mutual friends. It was enough that we took the high road and learned to enjoy each other's company and tolerated our individual cultures.

It was during this interracial-roommate experience that I learned to appreciate my natural beauty and the value-added beauty bestowed on another woman. I could get ready for class in less than twenty minutes. A five-minute shower, a two-minute facial wash (with lipstick applied), and five minutes to put my clothes on. Five minutes to take out my rollers and comb my hair. Two minutes to get my books and purse and walk out the door. Most of the time, I had a couple of minutes to spare. My finishing touch revealed a naturally pretty, young adult. My roommate: twenty minutes to wash, dry, and style her hair. It took her over thirty minutes to apply her makeup, artistically, with a touch of adequate precision. She was just as pretty when she walked away from the mirror. What a learning experience. I could not have learned this in any textbook. I didn't know it then, but I was being prepared for living and working in predominately White neighborhoods and environments. These experiences were no less of value; they were just profoundly different. My roommate and I embraced our differences, and the sun continued to rise and shine each day.

My boyfriend and I continued our nonconventional love affair. For him, the "just wait a little longer" had turned to "I promise I will be ready in a few more months." Then the time came. He stated, "I am ready to settle down into a monogamous relationship." I had a few more months at the Ole Miss academic campus, so I believed him and agreed to start a real monogamous relationship.

With a promise ring in hand to seal the deal, we took a road trip to the old, raggedy shack (barely still standing) where I was born. Although it was still standing, it was obvious that it was definitely primed for a demolition crew or a strong, fierce, windy moment. Just before sunset, we stood in the barren front yard, and he slipped a tiger eye promise ring on my finger. We took this as a symbol of embracing our earlier, unusual beginning and our promising dreams for the future. We left the place of my birth happily in love. As we traveled down the pitch-black, country, dirt road, we decided to pull over and stop in the heart of the darkness. When we cut the car light off, the moon shining down on the car became all the seductive light we needed. We crawled from the front seat to the back seat of his car. There we made young love and took our relationship to the next level.

Don't take my next statement to mean that being in love was not the most important emotion at this moment. I just learned another great lesson. There is a difference between "being in love" and sex. I *do* remember gently saying to him, "Is this what I have been waiting for?" I was disappointed that his sexual education had not resulted in more bells and whistles for me. By then, I *did* believe that sex was very important for a relationship, but also that it was not the "all in all" of a relationship for some people. I was hoping our relationship would be one of those. I was so in love that I was open to doing what it took to make the relationship work, as long as it was just between the two of us. I must admit, I wanted to yell and scream like he said all the other women did. Just a thought… *were some of them faking it?*

Love was buzzing in my heart. He had a 1975 blue Chevrolet sedan. His mother made sure he had transportation on campus and to get home to visit. We frequently took rides around the campus to see what was happening in our college lives. He loved that car and drove it with much care. His driving experience was way more advanced than mine. I had learned to drive, but didn't have much practice because I did not own a car. Therefore, I viewed him as the smarter, more expert driver between the two of us. This is why I *crashed* into a surprise one day when the accelerator on the car jammed, and the brakes when out. As the car went through the stop sign, another car T-boned us on the passenger side where I was sitting.

Seat belts were mostly for fashion then; we didn't have ours on. My body jerked from side to side. My vision became very fuzzy. Once I stabilized myself and got my vision back, I held my head up, only to see an enormous tree in our path. We hit the tree, which was in the front yard of a classic, big, white fraternity house. My head immediately hit the windshield. I bounced back in my seat with head and lip lacerations. My lips and scalp were bleeding profusely. When the car came to a stop, I opened the door on my side and fell out. The crowd was screaming. "Is she dead?" "What happened?" Photographers were snapping pictures like celebrities were on the scene. I guess we *were* university celebrities because we made the front-page headline of the university newspaper.

I write about this because I thought of so many things my boyfriend could have done to avoid the accident. Just to name a few: navigate the environment much better, turn off the ignition, or use the emergency brakes, among other things.

So, I could no longer deny I was just as smart as he was, and in some cases, even smarter.

Chapter Ten

DAFFODILS: UNREQUITED LOVE

Life kept getting in my way, and I kept getting in the way of life. The cycle just kept circling. I was trying to keep up. I was making progress, but just by way of taking two steps forward and one step backward. Thinking I was on track, I was intoxicated with the belief that I had finally landed the love of my life on mutually agreed-upon terms. For me, they were the normal and expected terms of engagement since the beginning of time: there shall be one woman and one man. I was happy until I was not.

> Daffodil symbolizes regard and chivalry. It is indicative of rebirth, new beginnings, and eternal life. It also symbolizes unrequited love. A single daffodil foretells a misfortune while a bunch of daffodils indicate joy and happiness. (The Meaning of Flowers, n.d.)

When I was happily in love, it took on the meaning of a bunch of daffodils. It didn't take long for that bunch of daffodils to dwindle down to the meaning of a single flower. Soon, a misfortune came to be foretold. The misfortune was wrapped with selfishness and broken love. As my story continued, the daffodil came to symbolize a naïve young lady who had the misfortune of accepting a dark daffodil-spirited proposal from a smooth-talking, debonair, narcissistic, and selfish playboy who wanted it all.

The promise of a future between me and my boyfriend had come to a point where he told me that he had broken his promise to me. He broke his promise because we were no longer on the same campus. His rationale was that the distance between us, once again, put a damper on his *manhood* and his *maturity* plan. It had not taken long for him to become unfaithful. Finding out that he didn't keep his commitment was crushing enough, but he did not stop there. He informed me that he expected *me* to take care of our financial future while *he* finished law school. Since I had graduated from nursing school, it was his expectation that my nursing salary would support us. He dared to shape his tongue to tell me that he would *not* start at the bottom of the job market. He would *never* work a *starter* job, such as McDonald's. No, he felt he had too much going for himself to lower his prestigious standards, especially since he was destined to be a trial lawyer. I guess he had forgotten, or perhaps didn't care, that I *had* started at the bottom. It felt like he wanted someone to take care of his daily needs while he put all his energy into studying. I had to refresh his memory and let him know that this sounds like when his aunt told the town I was not good enough for him because I came from the other side of the tracks. Her thoughts about me had surprised me because from my vantage point, we were on the same side of the tracks. His family was just able to purchase a sleeping car on the train, but my family had to sleep sitting straight up in the coach seats. Both families were still on the same train tracks.

The time had come for me to realize I loved him, but I had to cut the cord. The relationship had once again taken a turn back to the status quo. He was still sticking to the same reason not to give me what I needed and deserved from a healthy relationship. I had totally committed myself to him, only to find out, for what it was worth, that I should have been somewhere picking up daisies. I remember thinking that this is what I told my mother she should have been doing when I was conceived. Why was I not able to practice what I was preaching?

I reluctantly left the relationship. It was a struggle, but I started seriously dating other people for the first time in my life. That was quite an eye opener. I found out there were all kinds of characters out there. Most of them were just playboys like the one I had just walked away from. I dated an older guy who took me to a jewelry store and told me to pick out whatever I wanted. I was unable to connect mentally with him during our conversations. Plus, he didn't have the thirst for the answers to *Why* questions like I did. I didn't want him to purchase anything that signaled more than a causal relationship. Therefore, I chose something inexpensive, maybe worth a couple hundred dollars. Mentally, I was operating on a much deeper plane and had chosen someone who appeared not to know that a deeper plane even existed. It was easy to see that he was very superficial and materialistic. The men I was dating were not living up to the *brainy* stimulation I was yearning for.

It wasn't long before my ex-boyfriend had a new girlfriend, and he appeared to be serious about her. It broke my heart, but since we were on different campuses, the distance helped a lot. I had not settled into a serious relationship, so I found myself spending special times with him when he would come to Jackson, and when we were both back in our hometown. Keeping the cord cut was not working. I still thought, one day, he would become the one-woman marrying type. I wanted to be there to have first dibs on what had been mine and would be mine for a lifetime.

Six months later, the toxic relationship continued. Again, he made all the right promises. He said all the right things. One night while on school break, he came to my home in Clarksdale and gave me an Academy Award-winning performance. He led the performance with all the things he was ready to offer me. He also talked about the future power couple we could be. He threw in his dreams of becoming the President of the United States (POTUS). My ears perked up because these were big aspirations and that would make me the First Lady of the United States (FLOTUS). He was speaking the language of the two dreamers we had always been. At the end of his drama, he asked me to take him back.

The future I had dreamed of for so long flashed brightly and colorfully in my mind. In a "hope springs eternal" fashion, I said, "Yes, I will take yet another chance on us." I was ecstatic at the thought my knight in shining armor's coat finally turning a respectable white. My dream of a white, brick home with a white, picket fence, two children, and a dog was coming true, after all. Thank God, I kept his Academy Award performance and the thought of my future blissful happiness about it to myself. It only took him three hours to call me back and tell me over the telephone that he was getting married to the girl he had been dating for the last year. My knight's coat and armor were not only still black, but had invisible and painful thorns sticking out all around. I was beyond crushed, but my love for him still didn't lose its toxic strength.

He got married and moved to Columbus, Ohio. His mother, whom I had made a point to visit whenever I was in town, dropped me like a hot potato. A year or so after his marriage, I went over to visit her. She called me by his wife's name, "Martha." I thought it was a beautiful name because it was my great-grandmother's name, but it still hurt. I found the courage to write her a letter, telling her that I understood she loved her daughter-in-law, but calling me by her name appeared to erase my existence. She apologized. I should have understood that this relationship with his mother was not very healthy. It was not her responsibility to protect me. It was *my* responsibility to protect myself from such pain.

I was too young to take the high road and move on from the heartache. Contrary to all my teachings and values,

I went to visit him a few times in Ohio. I knew it was wrong, but I felt possessed by relentless love. We would sinfully spend the days together in a hotel and he guiltlessly went home to his innocent wife and children at night. Nothing felt good about these visits. Each time, I felt more dirty, used, and foolish, but my justification was that my definition of love was forever. He loved me first. He was my soulmate. *How could I give up on that dream?* I had tried, without success, to find my way out of this toxic emotional tornado. I was in a constant twister, causing me emotional turmoil and destruction. Like a cat, I was hanging on for dear life and would not let go. My heart was holding on to every heartbreaking lie he told me and holding even tighter to the desperate lies I was telling myself. Our song, *Always and Forever*, by Heat Wave, was adding the quicksand, anchoring me deeper into this ominous and destructive relationship.

When I returned home after the last visit, I found myself despising him *and* the person I saw staring back at me in the mirror each morning. Again, I reached down to pull myself out of the top of the gutter—at least it was not the bottom. I didn't receive much consolation from it being the top because I was still beneath the values which had built the fundamentals of my life. I longed for the strength to really break the cord forever. It took a lot of soul searching and professional help.

The professional help was not what I expected. I thought I would go into someone's office, lay on the couch, or sit in a comfy chair. They would not only tell me what was wrong with me, but fix it for me for an agreed-upon fee. How simple would that be? Fortunately, the experience was quite the opposite. There was no plush couch to lie on. I could not appreciate the comfort of the chair for the emotional pain. I learned quickly that when I was pointing fingers at him; there were three fingers pointing directly back at me. I had to deal with those backward-pointing fingers. I would never think of blaming someone else for finding myself in this predicament. The very hard work had to come from me. The psychologist was just the catalyst to keep me on the right track, dealing only with myself. That was enough to keep me busy for a lifetime.

After a lot of insight and hard work, I was ready to test the waters and let go of the long-lasting toxic relationship. I was excited to operationalize what I had learned. I was leery of how it would feel to cut out a part of my soul, although it was a toxic part of my soul. When that moment of epiphany came, I was standing at work, somewhat surrounded by several coworkers who were casually looking over at me. I didn't welcome the stares, but I couldn't contain my emotions. I exhaled and shouted, "Thank you, Jesus!" I started stomping my feet and dancing like I was Pentecostal instead of Baptist. I felt like I had been filled with the Holy Ghost, like the ladies in my childhood Baptist church. My coworkers kept staring, but none of them dared approach me. I guess to them, it looked like I was possessed or having an out-of-body experience. I had never felt so free, except when I was running wild on the open plains, back home in the backwoods of Mississippi.

Every time I thought about how good standing up and freeing myself felt, I shouted at the top of my lungs for days, weeks, and months. Occasionally, I still shout! The key was that I had finally learned to love myself. I had discovered that what I needed and deserved to have a healthy relationship *had* to start with me making healthier decisions. I was madder at myself for staying in such a toxic, "going nowhere" relationship than I was at him. My definition of love took a complete one-hundred-and-eighty-degree turn. The mature person who I had become realized it was *my* responsibility to free myself, not to depend on *him* to release me from his grasp. Just to recap, this transformation in my life was *not* easy, and it didn't mean I wouldn't find myself in unhealthy relationships in the future. It just meant that when I didn't die after this long overdue breakup, I realized I was a prime example of "what does not kill you will make you much stronger."

Still, to this day, he says he loves me. He has been married twice and divorced just as many times. I really don't think our definition of love will ever be the same. Years later, I asked him why he asked me to come back to him when he knew he was getting married. His response was, "I just wanted it all." So, I guess for a while, *I* was a sick part of his *all*. His answer surprised me, though. I expected him to say something like, "I was young, and if I had to turn back the hands of time, I would do it differently. I would have had more respect for your feelings." I guess that is why he was proud to share that there would be four of his ex-wives or girlfriends at his mother's funeral. At the funeral, I found myself being very nice to all of them. As I looked at each of the beautiful and intelligent ladies, I quietly said to myself, "Better them than me." The truth was… we all had fallen for a smooth-talking, debonair, selfish jerk. I recall several of his friends, old and new, coming up to me and saying he had lost a gem when he lost me. I kindly reminded them that his loss was my gain. I lost him, but I found myself.

He remains an acquaintance, but from a distance. There is no place for his romantic love in my life; it is truly wasted on me. I tell him so, and I mean it. My relationship with him gave me Post-Traumatic Stress Disorder (PTSD). If we see each other and he reaches to hug or kiss me, I get anxious and go into the fight-or-flight mode. I must give him credit for supporting my journey as a young girl while I searched for answers to life's *Why* questions. We faced the world looking for answers to questions that many people didn't consider as important. While my family members and friends were partying, not taking life seriously, we were studying and answering those challenging questions together. An analogy is that they were playing checkers, heading into life's experiences while we were playing chess. That remained the positive thread that was *stitching* us together throughout our extremely toxic relationship. I was intoxicated by his ability to stimulate my brain. That is a hard trait to match in a relationship. It is also an even harder trait to let go of, even when being with the person is otherwise toxic.

When I told him I was writing my memoir, he immediately said, "Don't let me have to sue you." I took his remark as a joke and told him it would be his version against mine. We are the only two who know what really happened. I suggested he would have to write his own book before I would entertain a discussion about *his* version of what really transpired. Strangely, he stopped returning my calls. Oh well, perhaps my getting ready to tell the world about our epic and toxic love was a bit too much for him. Maybe he finally agrees that his romantic love for me is truly just a waste of his time. Whatever the case, I have long ago taken him off my romantic love list, and now he has followed suit and decided to take me off his. At least, finally, we are singing from the same sheet of music.

Both my love life journey and nursing school journey subjected me to much joy and many thorns. The challenge was to travel such journeys without becoming jaded or cynical, or wallow in self-pity. The road to accomplish these goals is rough, but surely, we will discover some windows of happiness and, hopefully, bunches of daffodils along the way.

Remember, when you find daffodils in bunches, you are more likely to find joy and happiness; while a single daffodil foretells of misfortune.

Chapter Eleven

SNAPDRAGON:
UNDERESTIMATED UNDERDOG

Snapdragons can withstand a wide range of growing conditions, making them a symbol of strength and tenacity. This flower's ability to thrive in rocks and stones has been compared to a person's ability to overcome life challenges. ("Snapdragon Flower Meaning," 2022).

Snapdragons are plentiful in the South, yet not often spotlighted. In the story of my life, I compare the underappreciation I felt to the underestimated underdog. Yes, many people may have considered me to be an underdog. Little did those people know that my great-grandmother had equipped me with inner strength, endurance, determination, courage, and patience. Watching her handle life stressors with grace and ease mostly definitely allowed me to witness patience and wisdom daily. I also learned the importance of knowledge, self-reflection, and the power to overcome obstacles and challenging situations in my life by relying on deep courage and faith. I learned to bolster and fall back on my innermost strength in times of need, for the most part, during adverse situations. Sometimes it was the characteristics, defined by this flower, that pushed me to achieve my full potential.

I was still riding the highs of being in love and coming into the best version of myself. I left Oxford, Mississippi (Ole Miss academic campus), and started my actual journey in nursing education at the University of Mississippi Nursing School in Jackson. All I could think of was that I had made it to nursing school. Now, all I had to do was stay there and graduate in one summer plus two years. The summer was interesting. We started with fifteen ambitious and smart African American students. After intense summer courses of anatomy and physiology and pathophysiology, we had only six still standing.

I was not surprised that I was still there, considering I had graduated from high school and junior college with high honors. It was in my favor that they didn't require any sort of standardized entrance exam. What *was* surprising was that I started having problems before the nursing classes began, but I didn't have a clue as to why. At the end of my first semester, certified letters were sent home to my mother. My clinical/subjective grades were Ds. I knew nursing school had been a challenge when I had problems understanding the concept of the book, *I Never Promised You a Rose Garden*. I couldn't get beyond the first chapter. I later learned it was a book dealing with the challenges of mental illness. In my family, *that* was not a topic we had discussed *at all*. Being able to relate to or identify the different types of mental illness was totally out of the question. I also knew I had thought twice about nursing school when a mental health patient with Huntington's Chorea grabbed and held me hostage during my first clinical rotation. This progressive mental health disease ravished his brain, and sadly, there is no cure. I couldn't understand how he had randomly chosen *me* out of all the other students. At that moment, mental health was taken off my list of career paths

I wanted to pursue. But I thought I was ready to hang in there with the rest of the nursing specialties.

Which nursing career path to choose took a back seat to the most surprising factor, which was the supporting documentation for my D grades. I received unexpected feedback from my clinical instructors. The feedback included things such as the windowsills in my patients' rooms were not cleaned; the sheets on their beds were not tight; the furniture in the rooms was not properly arranged, and so on. I never gave it a serious thought that my housekeeping skills were a critical part of the nursing curriculum. Yes, I knew of the Florence Nightingale theory of cleanliness, but I didn't know why its unrevealed importance would determine my pass or failure. Until then, I thought keeping things clean was the purpose of the very important role of the housekeeping staff, as a significant part of the patient care team. The instructors never stressed that *I* had to be a good housekeeper or an interior designer in order to finish nursing school. If I would have known this, I would have paid keen attention to my mother's excellent ability to keep our house clean and organized.

My mother did not understand the need for me to be good at housekeeping. I think she would have asked me to reconsider my career path if she would have known the impact that my housekeeping skills would have on my finishing nursing school. She knew firsthand; I was not known for my domestic engineering skills. When the certified letters arrived, she and I both cried buckets of tears. We could not understand how a student with such past high educational honors could receive Ds and be teetering on the edge of a devastating and shocking failure. She really had a hard time officially signing for such awful grades. I told her I understood that I only had one opportunity to make this work. Since I didn't have much control over the subjective clinicals, I buckled down and earned an A in each of my objective classes. It took me a moment to realize that the other five African American students had parents who were pillars in their communities: bank tellers, schoolteachers, doctors, and lawyers. My parents were none of those. I started this journey with a Federal Pell Grant. If I failed, it would have been expected, and there would be no reason for further discussion. I guess I could have returned home and worked at the local grocery or bargain discount clothing store.

My instructors made it clear that they did not see anything special in me. All I knew was that I didn't have much time to think about why this was happening to me. I had to spend my time finding a way to succeed at all costs. My determination, tenacity, and *never-quit* spirit became evident. I worked harder than any other time in my life. My future livelihood was hanging in the balance. Fortunately for me, they begrudgingly graduated six African American students that year. However, there was something that I had no idea was front and center in their decision-making process.

It was only when I started traveling across the country presenting my research project that I ran into one of my former nursing school instructors. She looked at me squarely and told me that my misfortunes in nursing school had very little to do with my knowledge and abilities. She stated that she knew if I could get through the school-imposed discriminatory practices, I would flourish and become a damn good nurse. She told me the story of how six students were one more than the school needed to meet the federal government's quota for federal funding. The school did not intend to teach any more minorities (in this case African Americans) than they had to in order to receive guaranteed federal government funding. I couldn't help but come to the conclusion that they considered educating an *extra* African American student a waste of their valuable resources.

She informed me that when I walked into her class, her impression of me was nowhere close to the "junior to senior" report she had been given to describe me. She laughed, saying all she could see was that I couldn't roll my tongue and pronounce the word *specific*. It was noted that I pronounced it as *pacific*. The State of Mississippi didn't teach phonetics and enunciation in my country school;

therefore, I still struggle with the proper enunciation of certain words. She seemed to be almost as happy as I was that the University of the Mississippi School of Nursing had graduated six African American students in the Class of 1981. When this happened to me, she was just starting her university teaching career. It wasn't hard for me to understand that she was in no position to publicly fight my battle. She was no match for the commonly practiced black stains of Mississippi. Listening to her, I definitely got the sense that she had pulled for me behind the scenes.

It was Spring of 1981; nursing school was done. I had escaped that black stain of the University. We were all looking forward to the historical graduation luncheon. The high ceilings and brightly lit chandeliers in the luncheon venue were so out of my mother's league. She sat outside the room in the lonely and quiet hallway. I begged her to join me and the rest of the students at the beautiful and festive tables. The ambiance and food spread were like something me and my mother had never seen. Still, she firmly refused and told me to go and enjoy myself. Walking back into the luncheon without my hero was such a bittersweet moment. It was a hard decision to leave the person who had been my biggest cheerleader alone in the hallway. Afterward, I joined my mother and held her so tightly because she was the reason for my success. The school had only provided the rocky path for me to accomplish my success. My mother had not only walked the rocky road with me, but she had also helped to pave the road for me. The school was not only *not* cheering for me, but it had turned into my biggest roadblock to becoming a successful nurse.

I had completed the curriculum to become a nurse. I had also slowly walked across the stage and proudly shook the hand of many who had considered me a waste of their resources. Now, it was time to get a job as a Graduate Nurse Technician (GNT). It turned out that getting this job was a piece of cake. We, the African American girls, along with all the Caucasian girls, attended huge yacht parties, dinners at prestigious country clubs, and never-ending hospital recruiting parties. We were wined and dined to the hilt. The next hurdle to jump was passing the Mississippi nursing state board exam. This brings back my inability to excel on standardized tests. True to form, despite all my studying and praying, I failed the exam. I cried big crocodile tears, but they were wasted tears because I had to prepare to take the exam again. My coworkers were very supportive and showed sympathy and empathy. I was lucky I remained in the GNT role while I was studying to take the nursing board exam again. This role paid less money and caused me to briefly question whether I had made the right decision to become a nurse. My first and only shot at becoming a nurse was in grave jeopardy. I squashed the self-doubt and made studying my number one priority. I felt this had to be just a temporary setback—a setback that I would look back on as a challenge that made me stronger.

It was truly a challenging time for me. All but me and one fellow student had moved on to live their lives with great jobs, new cars, apartments, and some even got married. Two months later, I took the dreaded test again. When I got the results, the pain went from bad to worse. I had failed the exam once again. This time, I was beyond devastated. This time, the pay really dropped. Because I had failed the exam *twice,* the GNT role was no longer an option for me. Since there were no available positions, I not only had to leave my current place of employment as a GNT, but I had to take a position as a ward clerk at another hospital. These harsh times were very, very scary. I also had to leave my one-person apartment and move in with the other student who had failed the exam the first time. Believe me, I never would have mastered the skills as a ward clerk/office manager even if I would have been paid double my registered nurse salary. That just wasn't a strong skill set for me.

Another friend who had passed the exam called me and told me that everything, even getting nursing licenses, was political. She went on to say that she knew a friend who had the power to influence the state nursing board. I was desperate enough to meet with her friend. I met him at his prestigious home. He immediately began to drop names, ranks, and serial numbers of all his powerful and influential contacts on the state board of nursing. He preceded to tell me how pretty and fine I was, as he calmly offered his help in return for sex with him. My spirit was so low that I actually entertained the thought. I was contemplating selling my body for my nursing licenses. I had to choose between believing in myself and believing in a man who was asking for sex. I asked myself, *even if he really had the power to get my licenses, would it be worth keeping and living with this secret for the rest of my life?* I reached deep into my soul for my faith in myself and faith in the values that my great-grandmother had instilled in me. I found the strength to say, "NO" and "HELL NO." I left his home shaken to my core. I cried even bigger crocodile tears all the way home. Just thinking about what I very briefly thought of doing made me feel ashamed, dirty, and proud of myself all at the same time. I had come so close to going deep into the bottom of the gutter.

Well, I decided I would keep taking the exam until I passed it—even if it took me the rest of my life. I still didn't have any guarantee that I would pass the exam the third time around, but taking the nursing exam a third time was surprisingly more sobering. I found my inner strength to keep meeting my challenges and rolling with them.

It took all the strength I had to wait for the results of the third exam. I had been told that if the envelope containing your exam results was thin, you passed; if it was thick, you failed. The theory was that failed envelopes had all the paperwork to take the exam again. All my past envelopes were thick, and, of course, had instructions regarding how to reschedule and take the exam again. When the cheery mailman handed me the envelope, it felt thick. I stumbled and fell onto the closest car. I started crying again and asking God how He could do this to me again. The mailman was no longer cheery. He had stopped in place with a look on his face, as if he was wondering if he should approach me and offer his help or just keep delivering the mail. I'm sure he really didn't want to slow down his workday by getting tangled in my emotional drama. So, he just eased on around the corner.

When I opened the envelope, it read, "CONGRATULATIONS! YOU HAVE PASSED." I screamed with joy, and it sounded like one of those "let it loose" church shouts! I could feel blessings raining down upon me. I was thanking God for understanding that although I had talked a good game, I was not sure if I could have lived through another failure.

God's blessings kept raining down. My former employer had saved my job as a Registered Nurse with the same coworkers who had supported me through this very stressful ordeal. I happily worked with my friends and coworkers for two years. One day, I got the bright idea to apply for a promotion as a Charge Nurse on the evening shift. My supervisor had provided me with evaluations that showed I was well qualified for the position. Soon after I applied for the position, I went on a family vacation to Denver, Colorado. When I returned to work, my former preceptor (instructor) eased up beside me and put a registered nurse directory in my hand. With a sad look on her face, she folded my hands within hers and told me to take the directory because I would need it. This was a directory that listed nursing jobs available throughout the United States.

I thought she was such a coward. Later, I realized she had to decide between helping me or going against the establishment. The establishment was her invested bread and butter. I was an African American young lady who was just starting her career. She chose to bet on not upsetting the unspoken rules of Mississippi and maintaining the status quo. I didn't understand why she did what she did then, but after experiencing similar life experiences, I certainly understand now. I am sure that because I did not take part in pulling up chairs and getting coffee for the doctors, had something to do with how well I did *not* fit into this Southern culture and nurse and physician hierarchy. I liked and respected the doctors, but I did not see the purpose of waiting on them as if they were more important than nurses. I just wasn't wired that way because I wasn't raised to be subservient. I was raised to believe that although we had different roles; we were all to be respected equally.

One day, I dared to step out on a *Why* question to one of the senior doctors. I asked him why we were giving a patient seventy units of insulin.

He told me, "Because I said so."

Being a young adult with an equally intelligent, yet less-educated attitude, I respectfully replied, "Is there any reason I should deliver patient care and not understand what and why I am doing what I'm doing?"

I just wanted to understand the plan of care I was delivering to my patient. I didn't want to implement orders without knowing the rationale for why I was doing what I was asked to do. Again, I meant no disrespect.

I had also encouraged a patient to be more independent. I had shared with her that I was taught to do for patients what they could not do for themselves. She was not pleased in the least bit with me. When the doctors would refer to patients as *Colored*, I would fearlessly step up and ask them "what color?" Boy, looking back, I guess Mississippi was not the place for a young, little African American nurse to practice what she had been taught. The doctors and nurses must have thought I was "too big for my britches."

I had a serious conversation with myself and decided I had been in Mississippi for twenty-five years, and that was long enough. There was no need to continue to endure the wrath of the Mississippi (in my opinion "ass backward") culture. Well, it *did* help that I had met a man while on my family vacation. He tickled my fancy; therefore, I decided that I wanted to move to Denver, Colorado. I had held the dream of living in Denver since my first visit in 1970. So, this seemed like the perfect time to make this dream come true. In my opinion, I was just practicing my demand for respect and equality.

I had to take care of a few loose ends before the move to Denver could begin. I had an apartment full of new furniture and a new car. I called my parents and asked them if they wanted the new furniture. I told them the landlord would have the key to the apartment and if by chance they didn't come and get the furniture, he would be glad to claim ownership of it. I rented an on-top-of-car U-Haul. Once packed, my brother and I drove straight to Denver, Colorado. I didn't have a job waiting for me, but my uncle (with the chip on his shoulder) had agreed to let me stay with him until I found employment and got on my feet.

I worked hard to establish myself in Denver. I took a job at Fitzsimons Army Medical Center. I was looking ahead. Being unfairly treated was in my rearview mirror, I thought. But one day, while sitting in my apartment, watching the birds feed their young outside my bedroom window, the phone rang. The sound took me away from that precious bird-feeding moment. The person on the other end of the telephone shocked me. It was the associate degree RN whom I had worked with at my previous place of employment, Mississippi Baptist Medical Center. My immediate thought was, *What can I do for her?* She didn't waste any time and proceeded to tell me a Mississippi story that shocked me even more than her being on the other end of the telephone call. She told me she had been wronged and needed my help. I sat straight up in bed so my perky ears could hear the complete meaning of her saying, "I need your help." She told me that when I applied for the position of Evening Charge Nurse, she had been called into the office. The Nurse Manager had told her that all she had to do was apply for the position, and they would guarantee her the position before they gave it to me.

I was a degree-prepared (Bachelor of Science) registered nurse. Her associate degree didn't come close to being equal. She continued the conversation and told me that once I left; they reneged on their gracious offer. Now, she desperately needed *me* to help *her* get the job she deserved. She added that she was told she was a better fit for the charge nurse position because she was Caucasian.

WOW! This was a clear example of White privilege to the infinite degree. She was more than happy to accept a position she *deserved,* even though we all knew she was less qualified. The plan she agreed with worked for all parties involved until I (the human obstacle) had removed myself from the equation.

Of course, I strongly disagree that she deserved the position. I calmly informed her that I had no empathy for her. I heard complete silence when I told her I felt she was just as complicit as the others in the plot to keep me from a job I was clearly qualified for. I emphasized that I only wanted that job and any future job if I deserved it and was qualified for it. I wished her luck and told her I was making a conscious decision *not* to help her. I didn't care to look back in the rearview mirror. I was looking forward, and in my future, I didn't see her or the rest of those evil people who schemed to derail my career. I also felt compelled to tell her that I didn't know *how* they could sleep at night. I hung up the phone and said a prayer of thanksgiving because I knew I had made an excellent decision in leaving Mississippi. *I* could sleep at night; I had left the people who had no shame in their game when it came to devaluing People of Color.

Mississippi didn't have the monopoly on devaluing Black people. My life-changing struggles continued in Colorado. Although the struggles were more subtle, there were many. I must give the "no shame" Mississippians some credit. They are straight to the point and proud of their unfair dirt; therefore, you know what they are capable of doing. They let you see how they treat others. If you are smart, you know it is just a matter of time before your turn will arrive. Coloradans are different. You will not know what hits you until you have been knocked to your knees. They will smile with you, dine with you, work with you, and mow you down like you are a total stranger. That is the definition of a "silent throat cutter." By the time I arrived in Colorado, I was still shy, but I had found my inner strength and the ability to adapt to workplace politics and downright "watch your back" tactics.

It was not long before a mentor of a lifetime had found me. She literally pulled this shy wallflower off the wall. She saw my inner strength and adaptability. She began to expose me to the positive intricacies of Black and White culture, the importance of being connected and active in the community, and keys to dealing with workplace politics. I became a true leader (president) of national, regional, and local organizations. With her by my side, I learned to navigate my ambitious career ladder, which I knew would be a winding one. I just didn't know all the twists, turns, stops, and starts I would encounter along the way.

Over the years, I wrote and developed many hospital policies and procedures, set up many nursing programs (cardiac rehabilitation programs, cystoscopy clinics, initiated the first twelve-hour shifts, managed schedules, developed and implemented shared governance, etc.). Yet, when I applied for a nurse manager's position in a lackluster unit, they reluctantly accepted me on a trial basis. The unit was a medical unit that cared for the first AIDS patients amid the AIDS epidemic. No one had the courage to apply to manage this unit, except me. Even then, no one wanted me to have it. If the truth be told, they had to give me credit for being so courageous by applying for such an assignment.

I was offered a six-month trial with the understanding that my request would be reconsidered at the end of the six months. Because I had worked so well with my supervisor and was committed to being successful, three months after I accepted the trial offer, she officially offered me the position. I accepted the position and continued to work well with her. Just before she left two months later, she requested a promotion for me. The promotion was based on her submitting an outstanding evaluation for my commitment and hard work.

When that supervisor left, my new supervisor came in like an untamed lion out for Black blood. Her managing style was microaggression on steroids. She immediately asked me to withdraw my evaluation and change it to a satisfactory rating. I refused, and the battle was on. She began to embarrass me in front of my staff and blamed me for every error made by my staff members. She stooped as low as to ask me if I had any alcoholics in my family. I was strong enough to tell her, "It is my opinion that *every* family has an alcoholic, even if they are hiding them in the closet, only for someone to take a trip to the pantry late at night when no one is around as a witness."

One morning she was brazen enough to take me into a meeting room and begin reading me the riot act. She told me I was not qualified for the position, and I should resign, or she would make my life a living hell. I started crying a river of tears. She appeared to be pleased with her "down one side and up the other side" beat down as she stood over me with an air of superiority. But what she didn't know was that when a *Sistah* is crying a river of tears, it is not because your beat down is having your desired effect. In most cases (especially in *my* case), they were tears of anger. I was ready to fight and defend myself. I wanted to claw her eyes out. This highly educated Caucasian woman without any street smarts did not understand just how close she was to a cold-blooded, back alley, street brawl. But because professionalism had always been my beacon, I had to dry my tears and let my professionalism guide my next step. I decided that I had always wanted to work in the private sector. Therefore, I should pack up my office desk and make some calls.

After I called hospitals in the private sector to inquire about positions, of course, I called my mentor, and she came racing to my rescue. When she got there, I was in the middle of emptying my desk drawers. As I was packing my things into boxes, she was literally unpacking them. She looked me squarely in my eyes, held my hand, and told me, "You are not going anywhere if I have anything to say about it. You are just as smart and tenacious, if not more so, as all the other Nurse Managers in this hospital." This is when my two top career commitments: professionalism and leaving your place of employment on your own terms kicked in. With my mentor in my corner, I decided to stay. No, the private sector hospitals never called me back. I later came to believe that working for the government must have been my career destiny. It was at this point that my career became a joy—I served the veteran population with great humility.

Serving the veterans and climbing the career ladder did not get easier. My supervisor kept her promise of making my life a living hell. She even brought several other nurse managers into the fold. Their roles were to monitor my actions and report back to her. She would schedule weekly meetings in her office. When I arrived, she would continue her desk work and ignore me as I sat there for the entire hour. At the end of the hour, she would dismiss me and remind me when our next weekly appointment was scheduled.

Ignoring and disrespecting me didn't change my mind about lowering my evaluation rating. It just made me dig my heels in deeper to fight for what I deserved. My mentor and I had to strategize for the promotion that had been requested by my previous supervisor. We had to make sure my evaluation was reviewed when the people plotting against me were out of town. We couldn't take our chances and let them be in the building when I was up for review. If they would have been in the building, word of mouth would have traveled at the speed of lightning. The obstructers would have interrupted the one-hour nursing professional standard board review. We learned to call meetings and asked for explanations regarding why I was denied positions. This helped us stay one step ahead of the people plotting to hold back those they didn't like (those who were not part of their work cliques).

My mentor and I became a team to be respected and not to be taken lightly. Everyone knew they had to be prepared to answer the *Why* questions because we were going to ask them. There were Caucasians in hiring and firing positions who boldly told me, "I will see that you never get a position in my department." Others told me I was not qualified again and again, when I was most certainly qualified for the advanced positions. Eventually, I filed an EEO race discrimination complaint against my supervisor. Sadly, the truth of the matter is, this was the only way for me to be heard. My mentor and I fought the never-ending fights for my role as a nurse manager. By the time I became a nursing supervisor and Adult Nurse Practitioner, we had finally learned to outsmart our enemies strategically. When they would look for me, I would be two steps ahead of them. Most of all, I didn't use my energy looking back for them.

The unfair treatment was never ending, but my methods of dealing with it changed. I had learned to work smarter and not harder. This was all tested one day. The day arrived for revenge on my former vicious supervisor. She happened to be assigned a supervisor who gave *her* a beat down like she had enjoyed giving me. They were two evil people fighting for power. What did that have to do with me? Well, late one afternoon, coincidentally, we crossed paths in the very quiet and lonely hallway. It was the end of the day; therefore, it appeared as if we were the only people still hanging around on that floor. When I got close to her, I could see she was crying an ocean of tears. As she cried, she told me how she was being mistreated by her supervisor. This was my defining moment. I had a choice to make. Should I tell her, "Good for you. What goes around comes around. Be careful, when you dig a ditch for someone else, you might be the one to fall into it.

This is how *I* felt when you used your power and position to wrong *me*." Or should I offer her my shoulder to cry on? I chose to lean in. I held her like she was one of God's children, just like the rest of us. She continued to cry an even bigger ocean of tears on my shoulder. Surprisingly, this was not hard for me to do. In such a defining moment, I was again doing what my great-grandmother had taught me to do.

My commitment to professionalism was tested again and again. My former supervisor decided to retire, and on her last day of work, I stopped what I was doing and found my way to her office. Once there, I THANKED HER. I informed her that her harsh actions had forced me to reach deep and make it my mission to show her that I was destined for success. I also told her that she was one of the catalysts that lit the blue-flamed fire inside of me. She never apologized, but it was obvious she appreciated I had survived her intense wrath and torturous behavior.

The underdogs are ultimately the ones who confront and defy life's challenges to become the heroes of their own truth, even when darkness keeps the spotlight from shining on them. Their true victory is won, not simply by surviving and thriving, but by rising from the ashes. They go through the red-hot fires and the blue flames—eventually coming out on the winning side.

Like the Snapdragon, I had adapted and thrived through the darkest of times. This was done because I had the tenacity to slay the naysayers and triumph as the underdog.

Chapter Twelve

BLACK ROSES:
DEATH AND MOURNING "GONE TOO SOON"

The black rose can be used as a symbol of death and mourning... In contrast, the black rose signifies no return to the previous and living life without hope for life and happiness afterward… As a result, the black rose has become a symbol of death's tragic side and how loved ones mourn. ("The Black Rose," 2020).

We must look back on the impact the lives of our "gone too soon" family members have had on us. After all, we must listen to the drumbeats of our memories of them so we can hear the voices of those memories in our present and dance them right into our future. Only then can we begin to move forward in any kind of meaningful way and carry their memories in our hearts and minds every day. We can remember the lives their footprints touched, the differences they made, and the people they helped who were blessed to cross their paths. All of their life stories will assist us in creating a picture of a beautiful collage of lives well lived. Whether their lives were blessedly long or sadly too brief, the love stories we share will inspire others to understand the depth of the loss felt by those of us who must now live without them.

I made my sudden and painful entrance into the *Great-Grandmotherless* and *Motherless* Clubs, and a black rose was the only flower that touched the depth of the pain and suffering I endured. When I journeyed into the *Great-Grandmotherless* Club, I was young and didn't truly understand the pain that had been thrust upon me. But I *did* recognize that a different appreciation for loss had immediately engulfed me and taken away my ability to breathe. I was consumed with so much anger that having an appreciation for the contributions she had made in my life was not my first thought. I was emotionally crippled by the suffocating and blinding pain for a long time.

When I begrudgingly joined the *Motherless* Club, I was older and better able to interpret each slice of the knife that pierced my soul. It was at that time, that flashbacks and memories of how my deeply sincere condolences to friends and acquaintances who gained membership before me could not have conveyed the raw emotions they must have felt upon their entry into this dreaded club. I had to go back and find the last person to whom I had expressed my condolences. Once I found her, I gave her a "Now I *really* know what it is like to walk in your shoes" hug and a heartfelt apology. This was my way of confessing that my idea of how I would feel at such a moment hadn't come anywhere close to what I really felt. It didn't take long for me to learn that these were the toughest losses and crosses I would ever have to bear. Each episode of pain and loss left multiple holes in my heart that will never heal. I just needed to find ways to live, survive, and thrive with missing pieces of the soul of my life's tapestry.

I have told the end-of-life story of my great-grandmother, Martha Magdalene, in an earlier chapter. I will tell the story of my mother later. This chapter is mostly in remembrance of my Aunt Jessie Mae and my first cousin, Martha Ann, *a.k.a.* Kitty or Kitty Hawk.

My mother and her sister, Jessie, were *twins* who were born one year, two months and seventeen days apart. This is in defiance against nature, of course, but no two people could have been any closer. They were in the same classes in school. They shared the same dreams and sense of belonging. They also shared the same devotion to each other and their family. As adults, they spoke to each other several times each day. Together, they shopped the deep-dive bargain stores. In their presence, you could feel the synergy of the sum of two being greater than two separate individuals. They would part from each other for brief vacations only. Most of the time they found themselves either living across the street from each other or next door to each other in double tenant, one-bedroom houses. In the double-tenant houses, they would just swing around to each other's porch without using the steps. When I asked my mother where she wanted to be buried, she immediately and firmly stated, "In Mississippi, next to my sister." She didn't show much, if any, concern for the burial place of her husband or her three children. Believe it or not, knowing the closeness of their relationship, her emphatic response surprised none of us.

Auntie Jessie was my great-grandmother's oldest grandchild. Her father was not the "family leader" type of man. Therefore, she became the family matriarch by default. As a child, she was joined at the hip with her grandfather, Joe Bertha. She received her leadership skills and great wisdom from him and her grandmother, Martha.

Aunt Jessie carried the burden of holding our family together. She worked thirty years and never got a chance to spend one penny of her pension or her social security. Although she drove many tractors and steered many wagons as a child and young adult, she didn't learn to drive a car until her early forties. Most days, she walked two to three miles to work. She energetically hammered many nails and carried plenty of lumber as she assisted Habitat for Humanity in building the only house she ever owned. Before owning her home, she happily lived in the Chapel Hill Heights projects. She always made it clear to us that she was going to free herself and her children from the projects one day.

Aunt Jessie and her two sisters didn't fight often, but when they did, it was like watching the fight of cats and dogs. The baby sister, Jannie, was like me; she did not enjoy fighting. She only fought to protect herself when fighting was her only option. She once told me that my mother threw her clothes onto the ground and slapped her so hard that she stumbled off the porch. I often told her she missed a perfect opportunity not to *spoil* my mother by standing up to her and not letting her have her way.

The family began spoiling my mom as a child. By the time I was an adult, it was too late to undo her spoiled behavior. I was destined to live with it; however, I learned the tough task of setting limits as to how much of that behavior I would tolerate. When I learned to set limits with my mother, I was well on my way to doing the same with anyone who didn't care to be fair and honest with me.

Each sister had three children; Auntie Jessie later had a son to break the tie. The group fights should have been equal, based on the number of people, but because I was so reluctant to fight, my mother's side was minus one. That put them at a major disadvantage. I was the champion of getting people off me if they jumped me. Unfortunately, helping my mother's side of the family wasn't enough for me to share my fighting skills and defending myself during these family quarrels. First of all, I typically didn't understand what they were fighting about. My love for each sister was too great for me to pick a side. I would often go off to a quiet place near the railroad tracks and return when I thought the fight was over. Usually, by the time I returned, each side had convincingly claimed victory. Because I was not there to participate in or witness the drama, I had no way of knowing who had actually won or lost.

For me, when family members fight like this, the whole family loses. I was more stunned that a few hours later, they were laughing and talking as if nothing had ever happened. This behavior was foreign to me. Occasional fights to draw blood were a part of their lives, but the fights didn't seem to touch the genuine bond between them. Here was another *Why* question that needed an answer. *Why did people who loved each other fight to draw blood, only to come back together and confess or display their love for each other hours later?*

For example, my mother was very neat and tidy. My Aunt Jessie was more relaxed and accepting of a less tidy home. The tension would rise when Aunt Jessie would come over and do something—like stick her hot dog into the mustard jar. My mother would let her know that such actions were not accepted at 527 Indiana Street. Aunt Jessie would express her opinion about my mother's rule as she respectfully walked out the door. She would go to her own home, where things were not so restrictive. She ran a household where people could go into her kitchen and uncover the pots while she was cooking. This is just how different they were, although they were inseparable.

Aunt Jessie was sixty years of age when she retired after thirty years as an x-ray technician at the Northwest Mississippi Regional Medical Center in Clarksdale, Mississippi. The Friday after she retired, her goddaughter looked into her eyes and told her they were flaming yellow. She looked into the mirror and confirmed her goddaughter's observation. She drove herself to the hospital the same day. It was not long before the lab results revealed she had pancreatic cancer. For her and our family, the word cancer or tumor suspended in the air like rain in dark clouds waiting to soak the ground at any moment. It was the uncertainty that frightened us the most and let us know we were facing a mountain of a hard fight. From that point, the real fight was on.

The focus became that we needed to not only win the battles, but we had to win the war on cancer. We discussed several locations for treatment, such as the University of Tennessee in Nashville or the University of Mississippi in Jackson. But Aunt Jessie decided to remain in the small-town medical center for treatment with small-town doctors. I was in constant discussion or disagreement with the medical staff. I tried everything to convince them to treat her as if she would *live* instead of as if she were dying. It was amazing how the difference in ideology guided their treatment plan for her. Perhaps they were practicing rationalized medicine without saying that was what they were doing. I was quite suspicious when she received chemotherapy that didn't cause her to lose her hair or significant nausea. Sadly, these are the very common trademarks of effective cancer treatment.

When her platelets and other blood products would drop, the doctors would say there was no reason to give her blood products to keep her alive. They would also say it would only be a matter of time before the end would come. I found myself going head-to-head with her doctors, whom she loved and trusted so much. She had worked with them over the last thirty years of her life. But as a Nurse Practitioner, I could see they did not add their love and admiration to her treatment care plan. It was my professional opinion that it was obvious they wanted to save the resources and let her meet her Maker as soon as possible. Aunt Jessie didn't share my opinion about her local Mississippi doctors. This made the battles even harder to fight. She didn't seem to understand what all the fuss was about. Nor did she indicate she shared my point of view that it was important for the two of us to be of the same accord. Perhaps she knew something that I didn't want to come to grips with. Was it a fact that if I made a fuss, it would only make them feel intimidated and move slower to understand my plea to extend her life? She was the second-generation victim of pancreatic cancer in our family. Her mother's brother was the first known family member to struggle with this dreadful disease.

When she didn't get better at the local hospital, she agreed to travel to the Mayo Clinic in Houston, Texas. There, she received chemotherapy, and ironically, we began to see the normal signs of someone who was receiving chemotherapy. Her hair fell out, and she was very nauseated and pale. With the chemotherapy she got better, but decided she wanted to go back to our small town to take care of her home. There was no convincing her otherwise.

Once back at home, she had to be readmitted to her small-town hospital within two days. Her care there was the same as before. I started fighting for her once again. Aunt Jessie slipped into a coma and became too sick to travel back to Houston; therefore, we had her transferred to Memphis, Tennessee. The battle to win the war on pancreatic cancer continued. We not only had to fight the doctors, but we had to fight the nursing staff as well. She was living her last days, and they insisted on enforcing the fire marshal codes for visitors every second of the day. We told them to bring on the fire marshals and whoever they felt they needed to bring. We were a united force, and we made it clear we were not leaving her bedside. By then, we knew she was transitioning to heaven right in front of our eyes. From that point on, we could predict how the end would play out.

Just as we predicted, Aunt Jessie waited for her brother en route from Denver, Colorado, to get there and say his goodbyes. She also waited to say goodbye to her daughter, whose birthday was coming right after the clock struck midnight that night. When she was first diagnosed, I had consulted a renown oncology specialist at my workplace; he looked me straight in my eyes and told me she would be dead in nine months. True to his expert words, in nine months, Aunt Jessie made the transition from earth to heaven. On December 11, 2001, she closed her eyes and entered the pearly gates. When I arrived in her room to say my goodbyes, I saw that her body, especially her face, had returned to one of the most beautiful I had ever seen. The earthly lights had gone out for one of the three most striking beauties I have ever known (her, my mother, and my Aunt Jannie). My mother, her nature-defiant *twin* sister, did not come to say goodbye at the hospital, nor did she attend the funeral. It was difficult for me to understand, but she just could *not* face the fact that her human mirror image had been broken forever. She wanted to remember her the way she was. I was surely not in any position to pass judgement on her decision. It was like a part of *her* had died, and she just wanted to wait until she would see her dear sister again in heaven.

As the doctor whom I trusted predicted, Aunt Jessie had lived nine months, give or take a couple of days. I don't regret for one moment how hard I fought for her to live. We must not lose sight that our family members are human resources that are most definitely worth the fight. The doctors move on to save the next life after they lose a patient. But we must live with what we did or didn't do for our loved ones for the rest of our lives. Yes, I disagreed with much of the doctors' management of my aunt's care.

Yet, intellectually, I understood some of their decisions. The question remains: When working with limited resources, what is the value of treating a patient to hold onto hope for their family versus the value of saving resources for another patient and their family? I don't know the answer to this question. I still say that I would not change any part of the fight I fought for her.

My Aunt Jessie had been in heaven for fifteen years when another life-altering event struck. My first cousin, Kitty, was the third-generation member of our family to be diagnosed with pancreatic cancer. We had her to cherish and love for four years after her initial diagnosis. She left Mississippi and boarded an airplane headed to Denver, Colorado, the week of the Fourth of July in 2016. She wasn't in Denver seventy-two hours before she became sick and disabled with severe back pain. I had to take her to the nearest emergency room to seek help. Earlier in January, she had been told that her oncology follow-up labs results were fine, and things were looking up for her. When things were looking up for *her*, that meant things surely would be looking up for the family as well.

Kitty received the family name of Martha, even though she was the third granddaughter. I was surprised that the name was still up for the taking when she was born. She was lucky enough to escape the long middle name of my great-grandmother (Magdalene); she received "Ann" instead. Her husband was the only person who called her, "Martha." They had a bond between them that elevated her name to a spirit of beauty and pride. When he would call her name, most of us would look around the space to see just whom he might be speaking of. We were that far removed from her God-given birth name.

Kitty was another hard worker. She also worked at the Northwest Mississippi Medical Center as a ward clerk/unit administrator. She endured things that were only her stories to tell, not mine. Therefore, I will tell what I think she would have given me permission to tell. She raised three smart and ambitious sons: a professional health sciences provost (college/university senior administrative officer), a lawyer, and a certified public accountant. Believe me, she and her husband worked hard to provide opportunities for their children. There was not one opportunity that just *fell* into their laps. Their hard work certainly paid off. Their father was a high school instructor and an assistant principal. But Kitty's Clarksdale Community College degree and, most of all, a heavy dose of common sense contributed equally to the success of their children.

She could dance, dance, dance! She and my brother, Michael, would take the floor. We, as a family, would sit back and be thoroughly entertained by their swinging moves. Once they were on the dance floor, there was not enough room for anyone else. They used every inch of the dance floor.

When Kitty was examined at the hospital, the doctor said she could see there was so much love between us; therefore, she suggested I take some time off to spend with her. She went on to tell me that her labs indicated the pancreatic cancer had not only returned, but it had spread to her spine. When we requested her last lab results from her personal oncologist's office in Mississippi for comparison, it was clear that her cancer had returned in January, and she had never been informed. *What was I supposed to do with this huge bombshell?* I had been taught to deal with these types of issues with the family members of my patients, but the emotions of dealing with her as my beloved family member clouded the issue.

I called her oncologist and informed him of the situation. He asked me how I knew that her pancreatic cancer has returned. I told him that based on her history, it only took me two educated guesses. First, she had a known history of pancreatic cancer, and her back pain was severe and relentless. Second, reviewing her lab results from January, which his office had ordered, sealed my professional opinion. This was the weekend I had to make one of the toughest professional decisions of my career—to get pain medications for her. It was a tough decision, but I had to find pain relief for one of the greatest loves of my life.

When I informed her oncologist's office about her severe pain and asked the on-call doctor for his recommendation for pain management, we agreed on a powerful narcotic. A couple of days later, when I spoke to her primary oncologist, he stated that he wouldn't have given her the pain medication which the on-call doctor and I had discussed and chosen. Yet, he didn't make any alternative recommendation.

When I became assertive in my request for pain medication, he told me, "Don't make me have to get nasty."

Without hesitation, I told him, "Go ahead and get nasty. I will take a full dose of your nastiness, if it will help us get on the same page to extend her life."

I had to face the fact that he didn't seem to have a professional investment in her care. Again, the Mississippi doctors stood tall on the medical practice of treating people like they were dying instead of treating them with the hope of living.

Like the doctors who treated her mother, Kitty's oncologist did not agree with me. Surprise, surprise. I got the sense they felt that because she had defied the odds by surviving four years post diagnosis, why should we keep expecting more time? I was just asking for medical decisions that would increase the odds of her continuing to live, instead of decisions that sped up the odds of her dying. A great example was not providing timely treatment when her follow-up labs were positive for the return of the cancer. That was surely a missed opportunity, perhaps, to keep the cancer at bay.

They discharged her from one medical center, and a couple of days later; she was admitted to the University of Colorado. This medical team stepped up to the plate. They were late to the ballgame, but they played the medical game as if they were aiming for a grand slam, using all resources to save another life. As a group of caring and well-connected experts, they developed a plan of care that gave her all the necessary tests, along with the human touch that any human being deserved. Their caring philosophy was, "We are going to schedule what we think will save her life. If God takes her before all the tests are done, then we can just cancel the tests." This was hopeful and uplifting for her and the family.

I was taught to manage her pain and diabetes at home with the appropriate equipment. All the necessary agencies came to offer care that the living deserved. We didn't hold onto or live with the concept of dying while Kitty was working hard to live. So, this was a refreshing and comforting concept. She was discharged home. Sadly, less than a week later, she had to be readmitted to the hospital. The medical team didn't stop focusing on saving her life until it was obvious to all of us that the time of transition was more closely nearing every hour. The day before her death, family members called and assisted her in using FaceTime to say goodbye to those who couldn't be there. This was very sad and beautiful to watch at the same time.

After the FaceTime calls, she drifted off into a light sleep. She didn't sleep long because she was refusing to maximize the use of her pain pump, not wanting to miss a moment with her family. When she awoke from her light sleep, she told me, "I am dying. Get my boys and get my aunt and uncle." I called them all. They all came immediately and stood at her bedside, waiting for her transitional moment to take center stage. I also went to find her nurse and informed him of her declaration of dying. We reminded each other how often patients know when the moment of death is near, and they find a way to prepare their family members. This time, I embraced the warning. I didn't pretend it was not happening like I had once done when my mother was giving me a heads up. Kitty was getting ready to make her transition to heaven.

Again, her sister (for whom her mother had waited for before she closed her eyes), was still on her list of those she would wait for to come and say goodbye. I knew Kitty would wait for her, just as her mother before her had waited. When her sister arrived, she crawled into the bed with Kitty, and they both fell asleep. Kitty's husband and the other family members went quietly to sleep on the couch in the room. When her husband woke up and walked to her bedside, he found that Kitty's sister was still asleep, but Kitty had quietly crossed over into eternal life. I arrived as the rest of the family members in the room were saying their last goodbyes and began leaving the room.

When I walked into the room, I headed straight to her bedside. I hugged and kissed her and said my final goodbye. Once everyone was gone, I helped the nurses get her dressed for her trip to the morgue. I wanted her clean and fresh like a black rose, re-birthed in heaven. Again, I witnessed the return of the striking facial features of another beautiful human being shortly after her death. I walked by her side as she was taken to the morgue, and I told her we had gone our last mile together until we would see each other in heaven one day. She was so beautiful and appeared to have been covered in heavenly peace.

Black roses are ways of saying, "Things are sad and painful, but there's still beauty amid the pains of the world." Black roses can express this much more than words ever could.

As we manage our flower gardens, we must remember that although each flower seems to be standing boldly and saying, "Hey, look at me! I am the star of the garden," they all play a unique role in life's bouquets. As flowers fight with tenderness and mercy to survive and flourish, we must understand that we are going to lose some of our most precious and beautiful *flowers* in this life. God will hold our hands as we reflect on the lost flowers we loved. We will always cherish them and the heavenly, lifelong memories we hold dear. We must refocus our sight on the blooms of the flowers left behind. We must open our eyes wide enough to notice, consider, and love the ones still growing and flourishing here.

God reminds us that as we weep for our "gone too soon" loved ones, we water the earth with the tears of all our sorrows. We must also remember that although it doesn't feel like it, He is always there carrying us through our grieving pains.

So, whether we see our loved ones who have passed on as beautiful bouquets or gardens of flowers or not, I just want the world to know that *our* family loved our "gone too soon" loved ones to the depths of infinity and back.

Chapter Thirteen

GLADIOLUS: STRENGTH AND FRAGILITY OF FRIENDSHIP

The highlights and low points of my life have been more precious and less devastating because I shared them with my best friends. Just like other gems in our lives, we sometimes take for granted that our friendships will never end. You think they will endure through thick and thin. We don't learn to appreciate these relationships until we lose or almost lose them. Then again, sometimes, no matter how much we try to save the friendship, it slips right out of our grasp. Often, this is like trying to hold water in your hands. No matter how hard you try, it seeps through your very tight fingers.

"One of the most beautiful gladiolus colors, the yellow gladiolus flower, usually symbolizes positive energy, happiness, and friendship." (P., Rebekah, 2021). Reading about this flower revealed that it has complementary spikes. These spikes give credence to the staying power of the flower. In my life, I see this symbolizing patience and wisdom to either keep a friendship together or assist in severing the losses, no matter how bitter or sweet the end of the friendship.

I was striving for a lasting and deeply bonded relationship in which my friend and I would pierce each other's heart with love, compassion, and understanding. At one point or another, everyone goes through a problem they need to deal with. Having a true friend who appreciates and shares these problems makes these times more bearable. This is the person who is there for you when times are good or bad. The symbolism of the gladiolus has assisted me in illuminating my story of friendship as it helped me come to the conclusion that a "best friend forever" means that someone will pierce the heart of another human being with love and the two will never give up on each other. Let me tell you the bitter and sweet story of my heart being pierced with joy and pain, all in the name of friendship.

Friendship is defined in many ways. It can be defined as a relationship of mutual trust and support between human beings. I have always prided myself on being open to all types of people. But I am very selective about the people I invite into the deep, deep thoughts of my life. If you find yourself close to my heart, you can be lucky or unlucky. You're lucky if you like the absolutely honest, *real* Sherry. We become bonded to share love, pain, sorrow, and joy. That can be a heavy burden to handle. Unlucky are you if the truth is not your friend, or if you expect me to take the world as it comes to me. I have found some people to be very fickle, and that's fine with me. If fickle defines you, then you most likely would not be happy sharing my innermost circle.

I don't recall having deep, hardcore childhood friends. I was more of a happy loner. What I recall is me and my cousins hanging extremely tight. We stuck together and took on the outside world as a united force. When I look at it that way, I would say they were my first friends. Other than my family, I can count my friends on both hands, my best friends on one hand, and still have some fingers left over. My long and short definition of "best friend" is my partner in crime, my ride or die, a vault to bury my secrets, and most of all, someone who I can trust to have my back twenty-four seven. It is someone who has signed up to listen to me at any hour of the day or night. That person would do this for me because they know I would do the same for them. That commitment is the reason my best friends can be counted on only a few fingers of one hand.

Most of my few best friends have been very committed to this friendship mission. It is not uncommon to find a bond that leads to best friends as a result of tragedy, loss, or failure. This was how my "best friendship forever trio" came to be.

I met Carolyn forty-five years ago. We were both new nurse graduates and worked at the same hospital on different floors with different specialties. We had gone to different nursing schools. She went to Mississippi University for Women (The W); I went to the University of Mississippi (Ole Miss). One day, she asked to borrow some money, and I loaned it to her. We became inseparable after that. Shortly after becoming friends, we took the nursing professional licensing board exam—we both failed it. Failing that exam fostered a bond between us. It was both a bond of pain and failure. Being in close spaces together helped us support each other through the awful failure.

For the two years I remained in Mississippi, we were joined at the hips. We club-hopped together. After the night clubs would close, we would gather with other friends and have our *Waiting to Exhale* moments. Together, we weathered love relationships and endured the Mississippi-stained employment practices for African Americans. We were fortunate enough to be informally adopted by each other's families. I was in her wedding; I still remember the hat I wore. Wearing a green cone on my head as I walked down the aisle, had to be a symbol of deep friendship and love. Anybody (except a best friend) would have said, "No" and "Hell no," to wearing *that* hat.

We hung tight during her pregnancy and the birth of her son. Saying goodbye when I left for Denver was very hard, but by then, we had declared ourselves as best friends for life. Nothing or no one could come between us. She was our adventure planner; I just gave her my money and followed the plans she provided, including plans for traveling all over the United States.

When I moved my mother to Colorado, my brothers were very angry and refused to help me drive both my car and hers eighteen hundred miles from Clarksdale, Mississippi, to Denver. With literally a few hours' notice, Carolyn stepped up and told me to give her time to drive back to Jackson, Mississippi. She went to drop her car off at her home, and then met me halfway back to Clarksdale.

Once we returned to Clarksdale, we were off to Denver like *The Beverly Hillbillies* with an extra car and my mother in tow. My aunt and uncle drove the biggest Nissan Pathfinder SUV we could find. My mother sat in the back seat, holding tight to a cash box. I was too busy leading her to Denver, that I didn't have time to take an interest in what was happening with that cash box. We had luggage strapped down on the top of the huge SUV. My mother demanded we take *all* her stuff, including some eating utensils and cooking pots. Even though she knew I had plenty, she wanted her own.

My best friend and I took the road like pros and drove the hell out of my mother's little, red Honda Prelude. It was the classic 1983 Prelude with the flip-up lights like sleek headlights with flashing eyes. Only a best friend would jump right into this family crisis and feel right at home. I thought we had bonded during the failing of the nursing board exam experience, but this sealed the deal. Some would say this solidified our friendship.

Before and after this trip to relocate my mother to Denver, we traveled the country like we were *Thelma and Louise*, going from one adventure to another. We went on cruises to Alaska, Bahamas, Jamaica, just to name a few. We flew to New York several times to see Broadway plays such as *The Color Purple, Fences, Memphis, Lion King, Driving Miss Daisy, Cat on a Hot Tin Roof*, and others. In Harlem, the

Bronx, and Times Square, we ate the best soul food. We were Mississippi socialites taking over New York City like we owned it. I was paying with credit (VISA). She was just the opposite. As a Dave Ramsey scholar, she was a cash or money order carrying girl. That was just one of the ways we were different. She gave me a customized and embroidered tote bag that read, "Sisters." We were sisters with different mothers. We were the sisters that neither one of us ever had. On April 12, 2012, when my mother suddenly passed away, in less than twenty-four hours, Carolyn was standing at my side so I could cry on her shoulders.

I met Linda (the third member of this *sister* trio) when she started working on the same nursing unit as I did. By this time, I had known Carolyn for four years. Linda and I worked very closely together as two young nurses on the unit. She commuted at least forty minutes to work each day. One night, we had a severe thunderstorm. I invited her to spend the night with me in the city. Linda, Carolyn, and I became best friends after that. Linda had three sisters; therefore, she was not as desperate for sisterhood as me and Carolyn were. Their children were close in age, and they got along so well, like brothers and sisters. Linda's mother died a couple of months before I moved to Denver. She was the first to suffer the loss of a parent. This deep loss tightened the bond between the three of us. We joined together and grieved like sisters. Carolyn and Linda remained very close once I left Mississippi. They were each other's playmate parents and babysitters.

My leaving Mississippi didn't slow us down when it came to staying in contact. The three of us bought a timeshare property together for the purpose of traveling the world. The idea of buying the property was to make sure we had a place to travel to and stay together at least once a year. We would fly to Las Vegas and walk the streets, only to laugh and jump for joy and buy clothes at every T.J. Maxx and Dillard's outlet in town. We also ate at the best soul food restaurants in Las Vegas: Cosmopolitan, Lo-Lo's Chicken & Waffles, Hot N Juicy Crawfish, The Hush Puppy, and Ellaem's Soul Food.

Then, on one of our cruises together, something went wrong. A different reality stepped into view. Carolyn and I were traveling without Linda on this trip. To this day, I really don't know what happened. Every time I approached the subject, and asked, "What did I do?" Her response was always, "You know what you did." I apologized with an umbrella apology. "I never meant to hurt you. If I did something to hurt you, I am so sorry." Her response, even to this day, is "You know what you did."

Yes, I was blunt and very opinionated during our discussions, but I was always respectful and sincere. That is the nature of Sherry. Everyone who knows me knows that I walk daily in my truth. But I had always assumed, if we were *sisters* and *best* friends, we would endure anything and everything. I was banking on the fact that we would endure each other's differences (and faults, too) through this short and fleeting life. I never believed in cat fights or wallowing in the weeds. I believed in getting to the point and airing out your differences. I always thought we would sincerely promise each other that we would do better and get on with our lives. Boy, in this case, I was wrong.

We didn't get to make many promises to do better because we didn't have many of those "in the trenches" loving discussions. To the best of my knowledge, the problem began when I went gambling at a casino on the cruise ship in Jamaica and stayed too long, according to her standards. I was known, in the eyes of my friends, to do that. No matter how long I stayed at the casinos, though, I was always ready to keep my commitments the next day. I didn't drink enough to have hangovers. So, a couple of hours of sleep, and I would be ready for the next adventure.

On this day, I was a little slow getting dressed and told her that I was okay if she went downstairs to meet the rest of our party. When I got downstairs, they all were gone. I was not upset. Being the person I am, I stayed on the beach and enjoyed waterskiing with the men in skimpy bathing suits. When we returned to our cabin later that night, she was quiet and so upset that she declined to go to dinner with me. She continued to decline having dinner together for the rest of the trip. I was sad that she wasn't at dinner with me, but I surely enjoyed the good food and the attention of being alone with the flirty servers. They were very attentive to single women, and I just enjoyed that attention to the hilt. I would sit straight up in my chair and prop my ears open to hear every word they were lying about. Remember, I was single. It was easy to guess that I was not getting sweet lies very often from the flirty opposite gender back at home. I was not desperate, but flirting was half the fun on cruise vacations.

The following year, we went on a magnificently serene Alaskan cruise. As usual, for the sake of friendship, I participated in adventures that were not at the top of my list of fun. I went to a sunrise volcanic lava event on a cold bus. The temperature was even colder, close to the fence, watching the volcanic lava's roaring flames. Therefore, I returned to the less cold bus within a few minutes. It didn't help that I was sick with a cold. She didn't understand how I could decline to take part in this experience. On this trip, I also declined to go to a whale-watching luncheon that cost two hundred dollars. I decided I would rather spend my money at the casino. I knew she didn't like the casinos the way I did. It didn't help that she was further along into her Christian journey of walking the path with God than I was. But the most deciding factor for me was that whales were jumping up and down all day, every day, putting on a show of panoramic views all around the ship. The beauty of this was the *in-your-face* whale show from the ship view was free. Still, to this day, I think watching the whales for free was a good deal. Yet, after the fact, the question became "a good deal at what cost?" I once thought our friendship was priceless. It was sad to discover young friends didn't always know how to protect such a precious commodity as lasting friendship.

When we attempted to sort out our disagreements, I heard what I had done years ago. For example, once she went to the car and stayed there while I kept gambling until sunrise the next morning. Yes, I did this. I owned it. First, I felt Carolyn had a responsibility to tell me that she was ready to go. When she didn't do that, I felt we both owned the problem. However, as it pertains to things I did years ago, all I could offer her was an apology. I also stressed to her that if she would have approached me and told me how she felt years ago (about staying at the casino until daybreak), most likely I would have considered her feelings and taken her home. Knowing me, if I had wanted to, I would have dropped her safely at home and traveled back to the casino. We both would have been happy. I don't have a gambling problem, but I am always looking for a win-win situation. She wanted to go home. I wanted to gamble. There was a solution to make both of those desires a reality.

It was a year later before I realized that our excursions in Jamaica and Alaska had destroyed our relationship. By the time the word about a problem got to me, it was delivered by a person who had traveled on the cruise with us. Carolyn had informed her that she would never go anywhere else with me. The revelation that her sentiments came from another person made me question how strong our relationship was. Plus, I would like to think that if I had been made aware of such issues in a timely manner, I could have remembered enough about the event to sort out the hardcore necessary details that might have saved our relationship. I am *that* person who remembers things for a while, then I assign a value of archiving them or dumping them so new memories can enter my brain. I was looking forward to many more good times; therefore, I didn't savor the moments of the bad times. So, by the time this issue was put on the table for me to deal with, my memory of the bad things had practically faded away. I couldn't really defend what I did or did not do. If saving our relationship was going to be based on how much I remembered about the bad times, I didn't stand a chance. When I said, "I don't remember," I really *didn't* remember. I always thought a "best friend forever" (BFF) would want to refresh my memory for the sake of saving our relationship. Again, I was so wrong.

I was unable to refresh my memory regarding what I had done to destroy our relationship. However, we *did* agree to attempt to repair our relationship. I remember my great-grandmother telling me, "When things are tough, they can sometimes get worse before they get better. You just have to be willing to weather the storm." Our trio of *sisters* went to New York City to have some fun and repair a precious friendship. Yet, I had never felt so alone. Things got tough on the very first day we arrived. But for the sake of our friendship, I was all in. We lived in the same hotel suite and quietly and softly tiptoed around each other. I felt bad for Linda—she was *smack damn* in the middle of our silent but tense battle.

It was heartbreaking that they purposely bought last-minute tickets and went to a Broadway play without me. Once alone, I called the airlines to book a flight and make sure I was gone when they returned to the hotel. Good or bad decision, I didn't know which. The airline offered me an outrageous fare for a new reservation back to Denver. I later learned that all I had to do was request a change in my current flight reservations for a very reasonable cost. Well, maybe not being aware of that information was good and offered us more time to work through our issues. As fate would have it, I was still at the hotel when they got back from the play. Things were still so chilly and quiet that you could hear a pin drop. You also needed to search for a sweater to combat the cold, unfriendly environment. By that time, I had decided I could take anything for another twenty-four hours. We were leaving and going our separate ways the next morning.

I decided to go downstairs to exhale and get some much-needed fresh air. I left a well-lit room, only to re-enter in the midnight darkness. Carolyn had turned the lights out, knowing I would return. Even a small amount of light would have helped me navigate my way from the living room to the bedroom. She was sleeping on a sleeper sofa in the living room. Moving around without the light on was bad enough, but getting to the bedroom with no light was a daunting task. The lights were controlled by a lamp on the bedside table next to the sleeper sofa. Yes, we were in somewhat cramped surroundings, but that had never been a problem for us in the past. We had all come from less than modest means. Our love for each other always outweighed the limited spaces we had to maneuver in the past.

When morning came, we all went through the courteous, good morning routine. We were three strong-willed southern belles who were lousy at pretending and tiptoeing around each other. We walked strongly in our truth, just in different ways. I am vocal and respectful amid my truth. Carolyn is quiet and more subtle and passive in her truth-walking moments. Linda is vocal like me, but she just wanted to stay out of the line of fire as much as possible. She wanted us to deal with our issues as respectful adults.

Because the space was limited, I could hear snippets of their low-toned conversation in the suite's living room. After they finished their talk, Carolyn slowly came into the bedroom and stated, "We need to talk."

I responded, "Go ahead, tell me what is on your mind."

She began to "tell me about myself." She said I was selfish, not a team player, and a few other things as well. I patiently waited and let her completely empty all her thoughts about me before I spoke a single word in response. At least, I was proud of my ability to listen.

When she finished, I simply stated to her, "I am not going to debate what you have to say about me. What I will say is whatever or whoever you think I am, I have been this way all my life. I am not pretentious. I have always presented my true self. I have been this way for the entire thirty-five years we've known each other. If you don't like me now, perhaps you never liked me."

She appeared to be taken aback by my response. Perhaps she thought I would come out with all barrels loaded and ready to defend myself. Instead, I was humble and open to hear and do anything that would bring back the relationship we once had.

Yet, the rubber had met the road. At that moment, our relationship was like being at a Mississippi crossroads. We were at the fork in the road where we had to make a decision. I was not willing to sell my soul to deny who I had always been. I can't be sure, but I think she was blind to the *real* me, as if she saw me as the person I was not, never had been, or never would be. I decided that her perception of me was *her* issue to deal with. If she didn't like me after thirty-five years, my feeling was that I would never live up to her expectations. It was sad to find out that we had different expectations of me. The guiding beacon for me was that I love the fundamental *me*. I was not thinking for one moment about changing myself, although I am always looking for opportunities for improvement.

We hugged and genuinely said we loved each other. But at that moment, my heart began to ache for my BFF.

Over a period of years, I kept reaching out for the BFF I once knew. I kept apologizing for whatever I did to break the bond between us. Our conversations went from joyful to painful, and I just wanted to stop the pain. Finally, one day, I said, "God, I am turning our relationship over to You. You've got the power." I took her out of my favorite contact page on my cell phone. Then one day, about a year ago, my cell phone rang. I recognized the number, even though her name and number were no longer locked in my cell phone.

She asked to speak to me by my complete name, "May I speak to Sherry Henderson? Is this Sherry Henderson?"

I answered, "Hi, this is Sherry. How are you, Ms. Carolyn?"

We talked for a while, and then the elephant in the room came up.

I asked, "What happened to our relationship?"

She told me once again, "You know what you did."

So, I was still the blame for the melting of the bond between us. She acknowledged zero sum responsibility for the status of our relationship. It was still all my fault. At that point, I came to the conclusion that our relationship would never be what it once was. My definition of friendship was no longer a shared centerpiece of our relationship. I had to question if it had ever been a shared expectation. I made the crossroads decision and mentally split the fork in the road. I couldn't muster up the desire to put her back on my BFF list. This was a crushing, heartfelt moment for me.

I regret I was unable to salvage our friendship. Best friends lend shoulders to cry on without having to be asked. We had not looked to each other for that gift in years. But if I wanted her to accept me for who I was, I had to accept her for who she was. That might mean we are still *sisters* who are no longer *best friends forever*. Who knows if that is where our relationship will stay? But again, I had put our relationship in God's hands.

I put the relationship of my once best friend, Carolyn, in the hands of God. I decided to move forward. It turned out that my real, true "best friend forever" was someone from my past who had gone on with her life. We would meet for school reunions and family functions. But when the "shit hit the fan" with Carolyn, *she* was there for me. She never said, "I told you so." We picked up and carried on as if only distance had separated us. We are still BFFs to this day.

This chapter was meant to highlight the significance of at least one BFF to share the journey of life with—the good and the bad. Also remember, friends accept each other as they are. They must learn to put pride and egos aside. We must be honest with ourselves, so we can be honest with each other. As I matured, I wrestled with the growing pains of making tough decisions, but I found there is a silver lining in each dark cloud. The key is to do the best you can (at that time) while staying open to ways to become a better person. Most often, we think of loss as bitter, but sometimes the sweetness of our loss does not show its importance until later chapters of our life.

The take-home message is that most things don't magically last a lifetime—not even the deepest friendships. We must invest in and nurture our BFF relationships, just like we do for our romantic relationships. It is also true that we get out of our "best friend forever" relationships what we invest in them.

"Everything of value takes work, particularly relationships."

—Maya Angelou

Chapter Fourteen

COTTON THISTLE: PAIN AND AGGRESSION

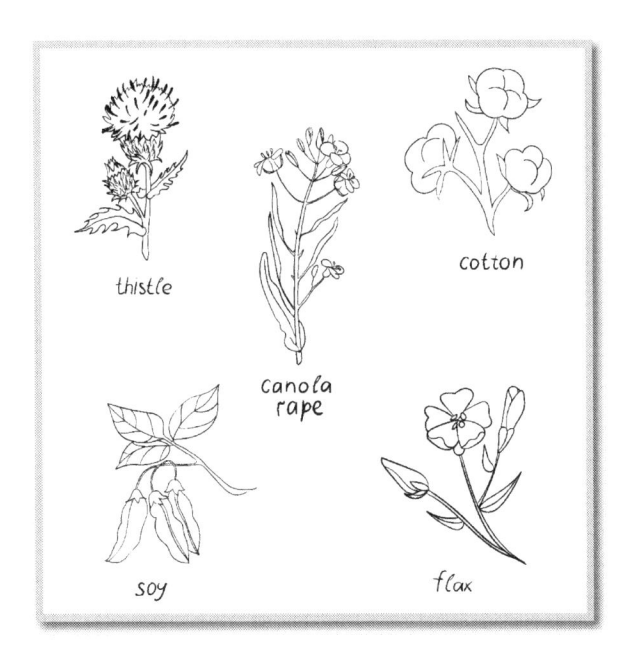

thistle

canola rape

cotton

soy

flax

I have experienced the loss of a thirty-five-year "best friend forever" relationship, but I did not let that stop me from reaching out and trying to help others. I kept traveling the path that was laid out for me. Yet, I still jumped in there and put twists and spins on my path from time to time. More times than not, they worked. There were times, though, when divine intervention would have served me better. One particular time, I picked up a cotton thistle that cut me and made me bleed.

The Thistle has a very thorny reputation. Some people even considered it a cursed flower. This association is understandable when you experience bristling thistles on bear feet. Scottish legends, however, paint a different picture. The story goes that a Norse army endeavored to sneak into a Scottish encampment by night. At least one of them was barefoot. Upon stepping on a thistle he yelled out, alerting the troops. As a result the invaders retreated and left for their home land with their tail between their legs. Historians believe this was the story of the Battle of Largs, and a spear thistle was the hero of the day. ("Thistle Meaning," n.d.)

Just like the pain of attempting to get close to the plant, one must take into consideration the thorns (fallout of the consequences) of attempting to help someone, especially those whom you are not qualified to help.

Well, I didn't go looking for a thorny cotton thistle, but one found me. Instead of leaving it where it found me, I brought it onto my path. It left me with emotional scars that healed, but will remain just one thought away to remind me forever that no good deed goes unpunished.

One of my good deeds emerged from my personal nurse-based sympathy syndrome. This syndrome has caused me to be oblivious that I was stepping on a path paved with ugly and vicious thistle plants. This phase of my life really began at nine years old. The son and daughter of my mother's best friend were attached to me and my brothers by the friendship and activities of our parents. We not only shared babysitters, but we also shared daily meals and toys. We lived across the street from each other, therefore; we grew up together. The son and I became early childhood sweethearts. I think back to him sneaking up on me and giving me my first big, juicy, smacking kiss. I remember immediately frowning and wiping the juice from my face.

As a family, they moved to Chicago when he and his sister were teenagers. He went into the military and while enlisted, he was misdiagnosed with a brain tumor. The ordeal of being told that he had a life-ending disease became a powerful catalyst for him to start using drugs. By the time his mother died at forty-eight from aggressive breast cancer, he was a full-blown drug addict. While I was in Chicago to attend his mother's funeral, he reached out to me for help. The naïve nurse in me felt that moving him to Denver, Colorado to help him was the least that I could do.

I felt there was no way that Denver could be infested with drugs like Chicago. My first thought was to bring him to a place of fewer drugs. The ultimate goal was to find better resources for drug abuse rehabilitation. He had put the house he inherited after the death of his mother into my name. This was to ensure that he couldn't sell it to support his drug habit. The house was deeded to him because he had helped his mother purchase it with his GI bill benefits. He had also received money from his mother's life insurance policies. He and my brother drove his brand-new Cadillac back to Denver. The car was the most beautiful, bluish-purple, with lavender leather seats. I do not like Cadillacs, but this one was very easy on the eyes.

Well, I put my plan in motion. The following morning, after they arrived in Denver, I called my insurance company and got a huge surprise. The insurance company informed me that we had to be married in order for him to receive drug rehabilitation benefits through my insurance. That was a big bone for me to chew on. We went to the park, and we sat there discussing the options as we both cried. At the end of the day, I decided to marry him. This was the only way I knew to get the rehabilitation help he needed. Remember, we were friends from a long way back. All I could think of was if anyone needed my help, he did. He had lost his mother. Who could help him more than a friend who was also an outstanding nurse? The agreement was sealed with a verbal promise that we would keep our marriage a secret since it was an arrangement and not a marriage in the genuine sense of the word. We reached out to my roommate, who was more naïve than me—if that was possible. She and her boyfriend became witnesses at the marriage ceremony officiated by the Justice of the Peace. Our quietly kept secret stayed between the four of us.

A couple of months later, we were both proud of his medallions of progress. He had successfully completed one of the most expensive drug rehabilitation programs in Colorado. We celebrated him achieving this milestone. One month later, he didn't come home all night.

I lived in a neighborhood where mostly senior citizens resided. When I moved in, they had baked cookies and brought them over to welcome me into my new home. That next morning after he didn't come home, as I was on my way home from work, I saw his car parked at a sleazy house in the neighborhood. This house didn't look like a place where senior citizens lived (or people who were committed to going to work every day to earn a decent living). I had used my insurance benefits and married him to help him; I had to save my investment. I went home and got my naïve roommate. Off to the unknown danger, we went. I didn't care. We had been on this undertaking from the beginning. We couldn't think of a reason to stop now.

She sat in my car while I went into the house to find him. The environment was just like *New Jack City*. People were sitting on the floors in the dark, bugged out, and smoking crack cocaine. I found him, took him by the hand, and led him out the door. He did not resist my insistence that he come home with me. Amazingly, no one confronted me or got in my way. They were too enmeshed in the activity of getting high to notice I was there. They certainly didn't care what I was doing there, as long as I didn't interfere in their high experience.

I still felt I could save him. I just needed to keep him away from that sort of environment. I brought him home and locked the doors from the outside. My naïve friend and I went back to get his beautiful Cadillac. When I got back home, the man who I had locked in the house had gone out the bedroom window. So much for two naïve girls who lacked street smarts. We were way out of our element. But worse than that, we had no idea how much fire we were flirting with. We had crossed over from the red-hot flames into the hottest of the hot-blue flames. Again, ignorance was bliss at that moment. We were terribly unaware of the danger that was awaiting us.

Not long after, on a delightful winter evening, I was walking to my car from the Aurora Theatre on Colfax. Parts of Colfax are known as the land of thieves and prostitution, but I was coming from a play at a respectable theater of culture. I happened to look up into the window of a consignment store and saw some familiar-looking clothes. As I took another look, I said to myself, "I have clothes like those." It took me another minute to realize that those *were* my clothes! Half of my wardrobe was on display for a second-hand store sale. He had stolen my clothes and sold them for a little of nothing! I went inside and told the store owner that the clothes were stolen. She informed me that she had no idea she had received stolen goods. She graciously offered to sell them back to me for what she had paid for them. They were Casual Corner outfits. Every woman of modest means knows the value of the Casual Corner department store to the fashion world. I didn't know then, but those clothes would become authentic antiques. I just couldn't bring myself to pay one more penny for suits and dresses I had already paid three to four hundred dollars for. Later, I found pawn receipts for other clothing items, such as my leather shoes and skirts. I had no clue that you could pawn items other than jewelry. This should let you know I had never seen the inside of a pawnshop before this experience. I walked to the nearby police station and told them about my situation. They emphatically informed me that because we lived in the same house, it was not considered stealing. Wow, what a learning experience.

Two weeks later, he broke the bond of secrecy. He called the nursing station where I worked as the Nurse Manager. He told the staff that he wanted to speak to his wife, Sherry D. Henderson. *Busted.* I denied it and told the staff he had to be someone playing tricks. I didn't know if they bought it or not. Lying was not my strong suit—I had lied and momentarily escaped the admission of the truth.

My mother arrived in town just a few days after that call. She was concerned about the extent I had gone to help him. When she started asking questions out of concern, he became angry. When I looked up, he was throwing the marriage license into her face, yelling, "We are married and there is nothing you can do about it!" *Busted again!*

The look on my mother's face was the most disappointing look I had seen or would ever see again. She shook her head and cried. This is the moment I fell off the pedestal my family had placed me on. I fell from grace as the beloved family princess, and I became a common peon. As I cried with my mother, I tried to explain to her that I just wanted to help him because he was my friend; he was a part of our family. I pled with her to understand that his mother would have wanted me to help him. *I had made a promise to a dead woman, who, if alive, would have told me to stay as far away from him as I could.* It was me and me alone who had needed to save him. The truth of the matter was, I was no match for such a complex drug abuse issue.

When I faced the truth and admitted that enough was enough, it forced me to pull the blinders off and bite the reality bullet. Finally, one day I woke up and told him I had enough, and I was on my way to the courthouse to correct this dreadful marriage mistake. I had learned that I could get an annulment. The trick was that I had to put the request in the newspaper and wait for him to respond. The bigger trick was to bury the announcement in the fine print of the least-read newspaper around, and most of all, not tell him about it. I had come to the painful understanding that I didn't have the skills to help him. *Had I been temporarily insane to think I could?* Yes, I was insane, simply because I had done an insanely crazy thing. However, just because I went insane didn't mean I had to stay that way one day longer. I made up my mind to cut bait, run for safety, and regain my sanity.

I left him in the house with my dog, Chris. Chris was a reddish-brown miniature Doberman Pinscher. His real name was Daddy Christmas. He was the apple of my eye. He was very protective and only had love for me. I made it clear to that man that when I got back, I would have simple instructions on how to have our marriage annulled. I was desperate to find a way to free myself from this hellish fire-and-brimstone nightmare.

On my way back home, I turned onto the street I lived on, and I could see a swarm of police cars with red and blue lights flashing. They had barricaded the entrance to my block. I drove my car as close as I could and got out, and began walking closer to my house. When I got closer, I could see the police squad and a SWAT team. The squad leader informed me they were communicating with someone at 1617 Lansing, who was threating to kill himself because his wife was leaving him. I calmly told the police officers to do what they needed to do, but "Please, don't hurt my dog." I had gone from a person trying to save someone from a life of drugs and crime to a person who didn't care if he lived or died. They eventually talked him into coming out of the house and going wherever they took him. I didn't bother to ask where that would be. I just ran as fast as I could into the house, hugged my dog, and exhaled. My dog and I were both happy to see the possibility of peace on the horizon. He was jumping for joy! It was hard to tell if the joy was for seeing me after such an ordeal or if he was just as glad as I was that the monster was gone.

My husband-by-arrangement came by my house a few more times, but I was spending my time working on saving myself *from* myself. I got a call one day from a police officer who told me that he had found someone trying to break into my house through a window. He said the person had told him that he lived there. He asked me what I wanted him to do with the man. Well, I told him to do whatever they do with all the other criminals. I hung up the phone and continued with my workday. He also appeared at my door one night and told me he was having chest pains and felt like he was going to die. I told him to get out of my yard, and I didn't care if he had a heart attack, as long as he didn't have it on my property. "The sidewalk and the street will hold your body until someone other than me comes to help you," I said. I went back into the house. I was in such a way that I didn't recognize the angry, bitter person I had become.

His sister called one day and said she was coming to get him. Her plan was to take him back to Chicago. When she arrived, we went to the pawnshop and got his car. It was so banged up from his driving without brakes and using the emergency brakes to stop. I imagined that sometimes he couldn't stop before plowing into something in his path, like a parked bench or whatever. In the long run, I did something right by having my name on his inherited house as collateral. I released my right to the house after he and his sister agreed to pay me for all my material loss. There was no price to put on the emotional adjustments I had to make to save myself. Eventually, everything was settled, and he was a distant memory back in Chicago. We didn't speak until the death of my family members. After all, we had been friends and family before we were enemies.

One night, he called and said he had gotten his life on track. He happily said God had told him to call me and sincerely tell me he was sorry. I told him I accepted his apology. I also told him I had one request of God, though. "Tell God I'm asking Him to tell *you* that you should never call me again." I guess my request was granted because he *never* called me again.

We saw each other at my mother's funeral. I was sitting there in grief when he waltzed to the podium and looked over at my mother's body lying in her casket. He told her that her son-in-law loved her and would miss her. *Busted—one more time!* Mind you, my best friends, Carolyn and Linda, were at the funeral. They didn't have a clue that I had been married. After the funeral service, I found myself voluntarily explaining my actions to them. I think what my ex-husband-by-arrangement had said went straight over Linda's head. I was sure it would take less than twenty-four hours for Carolyn to catch up to speed about the bombshell that had been dropped. Carolyn was the one who was always alert and astute about the dynamics of her surroundings.

My naïve friend who had been with me from the beginning of this nightmare was a part of the conversation to help me buffer the embarrassment. One of the secrets I thought I would take to my grave had moved from Denver, Colorado. This secret was now exposed to all of those I grew up with in my small town of Clarksdale, Mississippi. I didn't share this situation with many people, but I had never felt ashamed of doing drastic things to save someone in the past. However, after this, I promised myself that I would *never* do such a crippling Good Samaritan deed again. I had donated to the cause of trying to stomp out drug addiction. After that experience, when people with drug addictions approached me outside of my professional career, I immediately would go into one of those *Forrest Gump* moments and "run, Sherry, run" as fast as I could.

Even though I had learned to run away, when necessary, it didn't stop me from having to experience another momentous, life-changing event. One day, I was strutting down the work hallways, and a friend of mine stated, "Your legs are getting bigger and prettier. Are you pregnant?" I didn't understand the connection. But I *had* been feeling a little out of sync. Who wouldn't, while dealing with what had been going on in my life at the time? I just could not shake the weird feelings. I was not throwing up; I was not even nauseated. I was religiously taking birth control pills every day. Because I couldn't shake the out-of-sync feelings, I took a pregnancy test.

Damn. Damn. Damn. It was positive.

Oh my God! How many ways could my good deed cause me pain and punishment? I united with my partner in crisis—she didn't judge me. She agreed to help me with my plan. I had decided that I couldn't be connected to this horrible movie every day of my life. I decided to have an abortion.

Stop. I know what your next thought might be. How could I do this? How would I have felt if my mother would have aborted me? Well, you perhaps don't remember, but I told her more than once that I felt they could have been picking up daises instead of conceiving me; I sincerely meant that. I believe my mother would have had a better opportunity to fulfill her hopes and dreams if she had not been a child strapped down with a child. She made her choice with her limited knowledge, advice, and resources. Now, *I* was having to make a decision that I could live with. I will not get into a heated discussion about the right and wrong aspects of my decision. I will say that I am pro-choice. It is my belief that when I meet my Maker, I will stand before Him alone. I don't know if asking for forgiveness will save me. When I look back, I still do not regret my decision. Based on my truth and honesty, He will deal with me as He sees fit. In the meantime, I will put a period after the *Why* and *How could you* ask questions. I made the best decision for *me*.

Now I am ready to share how I survived this crisis—how *I* survived... *my* life. My friend in crisis and I got together and strategically planned how to do the best we could in order for me to come out on the other side of this as whole and healthy as possible. She drove me to the facility. I was shocked to discover where the clinic was located; I was dumbfounded to find that I had been passing by this place frequently on my way to downtown Denver. It was well-hidden behind a forest of trees. The protesters were very invested in their message with verbal chants and larger-than-life signs. I was emotionally torn, but I walked right past them because I had fallen on my sword and made my decision.

My partner in crisis took excellent physical and emotional care of me. We would speak of this situation briefly over time, but the secret remained between the two of us. She always made it clear to me that it was *my* secret to share or take to my grave. I decided to share with you because I know there are others like me out there with different names but similar situations.

My friend had asked me for help. I attempted to help. I paid a high price for my honest-to-God good intentions. If I could go back with the knowledge I have now, would I change anything? Yes, I would. I would recognize that I was way out of my lane—out of my league—to try to help someone without the proper educational skill set to do so. I would understand that "No" and "Hell No" would have been the right answer for such times. I would remember that a super nurse is one who knows when they are in over their head. They will know there is strength instead of weakness in saying, "No" and referring their loved ones to the appropriate experts.

My life was beginning to look like I was destined to walk a rocky path at every turn. I continued to be driven by my *never-quit* attitude and determination. These were the characteristics that kept me moving forward and not looking back. If I had looked back, I may have focused on all the bad things that happened to me. Instead, I chose to give more weight to how I was getting up and dusting myself off after each fall.

Chapter Fifteen

LOTUS:
SURVIVING AND THRIVING THROUGH VIOLENCE

The lotus flower is often associated with domestic violence and sexual assault and with purity, healing and enlightenment. This sense of purity arises from how it grows. It begins in muddy water, rises above it and turns into a beautiful flower that reaches light/enlightenment. The lotus flower is a symbol of strength, healing, purity, perseverance, promise and enlightenment." ("Logo, Mission," n.d.)

Rape (also sexual molestation) has long been considered a crime so unspeakable, so shameful to its victims, that they are rendered mute and cloaked in protective anonymity… The victims of rape must carry their memories with them for the rest of their lives. They must not also carry the burden of silence and shame. ("About the After" n.d.)

Often the flower petals are scattered in the memory of domestic violence victims because it exhibits characteristics similar to human behavior. Even when its roots are in the dirtiest murky river waters, the lotus produces the most beautiful, flawless flower. It only blooms in very swampy areas, so that represents the idea that out of ugliness, destruction and unrest, survivors can find their way to healthy relationships. "The flower goes through so much before it blossoms, so does the human consciousness before it can reach enlightenment." ("Logo, Mission," n.d.)

Without going through the difficult life lessons (the mud), a person would never reach a higher state of consciousness (the lotus). Like the lotus' refusal to accept defeat, it's almost impossible not to associate this flower with unwavering faith and inner strength within those that have suffered from domestic violence. It mirrors a survivor's journey toward healing and recovery. Like the lotus flower, domestic violence survivors have been at the bottom of the pond but have risen to show their worth, courage, and hidden beauty.

This chapter is another difficult chapter to write and even more difficult to share with readers. However, if I can provoke one person to pause and give deep thought to dangerously subtle moments in their relationship, it will be well worth it. These are the moments that will leave dark stains unless you use them as profound learning moments. There is wisdom in heeding the warning that it will be in your best interest to identify the signs and avoid the dangers of domestic violence. This can be done because you have heard someone identify the signs before life presents you with such a situation. You have the chance to be proactive and change the narrative.

If I had been proactive and learned from the wisdom of others before me, I certainly would have had the opportunity to change this part of the narrative of my life. My boyfriend and I had a house built together. He moved from a situation where he was renting a room from a friend and coworker. I left my first three-bedroom, one-bathroom ranch house and moved into a four bedroom, four-bathroom, two-story house with him. In our new home, we even had a winding staircase, a plush loft—all that, and more. Thinking back, we also got to choose our floor plan, color scheme, and multiple bathroom options, etc. The excitement of making those choices was over-the-moon exhilarating for us. If you were looking in from the outside, you would have sworn we were living the good life. We didn't have any major financial insecurities. What could be lurking just beneath the surface that you would not have been able to see? The alarm bells were so subtle; you wouldn't have heard them. Without a doubt, I didn't see or hear them.

We had been living together in a common-law relationship for approximately one year, when his mother, stepfather, and sister decided to visit. When they drove up and got out of the car, I sensed that they had hoisted all their pride onto him, making the house (*his* house, in their minds) a reality. I believe they saw him as the provider and main contributor to our success. I chose to give his mother and stepfather our master bedroom to stay in. One reason, of course, was they were older; the other reason was that I didn't want them to have to leave their bedroom to take care of their personal needs. I gave his sister a bedroom that had access to the shared upstairs bathroom. She had total privacy because she was the only other person upstairs. My boyfriend and I moved to the unfinished basement and slept on an air mattress. I don't think I could have been any more accommodating unless I had moved out and offered the house as an Airbnb. He didn't ask me to be kind to them. I did it out of the goodness of my heart. They were special guests.

His sister took one look at her bed and found tiny ink stains on the otherwise perfectly clean sheets. Yes, I studied in bed and was known to "ink up" some sheets. But these stains were barely noticeable—of pinpoint size. She demanded another set of sheets.

I looked at her and said, "If you want better sheets, you need to discuss that with your brother. He can get you whatever you need." Interesting enough, her brother, my boyfriend, didn't rush to her side and deliver new, crisp sheets. Either she didn't confront him with this *horrible* issue, or he decided she would be just fine on those sheets with the pinpoint-sized ink spots. I didn't see how sleeping on these sheets would change her life forever. In other words, she wouldn't get a disease or die from sleeping on lightly ink-stained, but otherwise perfectly clean sheets. What his sister didn't know (but he knew), was that when we moved in, my friends asked us why I was letting him bring his noticeably stained sofa into our brand spanking new home. I told them I felt he needed to bring some of his things to the new house. I felt this was a way of compromising until we could buy things together. I trusted that if my friends and I could sit on his stained couch, his sister could sleep on the sheets. I had no malice. I took as gospel that what was good for the goose was surely good for the gander. Perhaps she would pack a set of new sheets in her luggage if she ever had to come back to visit us. Our paths never crossed again; therefore, I will never know, nor do I really care.

It was clear, from the time they stepped foot into our home, that his family felt my boyfriend was in charge of the household. The environment soon became tense and obviously unevenly divided. It was them against me. I had voluntarily provided my brand-new Acura Legend for him to pick up his family from the airport. There was no way that four people could ride in his work car, which was a small Toyota sports model. There was even less possibility they would have any chance of riding in his classic royal-blue Corvette. Yet, I felt like the maid and transportation service in my own home.

My upbringing indoctrinated me with a dose of "how to behave at other people's houses." First, you do *not* have sex at someone else's house unless you are married. Even then, that is questionable. A hotel is always available if you can't wait until you get back home. This shows respect for the owner of the house and for yourself. His mother didn't feel that way when I was visiting her home. She had set up a lodging arrangement where we shared a bed in her home. I immediately told my boyfriend I was uncomfortable with the arrangements, but I would not raise the issue as long as he understood there was no way I would have sex with him in his mother's home. If he wanted to have sex with me, he would most certainly have to take me to a hotel of his choice. That was the only compromise I would make.

We weren't usually an argumentative couple. We certainly were not known for explosive arguments. Our issues were much more subtle. We argued over seemingly *crazy* things. For example, how many cans of tomato sauce to buy at a price of five cans for a dollar or how much to pay for mattresses for the bed. Mind you, I was buying these items with my own hard-earned money. And guess what? Most likely, *that* was the root of our problem. I was making twice as much money as he was. My rationale for bargain shopping was simply to take advantage of an opportunity to buy at a low cost, instead of waiting until the cost would be much higher. Even with my educational background in psychiatric behavior, it took me a while to realize that this was subtle control. Subtle, yet not one bit less dangerous.

One day, *all* "the shit hit the fan." A teenager in the housing complex came through and hit our old, raggedy blue pickup truck. We had paid for it with funds from the household account. We had a difference of opinion regarding what to do with the insurance money received to repair the damaged truck. I felt it was a *no brainer*. We should use the money to repair the truck. If any funds were left, we should put them back into the household account. If we agreed the truck didn't need to be repaired, all the money should go back into the household account.

When I reminded him that both our names were on the title to the truck, he informed me that he never put my name on the title. Therefore, he matter-of-factly told me that he had the right to do whatever he wanted to do with the insurance money. The temperature in the room started rising. It didn't take long for the verbal argument to become very heated. He pushed me. I felt I now had the right to hit *him*; therefore, I pushed him back. The shoving back and forth continued. Yes, he had violated my physical space first, but I made an awful choice. Remember, I was not at the peak of the maturity scale, and I was born a tomboy. I had never started a verbal or physical argument, but I prided myself on holding my own during either. It was like wearing and holding up a badge of honor. I had heard that some men never wanted to lose a verbal or physical fight. They feel they have to get in the last punch. When the shoving stopped, and when he suddenly punched the telephone numbers to call 911, I was surprised. I thought the fight was a tie at most. I really didn't think I got the best of him. This had to be his way of getting in the last punch.

When the police officers arrived, he told them *I* was the aggressor and was beating him up. They were more than ready to side with him. The rest of the conversation focused on arresting this woman for "beating up" a man. They kept saying things like, "Women are getting away with beating up men all the time," or "This is one time we'll make sure this so-called upstanding woman will pay the price for physically beating a man."

It was like I was starring in a horrible episode of *COPS* on the REELZ television channel. I was arrested, handcuffed, and led to the police car. They held my head down and pushed me into the back seat just like I remembered seeing them do to criminals on that show. *Wow! How had I found myself in a situation so out of character for me?* I was only defending and protecting myself. Yes, I could have left the house before things escalated, but I was holding on to my badge of honor and protecting myself. My driving thought was if a person hits *me*, I had the right to hit their ass back. With that thinking, I was now posing for my criminal glamor mug shots. I have taken pictures that looked like mug shots many times before, but this was the real McCoy.

This movie, starring the overly aggressive police officers, the rude check-in receptionist and the totally chaotic space where they treated people like they were less than dirt, brought everything into crystal-clear focus. I used my one phone call to call my faithful mentor. She came and bailed me out with *my* money, of course. Money well-spent, but an ounce of prevention could have saved me a pound of pain and a ton of shame and humiliation. I didn't dare call my family. I was too ashamed. They had put me back on a pedestal, and now I had fallen off again.

When I got home from jail, his family sat at our dining room table and ate as if nothing had ever happened. They never asked me to join them, nor did I make an attempt to. I was an outsider in my own home. After dinner, his mother had the nerve to stand in our kitchen and defend her son by asking me, "What does a classy young lady like you need with an old, raggedy truck?" *Wow!* All the principles I had been taught appeared to be missing from that question. I told her I was appalled that she was defending her son. It was my opinion that this was a perfect opportunity to teach him several lessons. The first was that *shared* ownership meant *shared* responsibilities. Another lesson was that lying about putting my name on the truck was wrong and a violation of the trust of our relationship. I also told her I could call *my* mother to defend *me*, but that was unnecessary. My mother and great-grandmother had long ago taught me the basics of right and wrong.

Well, it was good they had taken pictures of the house because it wouldn't be long before our home would become only a memory for him and his family. I did not feel safe. I didn't need this to escalate into my job or my family getting involved. My family could scold or discipline me, but they weren't going to have anyone else abusing me. For his sake, the sake of my family, and for my safety, I needed out. It didn't take long for me to start the process of going our separate ways.

Earlier, another situation regarding his subtle control involved mattresses for our bed. True to form, this situation also had aspects of attention seeking and was a warning of trouble to come. I had purchased new king-sized mattresses to replace the old ones on our bed. I didn't understand that the monetary or financial gap between us would cause deep problems. It was naïve to think it didn't matter who bought things to upgrade the beauty and comfort of our home. I had purchased the mattresses without a dollar from him. However, I had to solicit help from my brother and uncle to put them on the bed because he refused to help. This was a bit much for me and my family to understand. His control had seeped right out of the bedroom into the presence of my family.

That same weekend, he also wanted to control the cost of the food bought and served to my family. They were visiting to celebrate my Nurse Practitioner graduation, and I wanted to have a celebration dinner with them. The dinner was expensive, but it was for a special occasion. I had completed a major milestone in my life. I sensed, if expensive food was not costing *him* a penny, then he would enjoy the food and the company of my family in the spirit of happiness for my accomplishment. He refused to take part in the dinner I had planned in our home because he thought I should not have been serving them high-priced steak and lobster. His actions had nothing to do with the expense of the food. He had concluded my family was the center of attention instead of him. Things had gotten twisted. If logic had served me right, *I* should have been the center of attention because we were supposed to be acknowledging *my* graduation.

When we went out to dinner for another special moment to recognize the hard work and sacrifices I had made, he reluctantly joined us. He not only didn't pay for his meal, but he ordered the most expensive item on the menu: surf and turf. Perhaps he was not going to turn down the opportunity for steak and lobster a second time. It appeared to be the first whole lobster he had sat down with. Because of his lack of experience with eating it whole, it was clear the lobster was getting the best in the battle. (Oh, the things we do to keep peace in the family and keep our family from knowing the type of people we've chosen to share our lives.) I was already disappointed that he didn't take care of the dinner, or at least his and my portion, since I was the "Lady of the Hour." I was livid that he took advantage of the situation and ordered the most expensive meal on the menu. He knew I would have done almost anything to keep from acknowledging the white elephant in the room that everyone else saw, but chose to ignore. He was immature and not used to a decent life of *class*.

How could I explain his behavior and my acceptance of it? My family was smart; they didn't need an explanation. I can only imagine they were thinking, *how long will it take for her to wake up and do something about this bad movie?*

He clearly resented the love and closeness between me and my family. Yet, I can't blame everything on him. Being in a controlling relationship is something I had to take responsibility for. I had not mastered identifying subtle abuse. I was not interested in wasting more of my time to help him reach a higher level of maturity. Before I could help him, I needed to find a safe space and focus on helping myself. We could no longer be together; we could no longer share a home.

In addition to a memory, our home became a cash cow for him. I didn't want to move because I was in the middle of obtaining my Master's in Nursing degree and Nurse Practitioner certification. While being very busy in school, I had to find a way to stay in my home. The stress of moving and going to school was a combination that could certainly have derailed or delayed my educational goals. I consulted the realtor who had assisted us in purchasing the house. There was a good chance my boyfriend would trust the same realtor. I got lucky because the realtor helped me make him an offer he could not refuse. We had paid thirty-five hundred dollars each to purchase the home. With the advice of a lawyer and our trusted former realtor, I wrote my ex-boyfriend a certified check for twelve thousand-five hundred dollars. Strangely, he asked to ride with me to the lawyer's office. I happily drove us there. The radio was on, and I softly heard Mary J. Blige's single, *Not Gon' Cry*, with the lyrics, "I should have left your ass a long time ago." I turned the radio up to gangster jukebox volume. After all, we were in *my* car.

He had tripled his money. This was a better investment than he could have earned in the stock market on Wall Street. You would think that making more money than he expected would have been enough for him. No, it wasn't. He took me to small claims court. I was working days on my new job as a Nurse Practitioner, the job I had studied and worked so very hard for. The judge worked out a compromise, requesting that we meet in his courtroom in another city on the weekend. When I got to court, he had a beautiful, young woman sitting next to him. I immediately thought it was her brilliant writing and organizational skills that had prepared the well-written documents which were used against me.

When I told my family and friends about her being there, they immediately started asking questions, seeking to compare her to me. Their questions included: "How did she look? What was she wearing? Did you say anything to her?" My answers were: "Yes, she was pretty. No, I don't remember what she was wearing. No, I didn't say anything to her except *hello* when I spoke kindly to both of them."

In my mind, I was saying, *better her than me*. If I'd had a conversation with her, it would have been one similar to those my mother frequently had with me. My respect for myself and women, in general, would have ruled. I would have invited her behind the *shed*. I would have said, "Take a good look. Just think—it is *me* this time. Just consider that the next time it could be *you*."

The judge read the list of items he was suing me for, which included the ceiling fan and storm doors that were attached to the house, and his personal clothes stored in the garage rafters. When we got to the "forty-gallon containers," I told the judge that I did not recognize such items. My ex proudly informed me that they were THE GARBAGE CANS.

Shocked, I said, "Oh, okay."

The judge proceeded to say "Mr. Johnson, is that your signature on the settlement agreement? Were you of sound mind when you signed the agreement?"

He answered, "Yes," to both questions.

The judge slammed his gavel and stated, "CASE DISMISSED!"

I told the judge that he could have his clothes. I said I would give them to any friend of his whom I knew. I made it clear that he was not welcome back to my home.

After we separated, we lived in nearby neighborhoods. I saw him a couple more times in local stores. The last time I saw him, I was in a Walgreen's store; I heard a voice behind me call my name.

"Hello, Ms. Henderson." I looked back, and he was standing about ten feet away.

I said, "Hello, Mr. Johnson."

We chatted briefly about the status of our parents. He said his stepfather had passed away, and his mother was not doing well. He stated that he was moving back to South Carolina very soon. I wished him and his family well before he left the store to go to his car. I rushed the cashier along so I could peek out the door to see what he was driving. He wasn't driving anything special. I wondered about that classic royal-blue Corvette that I never got to ride in. I smiled and quickly made his business not my business. I could not wait to get home and tell my mother that I had seen him.

The highlight of the story was that I was able to tell my mother I didn't feel any love or anger for him. He had become just another human being to me. I was overjoyed by this feeling! I had handled the situation between us so well that when I went back to the courthouse to deal with some business for my mother, the bailiff told me that he remembered me. He told me that he was proud of me for how I respectfully took care of my business. That, in turn, made me proud of myself.

In the spirit of self-help, I attended domestic violence classes. There, I learned my actions were like bringing a knife to a gunfight—the odds were stacked against me. There was no way to turn my decision into a win-win outcome. Yes, I was a tomboy, but I had not been taught how to navigate such unforgiving and dangerous territory. So, I decided to turn this situation into a positive teaching moment by researching domestic violence for one of my graduate school presentations. Both the classes and the presentations were glaring eye-openers. I believe it is true that when you know better, you have the opportunity to do better.

Well, I embraced this learning moment. I recognized that the subtle danger I had not seen (or ignored) until it was too late was the fire that burned and scared the hell out of me for a lifetime. I took a serious inventory of my emotional maturity and discovered there was definitely room for growth. I had more hard work to do before I would be the person who my great-grandmother had raised me to be. That person was one who takes heed of early signs of control and subtle potential danger and runs quickly for safe and higher ground.

I made a well-thought-out and conscious decision to leave the relationship, even if it was at the expense of a financial burden. The cost of saving my life, or the life of someone else by making healthier relationship decisions and the rewards from the emotional growth was worth every penny. Going it alone left me with a luxury car note, an expensive mortgage payment, and sole ownership of all the other monthly household bills. But working hard to manage all this was more rewarding than spending one more minute in a jail cell. "Hindsight is 20/20."

In my mature opinion, relationship debates should not be about winning or getting the last word. Please consider them being about listening to the other person's point of view and getting your perspective across as well. It will surprise you how effective this can be. It might take a few days, but you and your partner will have time to think about the conversation and consider solutions to make the relationship healthier. However, you both should watch closely for improvement. Most people who are serious about respecting the feelings of others or improving the relationship don't go around saying, "I thought about what happened, and I am ready to sit at the table and talk about it." Instead, they get busy showing each other through proud actions what they have learned.

If love and maturity are alive in a relationship, partners will trade anger for understanding. Then, couples would be willing to take each other by the hand, caress cheeks, and wipe tears to soothe the hurts. The goal would be to steady each other's voices and avoid the rage. It was inspirational that, like the lotus, I rose above the water despite the darkness and suffering of domestic violence. It is seared in my memory that while I was in darkness under the muddy water, I was still a significant expression of beauty.

Although this chapter of my life was difficult, I managed to heal and blossom as a stronger, wiser, and more mature female adult.

Chapter Sixteen

PURPLE LILAC: FLOWER OF GROWTH AND CHANGE

"The lilac (Syringa vulgaris), which is an early flowering spring shrub, symbolizes growth. It stands for the change from ignorance to knowledge, from innocence to wisdom." (Stephens, 2020). I've learned that like many flowers, lilacs have several meanings. They symbolize spiritual growth and change because their beauty grows from the mundane to the extraordinary. I can relate lilacs to my growth because I have watched my life develop from mundane to extraordinary.

By this time in my life, I had learned so much from what I decided to call my *unforgettable* learning opportunities. I had experienced so many of these moments, that my mother told me she hoped I had earned a degree in "hard knocks and common sense." She was expecting our trips behind the shed to payoff sooner than later.

Reflecting and taking an inward look, the symbolism of the lilac confirmed I was no longer the person I was before my many pivotal moments. After these serious experiences, it is not a secret that I had become a more tough, hardy, and wise person. I had truly withstood the tests of time. As the lilac holds its own amid any harsh environment, I had continued to weather the storms, twists, and turns of my life.

Another incident that challenged my resolve to lean into maturity occurred when I started dating a guy who called me his "African Queen" the same day I met him. To be viewed as an African Queen was an honor in the world of Southern Black women. I took to the hype of this endearment so quickly that I became dazzled. As if that was not enough, he backed his easy-on-the-ears words with gifts, such as a beautifully framed picture of the lyrics to the iconic, *Lift Every Voice and Sing*, the Black National Anthem and the famous Brown vs. Board of Education memorabilia. He didn't know it, but those themes were very close to my heart. I have always been a champion of equal rights and the advancement of education. Meeting a charming man who embraced those themes and gifted them to me was like delicious icing on the cake. I couldn't think for one moment that meeting him was a mere, random coincidence.

He was very sexy, with a strut that looked the "Mr. Right" part as he held his head high toward the sky. His presentation was that of a strong and smoking-hot man who could have his choice of any woman. But he had chosen *me*. I could not stop looking at him as his alluring, grayish, super-expressive eyes gazed back into my inviting eyes. From the moment we laid eyes on each other, we were engulfed in easy smiles and laughter.

Once he wore a bluish-gray tee shirt, white knee-length shorts, black socks and gray sneakers for our run in the park. He matched these with a black cap and designer sunglasses. After our run, we both may have been sweaty, but I was too busy admiring the sweat stains in the middle of his shirt as we strolled through the trails in the park. The sweat stains reminded me of his strength and endurance. While I couldn't take my eyes off him, my brain was screaming, "This is too damned good to be true!" But my flesh was saying, "Don't sit this one out. Don't miss out on a golden opportunity to dance."

When I shared my giddy enthusiasm about my new friend with my mother, she immediately told me, "Don't be surprised when his *crazy* check pops up out of nowhere." My family on my father's side was planning a family reunion in West Palm Beach, Florida. Instead of a family reunion, the hostess (my aunt) had a brain aneurysm and died; so sadly, we had to prepare for a funeral. To take a break from the grief, I would call him and listen to how he was still impressed with me, his African Queen. His conversations would provide me a few moments of relief from my sorrow. It also gave me the chance to refuel the mental energy needed to console the rest of my family. I had no doubt that when I returned home, he would keep his musical words flowing, as I had become accustomed to them.

After I returned home from that grief-stricken weekend, I couldn't wait to stop by his place and decompress in his arms. When I spiritedly arrived at his home, he opened the door and asked me what I was doing there. I told him I missed him and had come to spend some time with him so I could recover from my recent family ordeal. Without an ounce of hesitation, he firmly slammed his door in my face. In a moment of shock, I dizzily stumbled a few steps backward.

My first and only thought was to pick up the biggest rock I could find. Boy, I found a big one. Led by my second thought, I picked the rock up and threw it. At that moment, I felt lucky. My perfect aim hit his storm door and cracked the glass. I went home with a sense of pride. I had shown him what could happen when I felt disrespected. At that very moment, I was sure that this relationship that had burned so brightly had been dashed out in one breathless moment. I gathered my thoughts and began planning how to pick myself up off the ground, dust off, and move forward, step by step.

About a week later, I received a business-like telephone call from him. During this call, he informed me of an estimated invoice to repair the glass on his storm door. He quietly mentioned that he just received his monthly check for mental health outreach services. *Bingo!* This was my mother's definition of watch out for his *crazy* check. My definition of mental health was not the same as hers, but for the first time, I could hear craziness in his now raspy voice and sense it in his demeanor. Wanting to speed up the process of taking the high road, I was eager to put this relationship "gone south" in my rearview mirror. I ended the conversation with a sincere apology for breaking the glass in his storm door. I gave my best wishes for his future endeavors. I was looking forward to practicing what I had learned about reflection and making better decisions. Yes, I had just made a poor decision, but I was deeply invested in early recognition of what I had done. I had been busy working hard to change my poor habit of making decisions that would cause me so much self-inflicted pain. I was determined to make better decisions in the future.

Strangely enough, the last thing I expected happened one week later. I got an unexpected call to report to the Director of Nursing's office. I couldn't think of any reason for the call. My work was not in question, to my knowledge. I stopped what I was doing and went to her office as summoned. When I walked into her office, my eyes traveled straight to the rock I had thrown a week earlier and cracked my recent ex-boyfriend's storm door. When the Director of Nursing asked me, "What happened?" I was honest and told her the complete story. She gave me a smile that made me feel perhaps she had found herself in such a situation at some point in her life. Then, she informed me that a mature person would have taken the high road that she had grown to travel versus the one she once may have traveled at my age.

Her advice was confirmation that I was on the right track and making progress toward striving for the high road of emotional maturity. I had been very reflective and had given my behavior much thought before I had a clue that I would find myself explaining my behavior to the top boss of the Nursing Service department. Therefore, I could honestly tell her that if I found myself in such a situation in the future, I would certainly travel the high road—the road less crowded than the heavily trafficked low road. I had put my reputation and my job on the line. *What incident could be worth a personal or professional tragedy?* NONE. None at all.

A year later, I saw him in a Walmart store. I spotted him before he saw me. Because the store was very large, I felt that turning around and going in the opposite direction to the other side of the store would be enough. So, that is exactly what I did. Once on the other side of the store, I kept shopping and put the thought of him at a full distance in my mind. As I carefully selected a bell pepper and turned to choose a good head of lettuce, there I stood, face to face with him. He told me that he was sorry he had treated me with such disrespect, and he had now chosen to live *his* life on the high road. He had recently been diagnosed with cancer.

I told him I was sorry and wished him the best with his medical challenges. It was refreshing to see that two people who had once taken the heavily trafficked low road had gone through life-shattering events that had forced life-sustaining growth and development upon them both.

Chapter Seventeen

JASMINE:
SEXUAL EROTICISM

A study that tested several men's and women fragrances for aphrodisiac properties found that the "winning blend" was the aroma of jasmine. Its rich, sweet smell has been used for centuries to improve libido and promote intimacy, which makes it one of the more well-known aphrodisiac scents. (Terjemahan, n.d.)

Ladies, this chapter is for YOU. Men, you should tread lightly if you have the courage to keep reading.

I had always been on the shy side when it came to life in general, but when it came to sex, my prudishness was off the chart. One day, I was sitting on my mother's bed eyeing her foot massager as it was hanging over her headboard. I really don't remember why I was staring at it. Perhaps I was wondering why it was hanging here. I had no memory of her doing self-pedicures. If that *was* the case, I thought the bathroom would have been a better place for it. I must have had an intense expression of curiosity on my face. My mother quietly leaned in and looked me straight in my eyes with a very broad grin on her face. She sheepishly told me that the foot massager was not *just* for her feet.

I thought about that for a moment; I didn't have the nerve to ask her to elaborate. Suddenly, the proverbial *light* came on for me. *Oh… oh! That's what she's talking about.* As mentioned before, my mother often made references to taking me "behind the shed" for teaching moments. This was a subtle teaching moment she offered without taking me there. The gleam in her eyes suggested that a foot massager could possibly enhance pleasure to other parts of your body— *sexual pleasure?* If this were true, I could only daresay your feet would be enraged with jealousy.

Weeks later, I was still thinking about it. *If my mother is happily open to an out-of-the-box sexual experience, why can't I be open to one?* I was not going to let the generation before me corner the market on sexual adventure and freedom. Sharing this rare, private moment with my mother made me recognize that I had a lot to learn. I used this experience to welcome the idea that women were sexual creatures just as much as men. Women may keep their desires private (at least some women), but I was glad to hear they were venturing out to find less talked-about ways to meet their sexual desires.

After I allowed the voices in my head to guide me to pursue my sexual *Why* questions, I ripped up the reasons *not* to think about exploring my sexual desires, and I replaced them with reasons to do so. *Why shouldn't I join the women who are making their sexual dreams come true? Shouldn't we, at the very least, consider opening our minds to discussions with our partners about what we want and need in the bedroom?* I found that sometimes, women may want to "open up" in conversations with friends they trust. Many times, friends have the same questions and feelings that we do.

Later in my life, I felt more comfortable with my sexuality and decided to venture into discussions with my "happy hour" friends. Our conversations would go where no straightlaced person would dare go. The discussions touched on almost anything and everything. Sitting at our favorite pub one day, they convinced me to have a drink I couldn't even pronounce. They were always ready to introduce me to another sweet drink that would take at least five minutes for the bartender to decide was a winner of a drink for me.

On this day, because the drink was mixed with one of my favorites (Grand Marnier), I was on board to try it. While enjoying this sweet and sour alcoholic drink and the reminder of the unspoken codes of silence, they asked me about my recent love life. By the way, the unspoken codes were, "If I tell you something, and it leaves this table, I will have to kill you," and "What is said at this table stays at this table." So, after a round of *pinky* swearing, I began "spilling the tea" and telling stories that were worth killing someone over if they spoke of any parts of our secret conversation.

One story hinged on folklore in the Black community. A well-known yardstick in our community is that the size of a man's feet will let you know what he is *packing*. Well, with all the odds of finding the man with the big feet *packing* the big *package*, I was batting zero. I am not going to tell you how many times I struck out. This losing record was my claim to sexual fame.

For example, I once spent time with a six-foot, three-inch tall man with a size fifteen shoe who was peacock proud when telling me that I was only dating him for his fantastic sex. I immediately pulled the covers back so both of us could view his sexual package at the same time. I lovingly pointed out to him that it *had* to be his stimulating mind that turned me on. If he saw what I saw, there wasn't an A+ package below to turn the average woman on by those means alone. Whoever coined the phrase, "It's not the size but the motion of the ocean," didn't have his motion for the poster representation. As Southerners often say, "I'm just saying." I was gentle and loving; I respected his feelings throughout the challenging conversation. I guess he had never been told the truth with love. The truth from me was that his ability to hold a stimulating conversation, his white Corvette, and his rank in the military were the obvious turn-ons he possessed.

Sexual turn-ons were still not coming easy for me. I couldn't blame it all on the men in my life. I had to admit; I had a responsibility to make sex (making love) enjoyable. One day, I met "Mr. Las Vegas" in the elevator of a Las Vegas hotel where we were both staying. He was a tall, light, milk chocolate cup of hot cocoa. He had muscles that stood up and smiled at me as he stood in a normal stance. When he took his bodybuilder's pose, his muscles displayed a *wow* effect that commanded the moment. He was six feet, four inches tall with a size fifteen shoe. As time went on, we developed a relationship that was packed with sexual desires, but never reached the next level during our Las Vegas encounter. We were both in committed relationships and decided not to cross the line, just to explore a moment of sexual pleasure. We *did* explore the bright, city lights together and had tons of Las Vegas excitement.

It was years later before our paths crossed again. He was passing through Memphis, Tennessee, where I was living at the time. We decided to share an adult night to remember. Committed relationships or not, we were *not* going to let the possibility of sexual bliss escape us a second time. In my mind, life was just too short to let that happen.

I hate to admit the truth about the disappointment that ruled that night. The *beef* just wasn't there. The motion of the ocean was once again almost nonexistent. This night was one more defiance of the yardstick myth as a measurement of what an African American man was packing. I didn't have the heart to tell him how unclimactic the experience was. By then, it was obvious that our best path was to stay friends forever. We are still friends today.

Those were examples of my batting zero to whatever. Then one day, a six-foot three-inch tall knight with a size sixteen shoe came galloping into my life. *Was this my turn to hit a home run?* Before his arrival, the most adventure I had experienced was twisting my body into a salty pretzel to accommodate a curved package.

Here he stood, with his appealing height and shoe size. He introduced himself with a flare of confidence. He told me he felt like a forty-year-old horny rabbit who could have great sex early morning, late afternoon, and bedtime, only to start over the next day. *Bingo!* It appeared the size of the shoe matched the size of the package! Immediately, I knew I had to get prepared to handle any baseball pitch he was throwing. He appeared to be packing in length, width, and depth. My research was on.

I grabbed my medical books, searched the internet, consulted my gynecologist, and talked candidly with my few friends who were not ashamed to discuss sexual issues. I went to Walgreens and made a sweeping grab for every cream, oil, and gel on the shelf to enhance the chances of a successful experience. My imagination took me to a world where I would have the opportunity to experience all the baseball-batting opportunities in the bedroom—from a single to a home run! I let my mind venture into the near future, where we could perhaps hit a grand slam in one night!

When he touched me, my body shivered with flaming-hot desire. He moved with a slow hand and a light touch down my spine. His touch made me yearn for this long-awaited and highly anticipated moment. The full moonlight coming through the high windows set the mood against my closed eyes. Our sweating and deep breathing made the covers feel damp, yet soothing. Each time I opened my eyes, I saw his piercing, light, cat eyes gazing down at me. I found myself trembling and clutching every part of his body with a tight grasp. The simultaneous sounds of harmony that escaped from both of us engulfed us and overtook the moments of mounting crescendo. It was an unvarnished, shameless moment when I was willing to overstep the boundaries of sinful pleasures.

For the first time, I didn't want the night to end. We lay (for how long I don't know), side by side, feeling the eroticism of desire. The shining fire in our bodies was smoldering. The deeper the burning flicker of fire, the greater the passion raging inside my body. I felt a kind of delirium during these unimaginably tender moments. I could not give thought to any inklings of sin in my heart. Each time he kissed me all over, it felt more delicious and enchanting than my favorite sweet wine. His lips were pleasingly luscious, like a bite of a chocolate strawberry. He held my breasts tightly, and they responded in blushful joy, standing at attention to his touch. We were enchanted with the physical and visual ambiance as we made an art of touching each other with thick, extra creamy whipped cream.

We savored this wicked ecstasy from the breath of the blissful moonlight to the early dawn. Without disappointment, the brilliant sunlight vividly pierced through the opened windows the next morning. For a short period, my sexual joy had reached its zenith. I was convinced that my scruples were indeed devilish, for nothing could feel more right than the sweetness I felt during each thrusting moment. I remember, as a young adult, I would sneak and read the Mandingo novels. But to have my own sexual experience that felt like it was lifted right out of one of the book's most erotic chapters was both sinful and satisfying. I felt as if I was living the experiences of the unashamed characters of those well-written books of the nineteen fifties.

Days afterward, I could still close my eyes, and with splendid clarity, recall not only everything I had experienced that night, but also what it would be like to have future moments of his lavish, indescribable sweetness. I felt an inner exultation as I realized I had sunk into a totally bewildered sexual abyss. I enjoyed this ultimate out-of-the-box experience. My whole spirit was compelled to remember the bliss and radiance of that deep intimacy. When I closed my eyes, I can see not only everything I did but also what I was thinking during each of those erotic moments.

As we got to know each other, the truth threatened to outstrip the joy of such an out-of-body sensation of ineffable inner joy. I discovered he was so good in bed because he was a kept man. He made a living seeking rich women to send into a sexual bliss. His mission and goal were to not fall in love with them, but for them to long for sexual satisfaction, so they would willingly share their sizable bank accounts with him. His night to remember would be directly tied to the dollars he could lift from their life savings.

I had to quietly and smoothly give him permission to move on to find another woman to take to sexual heaven and back. I had long ago learned that men love to leave women. Therefore, I created an invisible open door for him to walk through with his ego well intact. I decided that sex and money would not be a tradeoff for love and intimacy. I began to decline his offers of passionate sex.

One day, we had a serious discussion about how he didn't need to take such rejection from me because he had too much going for himself. I didn't participate much in that discussion. What was the purpose? I had learned to assess my relationship with him and make a sound decision regarding whether we were a good fit for each other. In this case, we were not. Finally, I had learned to cut bait and move on. Acknowledging my growth and development made me happy.

At the end of the discussion, I turned my head away. When I looked back, he was gone. I cannot forget how those intense sexual moments had unleased my sexual desire and quenched my erotic thirst. Although I had come to realize both the vanity of my desire and the rigor of my thirst, I was willing to let him go and take my chances of finding a combination of love and erotic sex one day. If not, I would still gladly choose a deep, loving experience over one that consisted only of erotic ecstasy.

Those precious moments shined with their own transparency, which did not allow our encounter to be diminished by any shame or regret. But when I write about this now, I still, for a fleeting moment, question if I made a mistake by not taking advantage of his services now and then. Then reality quickly comes crashing into focus. It reminds me that such a situation is still not worth the emotional risk to me. I had chosen a path that was the best fit for me, and I moved on with zest for my future.

Before you begin looking down at the shoes of every male who crosses your path, I would be remiss if I didn't inform you that the scientist in me sorted out the research. It reveals there is no evidence that a man's shoe size predicts what he is packing. I just got lucky for once in my life. I will wait for my heavenly sexual experience to come with pure love. In the meantime, I will keep my AA batteries ready to go—with a full charge.

Chapter Eighteen

PURPLE ORCHID:
LASTING LOVE AND REVERENCE

The road to finding true love had been just as rocky as it had been long. Taking a long time to find it is better than not finding it at all. The next step is to nurture and keep it.

For a mysterious and one-of-a-kind love, the popular orchid has been a go-to gift to represent refinement, luxury and mystery for years. This exotic bloom also symbolizes love, beauty and strength and makes the perfect gift to express how lucky you are to love your special person. ("15 Flowers," 2021).

Like most flowers, orchids have a variety of messages to convey. My conclusion after reading about orchids is that they symbolize an appreciation for thoughtfulness, beauty, strength, mature charm, refinement and security. That combination makes the blooms quite special and exotically unique. It is easy to see that what they symbolize are essential qualities to help us be successful in sustaining long-lasting relationships. I embrace the breathtaking beauty of orchids as my desire to stand tall for love and strength as I remind myself how lucky I am to love and be loved by that one special person.

Unlike the daisy, which is a flower that feels accessible to all… the orchid represents those things in life that don't come around easily or often. (Stanton, 2022). We must travel below the surface of our being to discover such rare gems in life. It redefines the message of how healthy, long-lasting relationships require dedicated practice in mindfulness and patience.

The orchid also inspires us to appreciate the power of togetherness and individuality required for a healthy romantic adventure. In relationships destined for longevity, we need to honor our own unique traits and those qualities that set us apart. While doing so, we need to embrace the love and reverence for our significant other who is different, yet very dear to us. Finding this balance is not only difficult, but very tricky. Regardless of our socio-economic status, ethnicity, physical or intellectual ability (or other qualities), the uniqueness of the orchid symbolizes the capacity for each of us to maximize our romantic dreams and connect with the rainbows of human colors and gifts. We must also seek spiritual enlightenment, a union with God or other positive sources in order to nurture our mind, body, and soul so we can nurture the same in our loved ones.

January 4, 2003 was a cold day, and finding the purple orchid of my life was a billion light years away from my thoughts.

A friend and mentor called me and said, "I just closed on a refinance for my home. Girl, the closing broker is tall, dark, handsomely hot and single. His lips look sweet enough that I could have walked up and kissed him. Too bad I am married, Sherry. I told him to call you and not to leave town without seeing you."

He promised her that he would have to take her advice and do that. I must stress that I had been taking a break from serious relationships. I was just working very hard on getting to know myself and how to identify and change my "how is that relationship working out for you," dating habits. I was also learning to identify when guys were nice, and sometimes even great, but were not a good fit for *me*. I was no longer willing to force square pegs into round holes.

I was moving from the home I had had built in 1992 to a new home to accommodate my mother's physical limitations. She had challenges that came with progressive multiple sclerosis (PMS). Because I could not have anticipated the future, my then *dream* home didn't lend itself to the safety and security of a person with such debilitating challenges. In the home I was leaving, my mother's bedroom was on the second floor. I couldn't keep living with the thought of impending danger coming upon us and we wouldn't have a fighting chance to save her because we couldn't get to her upstairs.

I was asked to contemplate converting my two-car garage into another bedroom. I was never in love with cars. I mostly saw them as a method of getting from point A to point B. However, I struggled with the thought of my beautiful luxury car being left sitting in the driveway to combat the undesirable elements day after day. So, I kept looking for another home. I found one that was handicap-equipped, just two traffic lights from my current dream home. The new home had a bedroom on the first floor.

The highly advertised handicap accommodations only included handicap bars in the bathroom across the hall from her bedroom. At least with these accommodations, I felt like my mother had a fighting chance to get out of the home if we encountered unforeseen danger.

I had made the final decision to move. On this special day, I was in full "elbow grease" working mode. My hair was standing on top of my head. I smelled like fresh bleach from my head to my toes. The movers had moved all our belongings from the old house to the new home. We (Aunt Jannie and me) were cleaning the old home when the telephone rang for the fourth or fifth time.

Once again, I told my friend/mentor that I didn't have time to be bothered with a man. My priorities were etched in stone for the day. She was relentless and wouldn't let go of the topic at hand. She firmly insisted I throw on some decent clothes and wait for his call. I relented.

When he called, he stated that he only had time to see me if I stopped by the airport. Auntie Jannie and I went into weighing the pros and cons of this adventure. We both were above the knees deep into the mission of getting the house cleaned so I could finalize my plans for my trip to Chicago the next morning. As the local Vice President of the National Nurses Union, I had a big career-altering meeting to attend. Anyhow, we decided to go to the airport and see this man because my friend just would not let me rest. I felt as if I had just drawn the short straw. She had won.

We figured the quicker I saw him, and he left the state of Colorado, the sooner I could get back to cleaning the old house. So, we would go to the airport, hide out behind some big white columns, and wait for him to show up at the Frontier Airlines check-in counter. When we saw a man who matched the description provided by my mentor, we would check him out. If he didn't pass the sight test, we would leave without an introduction. The only thing that would have been lost was our precious time. If he *did* pass the sight test, I would step up and introduce myself.

When we looked up and saw this tall, dark chocolate, slim and fine hunk of a man, our eyes lit up like Christmas trees. My aunt didn't try to stop me, so I eased over to his side and introduced myself. He was dressed in a well-fitted dark-plaid suit. I didn't like plaid, but his body made the plaid look like the suit had been tailor-made for him. We exchanged niceties, and time just snuck up on us. Before we knew it, it was time to say goodbye, so he could go through the security gates. He stepped up and, in a sexy, soft-spoken voice, asked if he could kiss me. I quietly said, "Yes." He leaned down and landed his soft, desirable and luscious lips on my forehead. He didn't know, but he had passed the first test. A sweet kiss on the forehead was better than him kissing me on the mouth or the cheek. I didn't like it when guys invaded my space without asking permission or gave me a big, juicy kiss at first sight. When he turned the corner and was out of sight, Auntie Jannie and I high-fived and gave each other a thumbs up, both agreeing, "That turned out to be a nice, fun-filled break."

He was gone as fast as he had come. During the past few years, I had decided to follow the man's lead. I was not going to call him. I decided that if he didn't call me, I would not pursue the relationship by calling him. For the next three days, he didn't call. I was ready to forget the fun-filled airport break and practice what I had committed to over the past few years when my telephone rang. It was him, calling to say, "Hello," and tell me he enjoyed the brief conversation we had at the airport. The more we talked, the more we discovered the things we had in common. He learned I was an employed nurse during the day and took care of my disabled mother during the night. He was single with two children, a daughter of fourteen and a son of twelve. I didn't hesitate to let him know I had no intentions of becoming a stepmother to kids the age of his children. It was a sensitive subject, but he agreed and stated he understood. I felt that children, (especially at their age), were too precious to be involved in relationships before the couple had a chance to get to know each other and make a conscious effort to plan a life that involved the innocent kids.

Approximately one month later, we decided I would come to Seattle, Washington, for the weekend, hang out, and do some serious sightseeing all over the town. I had never been to Seattle, but when I got there, it didn't take long for me to figure out that I didn't like the constant rain. No one used umbrellas; they walked in the rain without them as if it were not raining at all. The upside to this was that the grass was a beautiful, luscious green. The rolling hills lent themselves to majestically breathtaking views. I saw a very close view of this when he worked party bus tours during my visit, and I accompanied him. The enormous mansions on the hills had picturesque views of the mountains through one window and a clear, blue water view of the ocean from another window. Just to be in this mix was exciting.

One night, we went out to eat. When we arrived and found the restaurant was closing, he gracefully grabbed my hand, took me to the back door, and led the way right to the front of the restaurant. He softly asked for us to be served. The waiter was so amazed that we had found our way to a table; he couldn't find a way to refuse us. I was glad to see a man take charge and make things happen. He was not forceful or demanding. He was simply determined for us to get something to eat before they closed. You would have thought we had *old* money or prestige, but we had neither. We had determination and spirit.

As the relationship moved forward, we both were cautious and didn't want to rush to the next level. It was very endearing when he told me, "I don't take relationships lightly; I have to really think about what it means to take our relationship to the next level." It was refreshing to hear a man say, "Let's take this slow and make sure this is what we both want." With those endearing words being whispered into my ear, there was nothing else left to be said. He wrapped me in his strong arms and kissed me on my forehead. I peacefully lay there like I was wrapped in my Linus security blanket.

When our last night together arrived, it was time for an unspoken decision. He gently pulled me to his chest. Because I was willing to let go and respond to his unspoken language, it didn't take much of a pull to get me into a perfect position. The Pandora radio station happened to be quietly playing what became our relationship theme song, *Forget Me Nots* by Patrice Rushen. The standard hotel room became a place of imaginary blankets spread out in the woods. The birds chirped so sweetly as other wild animals looked curiously from afar. The ducks were taking flight with excitement, only to change their minds and return to the water with soft, smooth landings in a nearby pond. Moving to the next level had been simple and uncomplicated. Most of all, I remembered feeling very safe and happy. That was not a new concept for me, but letting the process work without taking charge every step of the way was most definitely new.

He had made the decision to invite me into his life with no "taking charge" from me. Talk about growth—I had come a long way, Baby! I had grown from a relationship of toxic proportion to one in which nature was allowed to lead the way. For once, I didn't try to oversell myself to a man, intentionally or otherwise. I let him see me in my natural comfort zone. When we made it to the next level, it was not because I did any heavy mental or physical lifting. We owned our commitment to move forward.

In August of that year, I had my forty-fifth birthday party. This was his first return to Denver. For the party, we were all dressed in fancy outfits. My mother was dressed in her elegant shiny, black dress and black high heels to match. The fact that her feet weren't going to touch the ground because of her inability to walk was not a reason for her not to be dressed to the nines. Because of the MS, it was difficult to get her into the limousine, but the excitement about getting to the party made all the challenges worthwhile. The limo ride was more for my mother than for me. She had never been in a limo that was not following a hearse to a funeral. My Auntie was not short stepping either. She was most definitely holding her own. Her feet *were* touching the ground and her high heel stilettos made her big, pretty legs appeared as if she was looking to give

Tina Turner some competition that night. It was also in her favor that she had facial features that resembled Tina.

The ballroom was lit with beautiful, shiny lights and joyous, bubbly smiles on the faces of the inclusive and diverse guests. I had the honor of hearing my guests say, "Happy Birthday" to me in their own ways. My mother did not hesitate. She was the first to ask for the microphone. She had nothing but great things to say about me. This was to be expected from a mother to her daughter on any given birthday. Even so, I was shocked and happy to see her take the initiative to do it. This was a "You've come a long way, Baby" moment for her, too. She was light years past the proud, but shy, lady who attended my nursing school graduation luncheon in the hallway many years ago.

Then, the moment came when my new boyfriend stood up and asked for the microphone. He surprised us all when he said he felt as if this was the family he had been searching for—and for a very long time. He also said he would like to stay around for a while. The DJ played all the right songs, and we danced the night away as the new man in my life had declared his place. What impressed me the most was his attentiveness to my mother. He anticipated her every need and saw to it that she was comfortable. I could visit my guests and know she was in hog heaven as he showered her with attention.

When the party was over and we arrived back at my housing complex, we were suddenly lost in the neighborhood. The limousine driver didn't know which way to go. I had lived in the twists and turns of our neighborhood for approximately eight months, but we had still gotten to a place where I didn't know whether to go left or right. It was not surprising that my mother and auntie looked to me for the directions. My new boyfriend stepped up without hesitation and gave the limousine driver directions as if he had been keeping us in his care the whole time. His attention to my mother was astounding, but his attention to detail that enabled the limousine driver to pull up into my driveway with no additional stops was remarkable. It was like he had a photographic memory.

His attention to my mother didn't end that night. He would call on holidays to say hello to me, and then ask to speak to her. They would laugh and talk for a while, and then it would be time for me and him to have a conversation. I found this to be quite charming and respectful. She was always smitten and enjoyed his company. He had lost his mother when he was seventeen years old. It was nice to see that he had the instincts of love and devotion toward a mother, despite his traumatic loss. This was working out to be a part of my wish to have someone who made a conscious effort to embrace my family instead of working hard to separate me from them.

He loved grits and frequently called me his "GRITS." True to my nature, I am sometimes *slow* to catch on. I finally told him that I didn't understand how the word GRITS related to anything other than an old-fashioned, Southern dish. He informed me that GRITS meant he had found his *Girl Raised in The South*. Wow, that explained a lot. He had not spent a lot of time with Southern girls. He was in awe of my honesty, realism, brain power, and my natural self. What he saw during these moments was what he would experience each moment of our relationship. When we visited Southern cities such as Memphis, Atlanta, and Clarksdale, he was like a kid in the candy store as he enjoyed soaking in the Southern heritage and culture.

I remember us going to Tupelo, Mississippi. He asked to stop by the Elvis landmarks. But when we got to a Southern home after a funeral, the thoughts of Elvis didn't come close to competing with the spread of Southern food. He had frequently declared his reasons for keeping pork out of his diet. On this occasion, however, I witnessed him take a perfect "Olympic 10" dive for greens (cooked with ham hocks) and well-seasoned peppers; green beans cooked in bacon grease; and cornbread that was swimming in bacon grease and butter. He was licking his fingers after each forkful of food. He laughed at me when I pulled out the greens and cornbread and ate them with my fingers. I explained to him that when you are among family, and feel "at home," food seems to taste better sprinkled with the deep, deep Southern heritage. It wasn't long before I could tell these Southern experiences were touching his soul, and he found my persona was just as pure and satisfying as the Southern food.

When we visited my childhood home, he was in awe. He was surprised how easy it was for me to seamlessly ease back into the southern environment. He pulled a chair up to the table and chimed right in with me and my stepfather as we talked about Southern culture: religion; the importance of voting; the fact that there is a world outside of Mississippi; and that Mississippi is not another state, country, or continent, but is truly another planet in the distant galaxy. The truth of the matter was that I had never *mentally* moved far from my Southern roots. I now knew the purpose of matching forks and spoons; therefore, I used them 99.9 percent of the time. It took a little time for him to get used to older Southern women telling him that he was handsome, tall and all of that, but also how they liked their men blacker than shiny black shoe polish. I guess that was a blow to his ego because his skin color had a way to go before he could compete with this beloved skin shade. When we went to my class reunion, he was struck by the relationships I maintained with my longtime ex-boyfriend's wife, ex-wives, ex-girlfriends and other admirers. He couldn't believe that for me it simply came down to: better them than me. He finally got the message that I meant as long as my ex-boyfriend was sweet on someone else, I wouldn't have to tell him, "No" and "Hell no," one more time.

Back in Colorado, we explored the mountains, as well as basketball, football, and baseball games. It was obvious we had a love of sports in common. The more we talked about sports, the clearer it became to see he was a huge Colorado sports fan. That decreased our opportunities to be sports rivals, but I was excited when we enjoyed watching the up-and-coming Russell Wilson beat one of my favorite football players, Peyton Manning, in a preseason game. I had been a Manning fan practically all my life; I was hooked on the family: Eli, Archie, and Cooper. We were all Ole Miss Alumni except Payton. He went to the University of Tennessee because Ole Miss was on a probationary period when it came time for his official enrollment. Not to mention, they lived down the road from my hometown of Clarksdale, in Drew, Mississippi. At the end of the day, we both saw magic in Russell.

Our first disagreement came when we were at a hotel in Memphis, Tennessee, attending a family reunion for my side of the family. When the disagreement kicked off, I said what I had to say, and he said what he had to say. Yes, there was some talking over each other, but there was also a great effort to listen to each other. Listening is an art that needs to be learned to have a successful relationship. The most impressive thing was that when the conversation got intense, he walked out of the hotel room. I stayed behind and didn't attempt to follow him. I didn't ask how long he would be gone or even if he was planning to come back. I stayed behind to process my thoughts. At first, I didn't know what to make of such a move. But as I thought about it, we were practicing time out—distancing ourselves until we could gather our thoughts. Again, I had found someone who was man enough to give up the last word for the sake of keeping peace in the relationship.

When he came back to the hotel, we were able to talk about our issues while respecting each other's feelings. We were learning to establish some rules of engagement. Setting equal time to get our points heard without interruptions, voicing only positive, uplifting words with the goal of strengthening the relationship. We had learned to grasp the concept of respecting each other's perspectives. Negative name calling, screaming and yelling, and pushing and shoving were not actions to be considered and definitely not tolerated. We both were learning to surrender control for the sake of individual and relationship growth. At that point, I couldn't speak for him, but I had proudly grown by leaps and bounds. Relationship growth can be such an invigorating sign of maturity when you recognize you are progressively becoming the person you dream of becoming. It is even sweeter when you have found someone who shares your level of relationship maturity. Make no mistake—GROWTH will make you uncomfortable.

I was always the serious one, but in this relationship, I found myself laughing at things I had never found funny before. One day, we were sitting in the car, and he was pointing out my country behaviors as he was *sawing* the meat off a chicken bone with his teeth. I had to let him know that I knew *I* was *country* and proud of it. I informed him it was my opinion that he was also *country* and didn't have a clue. I also told him, "On the day you discover you are *country*, too—I hope you will be able to handle such a rude awakening." It's funny when you call other people *country*, but it's not so funny when you discover *you* are *country* and *clueless*.

Our relationship became laced with more and more laughter and openness as we traveled through time. We would run through the streets, laughing at almost everything. He would pick me up and carry me across the streets instead of letting me walk. People would stare at us, but we were too busy having fun to care what they thought about us. We didn't mind sneaking away from everyone else just to get in a loud laugh. It was extra special when we were laughing about our inside jokes and everyone else around us was thinking we were weird and crazy. Yes, we were the good and innocent kind of weird and crazy. Thank God for private jokes.

As the years moved forward, I discovered he was a workaholic. He was driven by careers of intense pressure such as mortgage broker, high-end salesperson, etc. These were careers in which you had to produce so many widgets each hour of each day. Sometimes, making two hundred dollars per day and some days making five thousand dollars. My brain could not compute such pay disparity on any given day. The concern for me was that none of the amounts were predictable. I was comfortable taking care of so many patients per day and getting the same pay each day. Both our careers consumed a lot of our time, but he became more consumed with meeting intensely insane deadlines. That meant sometimes I would not hear from him for two or three days. His vacation times were inflexible. The words became, "I've got to meet *this* quota because it is the first of the month. I've got to meet *this* quota because it is the middle of the month; and last, I've got to meet *this* quota because it is the end of the month." At some point, it ran together to equal "all the time." It was okay until I retired. That is when I didn't want to do it anymore.

I shared my concerns in writing for a long time. Before this period in my life, I had been waiting for him to come into his own and be ready to take our relationship to the next level. Perhaps it was that I was the one who was not ready all along. I can't say I am ready now, but I now recognize that after learning to love and appreciate God's intelligent design (my perfectly imperfect self), I am in a much better spiritual position to love and appreciate another perfectly imperfect human being. So, I made the hard decision. I cut the strings of a seventeen-year relationship. I felt the pain of missing him and the whisper of the *What if* questions, like: *What if I would have stayed a little bit longer?* It was not a question of if he was a *good* man. I was not looking for a good man. I was looking for "a great fit for me" man.

Finally, in September 2021, I drew a line in the sand. I didn't get the sense that he felt I was for real. Who would leave a seventeen-year relationship? The answer is: an unhappy woman. I loved my career, even on the day I retired and left. I was damn good at my job. But I retired to spend the rest of my life being flexible and doing what I wanted to do. It didn't help that I was getting introduced to widget-based patient encounters and hated the impact this money-producing strategy had on the delivery of quality patient care. The introduction of this concept into my workspace was nothing like a high-end salesperson's career. Yet, I was being asked to care for so many patients in such a restrictive timeframe. Patient care became a high-cost assembly line that didn't reflect my high standards of care delivery. That made it clear to me… it was time to retire and go see the world. Then the damn COVID-19 pandemic got in the way of my traveling. We were both afraid to travel, therefore, face-to-face visits became limited to almost nonexistence.

His lack of response to my clear and well-written requests left me with no choice but to leave. I was done with the *Please release me* relationship songs and accompanying drama. I had always had the freedom and power to release myself. So, for once in my life, I used that power. I didn't leave because I didn't love him—sometimes, love is not enough to stay. At the end of the day, the portrait of my life's canvas might be *with* or *without* a man. However, I refuse to go through this mean and cruel life without a continuous search for mutual respect, love, and happiness.

He would text and ask me to stay in the relationship. He would also text me songs to tell me how he felt. Al Green's *Let's Stay Together*, Keith Sweat's *Twisted*, Patrice Rushen's *Forget Me Nots*, Jennifer Hudson's *The Christmas Song*, Otis Redding's *These Arms of Mine* and *I've Been Loving You Too Long*, to name a few. But he would not address the issues I put on the table. So, I didn't respond. I felt that if I was not worth his calling me and talking to me, then I was willing to carry on and look to the future.

He called one day. He sounded surprised that I answered the phone, but, at least, he had made the first step. He asked me to go to Hawaii with him. He was equally surprised when I said, "Yes." His stepmother had passed away, and he wanted to take me to meet that side of his family and say goodbye to his stepmother. He looked into getting the tickets and found they were too expensive—close to two thousand dollars per person to fly in and out for less than forty-eight hours' notice. Needless to say, we did not go to Hawaii. We immediately started having conversations almost every day, lasting one to two hours. I must admit, it was refreshing to talk to someone who could stimulate my mind again. For the prior six months, seeing Mr. Tall, Dark and Handsome, who could hold my attention, had been nonexistent.

It was so soothing to hear us thank each other for how we had managed to lace our actions and requests with love and sensitivity. Our relationship maturity was displaying the blooms of the seeds we had planted, nurtured, and committed to seventeen years ago. He sincerely reminded me how he loved hard and shared with me that my leaving the seventeen-year relationship had caused him much emotional pain. He couldn't believe that something so traumatic had happened to us. He asked me to reconsider: was there even a small window of opportunity for us to make an attempt at reconciling our relationship?

I was having a retirement gala in the next six weeks; I had a decision to make. I decided I would rather invite him to the gala, even if we didn't find our way back together, instead of not inviting him and we got back together—then he would have missed a major milestone in our lives. So, he accepted my invitation to be my escort for Sherry's Retirement Gala/Book Launch. We planned to spend some time discussing our relationship soon after the gala. I reminded him that I left the relationship for a reason. I was not willing to close my eyes, as if I had changed my mind about addressing my unhappiness.

I think we both had learned that when you feel appreciated, you will do more than expected. Perhaps my love has been by my side for the last seventeen years, and at last, I have the vision to see and appreciate him. But now, I also have the voice to stand up for what I believe in and the desire to listen to his spoken and unspoken requests. I have also found a way to meet his needs without compromising my own. One of the most importance aspects of the seeded blooms of our relationship is to never lose focus of our commitment to provide an environment for mutual happiness and respect. I am *peaking* into my own. That means I must strive to protect the sacred heart of another person, along with that of my own. That is what mature people do.

If we are to make it, we must listen to the pace of our souls. We can choose a life of courageous love over self-protection. We can also embrace the spirit to keep believing that it is not so much how high or low our experiences are… but how much we have learned from them. Hopefully, we will take the traits of the orchid flower and practice providing our relationship with proper care, increasing our chances of having a loving, happy, and long-lasting partnership. We must work hard at staying together, so we can grow together.

Chapter Nineteen

FORGET-ME-NOTS: REMEMBRANCE

Forget Me Not

I had reached the period of my life where I had weathered the storms. I had the career of a lifetime. I had emotionally grown by leaps and bounds. My mother was happily living with me. Yes, she would have preferred to live independently in her own home, but she had made reasonable peace with her narrow options. I couldn't cure her of the tragic plight of multiple sclerosis, but I made sure she had everything she needed and a lot of things she wanted. She couldn't travel the world with me as I had dreamed; I offered her all the possibilities her limitations would allow.

Forget-me-not flowers communicate a simple but essential message to a family: our loved ones live on in our memories. We tend to shy away from painful emotions that remind us of the loss of our loved one. For this reason, we often avoid the topic of their death with the intention of sparing our family additional discomfort. Silence becomes a common practice.

"The forget-me-not communicates this simple but essential message to a family your loved one lives on in our memories. We tend to shy away from painful emotions, and for this reason, we often avoid the topic of a loved one's death with the intention of sparing the family additional discomfort. We stay silent because we don't want to remind the family of the loss of their loved one. While this approach is well-intended, it's often unhelpful. Tell stories, share memories, and talk about the positive attributes of the loved one. Remind the family that their loved one has impacted the lives of others." (Kessler, 2017)

While researching material for this book, I read an article about grieving that suggested we must go backward before we can go forward, and remembering is one of the best ways to take a healthy step back. Dr. Wolfelt, a grief counselor advised,

> After all, we must listen to the music of the past so that we can sing in the present and dance into the future. We can't start this process until we take a step back and reflect on where we have been and what we have lost. Only then can we begin to move forward in any kind of meaningful way. (Kessler, 2017)

The forget-me-nots of my life include my great-grandmother and my mother. In their own rights, they are both unforgettable. They were both fiery and forces to be reckoned with. My great-grandmother was very quiet, but as I have mentioned before, when she spoke, it was in our best interest to listen to the message and follow the instructions. She was a case in point for the truth that you don't want to make a quiet and even-keeled person angry. It's like you have caused them to deviate from their comfort zone. Boy, they will make sure you never forget… they don't like that at all.

Unlike my great-grandmother, my mother was very opinionated and entitled. She expected the world to revolve around her. Her siblings, my brothers, and I never stood up and challenged her with the idea that her expectations were unrealistic. We jumped to meet those expectations as fast as she shared them with us. This resulted in us always searching for a balance of meeting her needs to please her and getting our own needs met as well. While my great-grandmother was quiet but fiery when pushed, my mother was fiery twenty-four seven. Fiery was the one and only gear that defines my mother's legacy. To say she was complicated is an understatement. She was loveable, yet demanding. In hindsight, I would say she was introducing us to a concept that later earned the title "tough love." We didn't appreciate her method of parenting at the time, but me and my brother speak of how much we appreciate and thank her today. We became independent thinkers and self-sufficient adults. We entered adulthood, respecting education and gainful employment.

My mother was not a domestic engineer by choice; she was always looking for a job outside of the home. The upside of her being a domestic engineer was that she was home when we went to school and there waiting for us when we came home. We didn't have the latchkey kids' experience. We at breakfast and lunch at school, and she had full meals for dinner, prepared for us when we came home each day.

My mother didn't have an opportunity for a formal education or a professional career. However, she took part in many job and training programs in Chicago and in our hometown area. Job Corps was the farthest job from home she ever had. When she went away to Job Corps was a very emotional time for my brother, Michael. He recently told me about his experience. While she was away, he feared the people they stayed with in Chicago wanted to adopt him. He felt Mom had agreed to such an arrangement when she didn't come home for several weeks. When my Aunt Jessie came to visit him in Chicago, he thought it was Mom returning from Job Corps. But when he didn't see her, he was disappointed and began to cry. When Mom stepped from behind Aunt Jessie, he later described it as the most beautiful moment of his life. Though that had been many years ago, we cried together when he recalled this intimate moment, and we remembered our loving and complex mother. Just the opposite of my great-grandmother, she was always fussing and yelling about something. She loved attention, and we learned that life was a lot easier when we lavished it on her. As long as she was fussy, I was okay. When she became very quiet, I got very nervous because I knew she must be sick. During the quiet times, if I had to, I would crawl into the bed with her and listen to each breath she took.

When I got my first job after nursing school, I began giving back to her immediately. That seven dollars per week she provided to me had been a good investment for the both of us. I looked around the house and started buying her things such as new cookware, her first microwave, and tons of clothes. When I bought clothes items for myself, I bought another one in her size. This became funny when she came to live with me. As I walked out of the house to go to work, she would humorously say, "Hey you! Hold up! Hold up, come back here, and pull off my clothes." I had to laugh out loud and remind her that we had many matching outfits. She would just laugh and say, "Just be careful, because you know I don't want anybody wearing my clothes."

She was a fashionista, and she made dressing like a queen bee a top priority. My mother would frequently remind family and friends that she was once built like a Coca Cola bottle; therefore, everything looked fabulous on her, even in her seasoned years. When she went out of the house, she was certain that she was dressed to stop traffic. When she became confined to a wheelchair, she refused to wear clothes that were not her exact size. My mother wouldn't have anything to do with the fact that clothes had to be at least one size larger to fit a person who required assistance with dressing. I got smart and would cut the sizes out of her clothes. The nurses and doctors could not wait to see what she would be wearing at her medical appointments. I made sure she didn't disappoint them. Exercising was also an important part of her daily activities, even as she spent the majority of her days in the wheelchair. Before she was diagnosed with MS, she had been known for walking five miles a day and then turning around and riding her stationary bike ten miles. (I can still only do one mile per day on my treadmill.) For the last ten years of her life, because of that dreadful disease, she had to see the world from her electric wheelchair.

Before the dreadful fate of MS, she had added *successful* beautician/cosmetologist to her résumé. This career brought her great happiness. Earlier, I shared the adventure of her holding tightly to a cash box that she kept on her lap during the trip to Colorado. Well, when we arrived in Denver, she handed me the key to the box. I opened it and found ten thousand dollars in fives, tens, twenties, fifties, and hundred-dollar bills. This was her life's savings from working as a beautician. She washed and set hair for five dollars and perms were fifteen dollars per head. Once she moved to Colorado, she started receiving an old-age pension check for six hundred dollars a month. My God, by her standards, she was rich! Boy, when I asked to put the money in the bank, she put her foot down with a hard,

"NO." I nervously and reluctantly accepted the money being kept in her room under her supervision.

I came home one day, and we couldn't find the money. By this time, it was approximately twelve thousand dollars. She had spent down by buying essentials such as a bedroom set, loans to family members, and carpet for her room. Yes, she had to have carpet (so she could waste yogurt on the side of the bed that was so close to the wall that we couldn't vacuum). I beat myself up and regretted every time I stopped myself from putting that money in the bank, even if it was against her wishes. We had so many people coming in and going out of the house. It was all a necessary part of the excellent care she needed to provide her with such a high level of healthcare, three times a day, for seven days a week. I didn't want to think about it for a moment. But I couldn't help but be reminded of all the windows of opportunity for the money to walk right out the door with one of the employees who could not resist the temptation. There were plenty of opportunities for our minds to wonder what could have happened to the money. Now, I was consumed with the thought of how I was going to replace her money that I hadn't protected by taking it to the bank.

The thought of what happened to the money haunted me daily. Then one day I came home, and it was like money had rained all over her room. Bills were everywhere. Once I thanked God, I gathered the money and told her I was putting it in the bank that same day. She still gave me a hard, "NO." I called her brother and sister and asked them to manage her money, or it was going into the bank. Each of them declined. Well, the money went into the bank and for the rest of her life; she told the family I was gambling her money away at the casinos "up yonder in those hilly mountains." I didn't care what she said about me. The money was safely in the bank. It was available to make sure she had everything she wanted, including the proper burial she deserved.

She was very helpful in making a proper burial for herself possible. She had the old JC Penny insurance policy through Stonebridge. Yes, it was from the stone ages. With that said, I am sure like most people of her era, she had paid three to four times the value of the policy in unwavering, reliable, on-time monthly payments. Another insurance company called one day. She answered their required questions. The one question that stood out was whether she had any pre-existing conditions. Her response was, "No." I'm not sure if she understood the definition of "pre-existing condition." Perhaps they reached her at a moment of denial. I don't know because I was not part of the conversation. I knew she didn't tout her health problems with a badge of honor. Whatever the reason was, I also knew the insurance companies didn't usually approve people with pre-existing conditions. Moreover, I was sure they had weighed her age and health status for approving the insurance policy. I was convinced that when I called them, they would understand that she communicated the wrong information; therefore, they would terminate the policy.

Because I didn't think she would leave this earth anytime soon, I never found the time to cancel the policy. Well, she died eight days before it was fully vested. I knew this was another reason the policy would be null and void. I was expecting them to return the money we had invested in monthly payments. Surprisingly, they fully honored the three-thousand-two-hundred-dollar policy. She had managed to add to her burial funds. I purchased a full "Betty Boop" ledger (grave marker) for her burial site. It was also inscribed with, "We will always love you. -Brown, Ronnie, Michael, Sherry." It was amazing that she had provided herself with such a beautiful final gift at no extra cost to the family.

My mother had smoked for several years. Her pack per year was low because it took her at least one week to smoke a pack. I remember religiously going to the store to buy the Kent cigarette brand for twenty-five cents per pack. Five months before her death, she was diagnosed with lung cancer. Then, she had an added bitter pill to swallow—MS and *now* lung cancer. They discovered the cancer while she was getting tests for a routine MS follow-up. She didn't have any symptoms. Yet, when the oncologists reviewed and discussed her case at length, they informed us that they didn't feel she was a good candidate for treatment. I was devastated. She didn't seem to be bothered about their decision. I gathered my wits about me and did what I had always done. I got busy and did my research.

I read all I could about the surgical procedures and the recovery phase. I tapped my trusted Veteran's Administration (VA) doctors once again. They reviewed the x-rays and confirmed the diagnosis. The VA doctors were wonderful. They not only gave me their medical opinions, but the chief of the department would always add a loving hug for moral support. We were so blessed to have access to such a wonderful group of caring and knowledgeable doctors.

When I returned to the cancer specialist's office, I was loaded with courage, knowledge, and determination. I was ready to stand before God and these doctors and fight for my mother. I sat there quietly, waiting for my turn to speak. When the radiation oncologist spoke, his first sentence told me that God had been fighting her case, and we didn't have anything to worry about. He said in no uncertain terms, "Mrs. Brown, we are going to treat you, and this is how we are going to do it." They laid out the best treatment plan I could have asked for. She still appeared not to be bothered.

It was as if she knew God would take care of His faithful and dedicated child.

She would look forward to her treatment visits. The day of the treatment, she would awaken early, bright-eyed and bushy-tailed, waiting to get the show on the road. The doctors were amazed by how well she tolerated her individualized treatment plan, on time, and without a single complaint. Two months later, they told her that she was free of lung cancer. Still, she looked as if she had no doubt that God *had* her all throughout this journey. She was born a trooper, a high maintenance one, but yet, a trooper.

Approximately two months later, after she was cured of lung cancer, my Aunt Jannie called me and told me it was an emergency. She screamed for me to come home *now* because my mother was in a deep sleep, and she couldn't wake her. When I arrived, I couldn't wake her either. I called 911. Before they got there, I was in the worse medical crisis of my life. For the first time in my career, I had to use the sternal rub. This is the application of a painful procedure, very firmly using the knuckles of my closed fist to the center of her chest. I was checking to determine whether her brain had the capacity to function and keep the body's activities working properly. Her body's response was questionable, and I didn't have my fantastic medical team from work by my side. I was alone, and it appeared as if my mother was dying in my arms. Then, my action woke her up! I had started an IV. She was alert and ready to go when the ambulance arrived. I helped them put her on the stretcher and into the ambulance. Off to the emergency room the paramedics went; I followed very closely behind.

Once she settled in, I was expecting to wake up to another ordinary day in the Henderson/Brown world, as I had over the last ten years. Because of her diagnosis of multiple sclerosis, we had been to the hospital many times. The routine was virtually the same. Mother would be admitted, treated for a urinary tract infection (UTI) and sent home smiling. Each visit, my aunt and I took turns spending the night with her. Even though it became obvious that within twenty-four hours she would have the nurses and doctors wrapped around her finger, we felt we didn't dare leave our precious spoiled gem alone. It usually wouldn't take long before she would have the nurses requesting to take care of Ms. Brown because she was so funny and kept them laughing throughout their shifts. What they didn't know was that there were several times she would make me mad, and she would say something so funny that I had to turn my back or leave the room so she would not see me bent over belly laughing.

No, the television series, *Meet the Browns* didn't have anything on the two funniest people in our family: my mother and my brother, Michael. Their Academy Award comedy performances would have the family belly over in laughter with tears. Only a small taste of this brought pleasure to the hospital staff, who felt lucky enough to take care of her.

Sadly, this last admission was different from the very start. She was having episodes of deep sleep that I didn't understand. She was admitted to an observation unit with other patients and a nurse present at all times. My aunt and I were not allowed to stay with her, but we came and spent all the time the nurses would allow. We would then go home at night and start the routine over the next day. We were comfortable with this because in this situation, she was never alone.

Two weeks before this hospital admission, my brother said to me, "You know, Momma has started talking to those who have gone on to glory."

I said to him, "You don't know what you are talking about."

I simply moved on into the distant depths of denial. I couldn't wait to dismiss the thought that she was beginning her journey to leave us. (*I have to stop writing now because the pain is too much, and the tears are clouding the computer screen.*)

As I begin writing again (four hours later), I recall that two days after my brother had attempted to get me to face reality, my mother was sitting at her chosen spot at the kitchen table. I was sitting in the den watching television. She suddenly started talking to her sister and others who had passed on. I was too afraid to get close enough to hear everything she was saying.

I said, "Momma, I don't understand what you are saying or if you see those people you're talking to."

She turned and looked boldly and squarely into my eyes and said, "But I do."

I still stayed in the realm of denial from a distance. I could not, for one moment, embrace the fact that God was telling me that I was losing my mother.

She was treated for a routine UTI as expected. She returned to herself with flying colors, except she was still having deep-sleep episodes. I didn't understand, and the doctors told me not to put much stock into this behavior. They expected her to make a full recovery. Three days before her scheduled discharge from the hospital, she was moved to a regular room. The regular routine that included me and my aunt taking turns spending the night with her began again. The first night went well, except my Aunt Jannie was so concerned about my mother. She kept asking me if she was okay.

She said, "I have this strong feeling that something is not right. Are you sure she is going to be okay?"

I calmly said, "Yes, she is okay and ready to go home in a couple of days."

I could not understand how my aunt could be questioning me and the medical experts. I was a legitimate member of the medical care team. Nothing (I mean nothing), happened without my input and approval. I was definitely on top of her care. *What could my Aunt Jannie have known that the medical experts, including me, didn't know?* It turned out that she had a restless spirit and God was preparing her for the loss ahead of time. Her kindred spirit with God was much stronger than mine. She was attentively listening to Him.

A day or two after my mother's death, Aunt Jannie told me of some strange things that happened early on the day before her death. My mother was observed waking up from a deep sleep, and asked the nurse, "Am I dead? Am I in heaven?"

The nurse responded by matter-of-factly saying, "All I know is that you are certainly *not* dead, and this is *not* heaven."

My mother then said, "There is my casket over there, and it is not green." (Lime green was her favorite color).

Ironically, she was buried in a mahogany casket. I just couldn't find a decent green one. I was told that the strange conversation became stranger when the doctor came into her room later that morning. She told him that she would never be coming back to the hospital. She said she would never have another UTI or have the need for another catheter.

The day before the morning of her death, there was a tornado warning in the area that included the VA hospital (my place of work) and the Aurora South Hospital (the hospital she was in). I called her on the telephone while the unit staff and I were standing in the hallway of the hospital, according to the hospital tornado protocol. She was in her comedic mood. I put her on the speakerphone for what (little did I know) would be her last Academy Award comic act. She thoroughly entertained the staff as we waited for the tornado warning to end. I can only image that those who were in her room were equally filled with the joy of her raw humor as they listened to her entertain the captured audience at my place of work.

When I got off from work, I headed to the hospital to spend the evening with her and get her ready for her early morning discharge. The Denver Nuggets were playing a basketball game that night, but the hospital's television didn't have the station for me to watch them. I thought for a moment about what to do about this dilemma. I concluded that she was fine, and just waiting to be discharged in the morning. I made a conscious decision to go home and watch the game. As I was getting ready to leave, she started fussing and threw an award-winning temper tantrum for a Babe Ruth, her favorite candy bar. She was famous for having her "I'm getting my way" temper tantrums. But all of this was my barometer of how well she was feeling. Her actions confirmed that I felt she was ready to come home the next morning. When she was feisty, to say the least, I would not be worried about her. I would just make sure all her needs were met and respectfully go on about my business doing my thing.

On this occasion, she had plenty of pep in her step. I was happy to have her controlling me like I was a child again. It brought me so much joy to see her returning to normal. Yes, she could be an adult, spoiled brat, but she was the brat whom my family had created before I was born. Who was I to try to stop this spoiled freight train? It was my cross to bear to keep the spoiled brat as close to manageable as possible. I speak candidly about her personality, but really, I admired her for living life on her terms. She always found a way to be the center of attention, by crook, hook, or by sheer manipulation. She was smarter than I ever will be, and she maximized that to her advantage. Don't get me wrong, she was a beautiful soul. It was her *realness* and her ability to fully be herself that I deeply, deeply admired and loved.

Back to that night… I went to the vending machine looking for a Babe Ruth candy bar. I looked in the vending machines on her floor and the store in the main lobby. I could not find one. I asked her to just hold on until tomorrow. I promised her if she could do that, I would get her all the Babe Ruth candy bars she could eat, plus some when she got home. She forcefully grabbed a package of graham crackers and tore the package open with her teeth. As she put the graham crackers in her mouth, a blind man could see that she was unhappy. But the promise of plenty more of something if she would just wait a little longer worked as it usually did.

I kissed her forehead, fluffed her pillow, and elevated her head to make her comfortable. I walked to the door and found myself coming back again to kiss her again on the forehead. She had calmed down and looked so peaceful and beautiful. I had the adult spoiled brat my family had created back. I had supported and loved her through another hospitalization and was ready to start our precious daily routine again the very next day. I went to the door again and, for some reason I will never be able to explain, I went back and kissed her on the forehead a third time. I had never kissed her *good night* three times in my life. Yet, I didn't think much of it. I had no way of knowing those would be the last kisses I would give her while the blood was running warm in her veins.

I went home and watched the Denver Nuggets beat the Minnesota Timberwolves, 113-107. The Nuggets' win made it worth coming home to watch the game. I am such a sports fanatic. Before I went to bed that night, I mentally planned to pick her up from the hospital and bring her home before I went to work. My boss was always understanding, and he knew that at this stage of my life, my mother came first. He also understood that when I got to work, I would not leave until my job was done. He realized my dedication meant I would be at work way into the middle of the night if necessary. I was at peace and convinced that my mother and I were ready to face another episode of our usual routine. A good life, a funny life, a life free of lung cancer until another episode of treatment for a UTI.

When the phone rang at 5:30 a.m., I froze and didn't answer it. *Who could want something from me at that time of morning? Momma was in the hospital doing fine. Who else could be having a problem at this time of morning? It could be someone who dialed the wrong number. If so, they would realize that and not call back*—that was the thought I choose to stick with. When the telephone rang for the second time, I answered it. A friend whose niece worked at the hospital was on the other end. She informed me that her niece had called her and told her to have me get to the hospital NOW.

I hung up the telephone and started turning in circles like a dog chasing his tail. I couldn't decide to put clothes on or take off at a speed of one hundred miles per hour in my pajamas. I just jumped into my car with my pajamas on. At least if I was stopped for speeding, my thought was that indecent exposure would not be added to the ticket. When I reached the major turn to the hospital, my phone rang again.

My friend's niece asked, "Where are you?"

I told her where I was and then said, "You are not telling me what I need to hear."

Her slamming, life-changing, and heartbreaking response was, "Because I can't."

I dropped the telephone and floored the car's accelerator. In seconds, I pulled up to the front of the hospital. I jumped out of the car with the doors opened and unlocked. The engine was still running. I was on a mission. If I could get to my mother before she took her last breath, I would save her. I had to save her. I was trained to save lives. There was no life more important for me to save.

I ran up the stairs because I couldn't wait for the elevator. I couldn't stand still for one moment; I had to keep running to her rescue. When I reached the nurses' station, I could see the doctors coming out of her room. I used the wall to slide myself to the floor. I cried as softly as I could. I didn't want to wake the rest of the patients. The doctors and nurses picked me up and took me into a private room. Once I was in the room, I started screaming at the top of my lungs. My world had just suddenly stopped, and I had no control or say so about what had just happened.

Once I regained a bit of control, all I wanted to do was to see my mother. I stepped into her room and fell on my knees at her bedside. Her body was still warm. I laid my left arm over her chest and right arm under her head. I said to her, "Mother, all I have to say is that you knew I loved you. I will always love and miss you. I was on my way to save you, but God took you before I could get to you."

It was at that moment that I went on another long journey of being angry with God. This time, I was an adult. Yet, I still had some of the same questions. *How could He do this?* My mother still added so much joy to our family and especially to me. I was keeping her alive, waiting for the first MS cure. *How dare He take her?* He had no right to cause me so much pain after all I had done to prolong her life. In my thinking, laced with extreme anger and unforgiving pain, He was like a thief in the night who came and claimed what was mine. *I* had done all the hard work. *Again, how could He take what was my most precious joy?* There was no room for me to recall that she had belonged to *Him*, and she was only a loaner to me.

Although I had immediately started my long journey of being mad with God, I quietly spent every moment the staff would allow me to spend with her. When they came into the room and asked me what arrangement I wanted to make for her body to leave the hospital, I instantly went into *automatic* mode. I began to just put one foot in front of the other. When I got back to the family lounge, all my family and friends were there waiting to console me. They did the best they could, but my pain was too intense for any human being to handle or console me. When I got home, I threw up, uncontrollably, as if I had symptoms of food poison. My whole body had gone into disbelief and shock.

I stayed on that automatic journey for months. With the help of my aunt, I made all the arrangements. I honored my mother's request and had her flown back to Clarksdale, Mississippi, to be buried as close to her sister as I could make it. It didn't take long to find out that the plot next to my Aunt Jessie had been sold, and I didn't own it like I had been told. On the plane traveling home to celebrate her life, I sat next to a lady who engaged me in a conversation related to the purpose of this plane trip. She gave me comfort when she told me my mother would be proud of how I would keep her legacy alive through the beautiful person I had become. It was like she was placed in my path when I needed such spirited inspiration. Her words still to this day make me cry when I remember what she said.

My mother didn't wait for others to keep her spirit alive. One night, I was sitting in my bed downstairs watching television. Other family members were upstairs watching television. I decided to turn my television off and go to sleep. When I turned it off, it came back on about a minute later. I thought I had hit the wrong button on the remote control. So, I hit the *off* button again and the television once again turned off and came back on again a minute or so later. I called upstairs and asked my family if they were having problems with the televisions upstairs. They all denied having problems. At this point, I turned the television off again. I threw the remote control across the room to make sure I didn't hit the *on* button by mistake. With the remote control across the room, the television came back on for the third time. Just for clarification, there was no timer set for the television. I surrendered and said, "Okay, Mom. It's okay, I am not afraid. I know you are here to let me know you will never leave me if I am open to your presence." I told her I was open, then, and I would always be open to her presence.

Her birthday was two weeks after her death and Mother's Day was the following week. Not only had I entered into the *Motherless* Club, but I had unwillingly fallen into a triple painful three weeks for the rest of my life. On her birthday, my aunt bought green and purple balloons and two birthday cards. Before I opened the birthday card, I said, "Mother, all I have to say is that I love you and I miss you." It was basically a repeat of what I had said on my knees at her bedside the night of her death. When I read the card, they were almost the exact words I had said before I opened the card. I could feel her presence and her spirit.

We went out onto the patio to release the balloons. My aunt released the ones in her hand, and they just drifted forward into the distance, as we expected them to do. When I released mine, two of them followed the route of the ones released by my aunt. This is the *God's honest truth*: the last balloon went out, suddenly changed directions and came back toward me. Then it changed directions again and went forward for a few moments. Yet again, it changed directions and took a straight aim for the military airplanes that happened to be flying high overhead at that moment. I live in full view of Lowery Air Force Base, with planes flying over my home. But when the balloon found its way amid the Air Force planes high in the sky, it was just like an honorary military flyover in my mother's honor. I could see and appreciate this view, which was seared into my memory.

From where I stood, I also saw a few shiny silver objects that appeared to me as stars off to the right of the balloon, and the military airplanes were still in my view. When I turned and looked to the left, I saw approximately twenty more of these shiny objects. At that moment, I was fascinated and filled with pride. I didn't give much thought to the dynamics of what was happening right then. Two days later, it came to me that I had never seen stars in the daytime. I immediately took to the internet and verified that stars are not seen in daylight. When I got to work, I asked all my coworkers if they had heard of stars being seen in the daytime. Each of them confirmed that stars or shiny objects that look like stars were only seen in the darkness of the night.

I later came to believe that these were spiritual images of the people my mother had been talking to and had come to welcome her to her heavenly home. The few shiny objects on the right were just enough to represent her sister, Aunt Jessie; her Grandmother, Martha; her father, Doe Henderson; and her mother, Mary. I feel the other approximately twenty shiny star-like objects were our other family members and friends who had come to meet her and remind me that God had her. They were His angels, sent to walk side by side with her through the pearly gates of heaven.

Later on, I began to have strange, quiet thoughts. Thoughts of reason that most definitely didn't seem like thoughts of my own. Just to share a few… It was my birthday, when a thought came to me and told me that my family was going to give me a birthday party. Approximately one hour later, my family and friends showed up with happy cheers and everything they needed for my birthday party. I didn't hesitate to tell them that my mother had told me all about their plans. I was still surprised, though, because this was the first time anyone had ever given me a birthday party. Another clear example is that there came times when I couldn't find certain items after tearing the house apart. I would look in almost every place in the house. The quiet, "not of my own" thoughts would come to my rescue. Once, I had forgotten where I put one thousand dollars that I had been entrusted to keep. I tore the house up on every floor. I conceded that I had exhausted my efforts to find the money. I went to my room and lay down to take a nap. When I woke up, those quiet, captivating thoughts that didn't feel as if they belonged to me made me sit straight up in my bed. The thoughts told me exactly where to go to find the money. Still skeptical, I got out of bed and followed the quiet instructions offered by the quiet thoughts. I didn't have to look around for the money at all. I found it precisely where the thoughts had taken me. When I opened the cabinet where the quiet voice had led me, the box that held the money was in plain sight.

Some people tell me this is not my mother. But I feel they would have to experience this situation for themselves before I will embrace their opinions related to this subject. If it is not my mother, I will still take it because it comforts me to believe that my mother is still watching out for me. It has been this comfort that gives me peace and has helped me to stop crying my eyes out every time someone approaches me with thoughts of her. As long as it is not unhealthy or harmful to my mental or physical health, I will take peace regarding my presence in the *Motherless* Club in any way I can get it.

Reading *Letters to Mom*, by author, LaNette Kincaide (my writing coach), has reinforced that our memories and love for our mothers will never fade away. It is just the opposite. The light in our hearts will shine brighter and brighter. If we are open to their spirits, they will help to guide the path of our future and join the entourage that will come to escort us through the pearly gates of heaven in due time.

I still owe my coworkers and friends a big "Thank You" and an apology for not saying it earlier. I am still unable to read the cards I received. It has been ten years, but the pain is still raw. Some might say I act as if I am the only person who ever joined the *Motherless* Club; I know I am not. I feel for each member of this club. We share an experience that has ripped our hearts out of our bosoms, only to leave holes that will never heal.

We all grieve differently, but we must remember to go at our individual pace. We must be patient with ourselves as well as others who are on this lifelong journey. Neither of us loved our mothers any more or any less—just differently. The pain from the loss took away many of my heartbeats and frequently caused me to hold my breath as I experienced many skipped beats. I feel that the experiences of each other's pain are intertwined. Recognizing this is the key to not only surviving this catastrophic loss, but learning to smile amid the tears. We all are just on a mission trying to make the best out of this thing called life.

Mom, like Randy Travis says, "I'm gonna love you forever and ever, forever and ever, amen."

Chapter Twenty

FIRE LILY:
FLAMING FIRE

Flame lily
Gloriosa superba

I was born a pistol. Quiet and shy in the company of people, yet I was a pistol waiting to be loaded and fired for the world to see I could make a difference. I do not remember ever changing the fundamentals of my life; I just remember thirsting to satisfy my curiosity and embracing my growth and development. Today, I look back and appreciate how my many triumphs and tragedies have brought me to this moment. It's too late to spend a lot of time thinking about regrets or wondering why it took me so long to grow out of my shyness and find my voice. I hope for a great number of years in the future, but I choose to stay *woke* and smell the roses of the present. I have been through the rain and the storms, but I made it.

"Rising from the ashes after fires, the fire lily creates vibrant red and pink displays across the Cape Fold Mountains of South Africa." ("Fire Lily," n.d.) The pictures of the fire lily reveal huge patches of bright red blooms, which literally look like they are on fire. As I gaze upon on the beautiful image of the fire lily, it reminds me of the realism, fiery spirit, simple grace, and elegance of how I would speak about myself in the third person. I literally feel like, *This Girl is on Fire*. The symbolism of the fire lily in my life comes front and center, as I feel the burning fiery desire in my soul to champion an emotionally rich and love-filled world for humanity. I yearn to learn how I can share my authentic perspective of equality for all.

I hope, by now, you can see that I was an intuitive, critical thinker as a child. I got stuck on *Why* questions and would never let go until I found the answer. Sometimes the answer was as simple as, "The answer to that question needs more research and you are just the one to keep searching for the answer." I hope my story has spoken for itself, and I have left a few unanswered questions. I hope I have answered the ultimate questions: *Who am I? What is my well-thought-out life purpose?* I anticipate you will agree that I am the truth I speak and the walk I walk. The genie (Sherry) is out of the bottle. I couldn't get her back into the bottle if I wanted to. The reality is, I *don't* want to. I don't need a "do over." My life has been a very inspiring and rewarding journey. I have not only surprised myself, but inspired myself as well. My wildest dreams have come true many times over. I quietly reached for the outer limits of space. So far, I have landed in the orbit of bursting bright stars. Being a positive role model who attempts to inspire others who have crossed my path makes me most proud. My family members who admire the world are living legacies for the world to see how *their* life journeys have been influenced by my blazing a well-lit path for them to follow. These days, that once shy and introverted young girl does not meet a stranger. Now, everyone who crosses my path becomes an opportunity for me to be a beacon of light that spotlights kindness and hope for world peace and unity. Not in the near or distance future, but NOW. I know I have made my great-grandmother proud.

If my memory serves me right, there was never a time in my life when I wasn't striving for things to be simple and equal. No matter how complex things became, I was always searching for the simplest and less complex solution that was laced with inclusion. I laid eyes on Dr. Martin Luther King, Jr., when I was ten years old. He visited our small town without media attention, before traveling to Memphis, Tennessee, the next day. Having been in his presence the day before he was assassinated left me with the impression that I had a responsibility to *do* something to make a difference for equality, no matter how small.

The road to fighting for equality and justice was paved with a thought planted by my great-grandmother. I had learned that my family once lived in the middle of a cow pasture, and I had received seventy-seven cents for picking a very heavy sack of cotton. So, Dr. King's presence and hearing his mission and passion at an early age watered that seed my great-grandmother planted. My promise to society was that I was going to show the world that you can oppress a people, but you can't keep them down forever. Also, I would show that the inhumane treatment of my family was downright wrong and a disgrace to mankind.

As an adult, campaigning for Charles Evers in Philadelphia, Mississippi, I started nurturing the seed of equality. He was a Mississippi civil rights and political icon. He was also the brother of Medgar Evers (Field Director of the NAACP in Jackson, Mississippi, who was assassinated right outside his home). The seed bloomed, and I began to see myself as deserving of equal opportunities, as well as having the desire to provide the same equal opportunities for others. I was merely seeking to take advantage of all the colors of the wind that life had to offer me. Equality is just one of the wind's colors held close to my heart.

Sometimes, it would be easier to surrender to the path of least resistance. I have had to face many dark characteristics, such as being jaded, cynical, or spending time wallowing in self-pity. But like my mother, I am not about *easy*. Plus, I find these things to be a waste of precious time. I am about peace of mind, empowerment, and inclusion of others.

Nature became my best friend as I roamed the plains of the countryside. I don't see myself as *pretty* nor perfect, just perfectly *imperfect* with a fiery fight. I strongly believe that beauty is in the eye of the beholder. In my opinion, my pure and vibrant natural beauty is an extraordinarily rare treasure, originating from the inside, only to blossom outward, like magic. This classic beauty becomes rarer because "beauty in a jar" has taken over mainstream society. Unlike too many of today's women who are eager to use their faces as canvasses to paint portraits that are sometimes unrecognizable, I mainly prefer to start and end with my God-given natural beauty. That means whatever makeup is taken off or put on still leaves a recognizable person (me).

Don't get the wrong understanding. My self-esteem is not low, nor am I "Debbie Downer." Far from it, I am so comfortable in my skin. Time spent measuring my beauty is a waste. Beauty starts and ends with how my inner spirit guides me to be my *true* self. Listening to my own heartbeat lets my commitment to authenticity come shining through.

My story reads like a book of a million Kodak memories, with my great-grandmother as my North Star. When asked to go back to a quiet and serene place, most people choose watching the sunset at the beach, sitting next to a cozy fireplace, etc. I choose those moments sitting so close to her on the porch of our raggedy house without any room for air between us. Holes must be in the floor of heaven. When there is a heavy rainstorm, I imagine she is crying tears to let me know she misses me, and she is watching over me as she waits for me in heaven.

Nothing was more real than the day I became conscious of living the last days of my lifecycle. I most definitely have more years behind me than in front of me. This realization doesn't cause fear or major disappointment—just the opposite. The value of every breath I breathe increases substantially. Taking pride in who I am and staying engaging in only endeavors that bring me pleasure instead of pain are my top priorities.

Like the fire lily, I have risen from the hot ashes and red, clay dirt of the backwoods of Mississippi, into a world open to my roaming desires. I feel I am the poster child representing the belief that no matter where you come from or what mistakes you have made in your past, there are always opportunities for redemption, as long as you have pure intentions. It is a plus to be committed to good deeds. Furthermore, like the fire lily, I am hardy. I don't require a lot of maintenance, and I'm extremely adaptable to what the forces of the wind blow my way.

With that said, I still feel this girl continues to be on fire with a raw sense of humor that captures the essence of her being. I have climbed the ladder of success and firmly landed in a good spot (like a fire lily in good soil) to reap the benefits of my labor. This is another way to acknowledge that I have sustained fiery purity and passion. I raise my hands to the heavens with joy and let the world know I am still not only standing, but I am amazingly thriving. I have survived too many storms to be afraid to embrace a few raindrops. I stand tall and own my humble roots, while keeping my feet flat on the ground.

As a woman with a fiery character, who respectfully expands the whole gamut or spectrum of personality, this once shy country girl can proudly take her seat on a clean floor in the backwoods country homes of America. With my *Cinderella* shoes on, I can comfortably wine and dine at the table in the fancy antique oak chairs of the White House. At first, I might not know exactly what to do, but by relying on all the things my great-grandmother taught me, I will do fine. She taught me to sit quietly, look, and listen, and remember to always consider, "When in Rome, do what the Romans do." The caveat is to leave with your core principles intact and to have learned something that adds value to your life. This idea has gotten me through many fancy events and places far away from the backwoods of Mississippi. It's true that, "You can take the girl out of the country, but you can't take the country out of the girl." My heart and soul—country proud.

Truth can be stranger than fiction, but you can always remember it is truth because it remains the same. I once had an African American friend tell me several times to my face, "I don't believe you when you keep saying all those things happened in Mississippi. That couldn't have happened. I also lived in Mississippi." What she didn't know was, historically, North and South Mississippi were as different as night and day, even for Black folks. In South Mississippi, Black people owned land, and some of them even owned slaves during that horrible time in history. They used their land to establish generational wealth and build a future of hope and dreams for their families. For many, their dreams became realities. Their parents built strong, beautiful brick houses on their land, not very far from the white, sandy beaches. Their homes had enough bedrooms for the girls to sleep, separated from the boys. In most bedrooms, everyone had their own beds. They freely enjoyed walking and running to the beachfronts, fishing and picnicking at their leisure. Even the weather in South Mississippi was mostly warm and inviting. The use of an overcoat was a rarity.

Just to note a startling contrast, in North Mississippi, *we* didn't own any land or houses. There were no exceptions to Black people experiencing life as enslaved people. We weren't even the first owners of the raggedy clothes on our backs. Ditches and shadow fishing ponds were as close as we came to beaches. Thick, reddish mud (clay) was our sand. We didn't have the overcoats to protect us from the wet and piercing cold. I ate so much of the reddish mud that I developed a cast iron stomach. If my African American friend views my life as a horrible fantasy, how could I expect the world to see me as *An Unequivocal Southern Belle*? I kindly disagree. It is instilled in the fabric of my soul that I mattered equally, in contrast to what others might think. Maybe now that I have taken the time to put my story in print, my friend will decide that my bravery in sharing my story with the world is potential proof that I just might not be lying. May God bless her soul.

As a child and young adult, I didn't dream of being married or following the typical female path. No disrespect, but I didn't want anything to do with limiting my dream to an era when a woman was seen as being "confined to the kitchen." I didn't like the confinement, nor did I like that society saw my place as being in the kitchen. *I only have a kitchen because it came with my house.* When guests arrive, the tours start with me highlighting this rule of the house. I didn't care to keep my dreams at bay for the sake of a husband and family. No, I was destined to have it all. Things didn't quite work out exactly as planned, but I never compromised my dream.

I was often told that I missed my calling as a model or a pianist (a pianist because my fingers were long). They are both respectable careers, but there are a couple of events that proved my seeds were planted exactly where I landed. I got an organ keyboard for Christmas. I learned to play by the numbers instead of the notes. My fingers didn't move across the keyboard with grace; therefore, my touch was hard and firm instead of soft and graceful. Neither did I have the innate or learned ability to appreciate synchronizing harmony. Now that spoke volumes. Being a model was less of a tangible dream. I didn't know any Black professional fashion models as role models. Honestly, role models or not, I didn't have the confidence to hold my head up high and strut the red carpet until later in my life. Regarding the modeling business, it is never too late.

My story is laced with a heavy dose of naivety. Most of this naivety has been a part of the naturally delayed development of my emotional maturity. Being a late bloomer meant that it often took me longer than most people to find comfort in owning my place in life. This lent itself to needing more time to process and figure things out. But when I did, the fruit of my solid thought process stayed with me for a lifetime.

I would go outside when I was young with the feeling of being free to roam endlessly. But the real appreciation of exploring the depths of my being free didn't hit me until my late forties. I don't get out much now, but when I do, I am so much into letting my sense of "doing what I want to do" take over. I now live and let live as I have the time of my life. I long ago committed to being naïve instead of being jaded. The trick is to find a happy median. I have made great strides, but there is always room for ongoing growth. I am still steadfastly committed to the idea that if I have the chance to dance or sit it out, I will choose to dance.

Long ago, I put my *Cinderella* slippers on and went to a party outside the *country* of Mississippi and never mentally took my slippers off. I purposely walk the world in those slippers every second of the day. That is no lie, no bragging, no boasting—just a cold, hard fact. I live to be energetic, silly, funny, strong, capable, and kind. Adaptability is my halo and super trait. Without the ability to adapt to my environment, I would have mentally died a long time ago. I would not have survived... let alone thrived. Because of this, the bouquet of flowers in my life continues to blossom and thrive in any environment I encounter. I do not ask God to remove the obstacles in my life. I don't feel alive if I don't have healthy growing pains; therefore, I ask Him for strength and wisdom to navigate my path around them.

My most important message in writing this book is to highlight if I can do it, so can you; especially for the younger members of my family. The voices in my head kept speaking to me from the first day I created the email address, "Black Magnolia" at least fifteen years ago. At that time, I had the insight and envisioned the title *Black Magnolia: An Unequivocal Southern Belle*. Several times, I wrote the first chapters, only to move into another house. When I got to the new house, I never knew where I safely packed the valuable beginnings of my story.

Recently, I stumbled onto a writing coach by mere coincidence (she calls it no accident). I call it another day that my curiosity yielded a path for me—this time to establish a creative writing relationship. The relationship has consistently encouraged my taking to pen and paper to discover my creative writing skills. Her guidance and coaching have resulted in me humbly sharing my story with you and the rest of the world. The experiences of my story do not have one-of-a-kind uniqueness, but I always wanted to share my story in print. There are plenty of stories more fascinating and uplifting than mine. It might be *your* story. It could be the story of the person next door that the world is waiting to read. Your story could light a fire to blaze the path for the next generation.

I love interacting with all types of people of all nationalities. However, if the truth be known, I am most happy when alone. Some people feel you must be lonely if you are alone. On the flip side, some people are lonely among a crowd. For me, I make my inner peace with the resources I have to work with. That *is* my true essence, but it is not the completeness of who I am. Maybe being such a loner is the reason I didn't know I was Black or African American and different until the world told me I was. I prefer being addressed as African American because Black does not embrace my African heritage. The world has not only attempted to never let me forget it, but also made an effort to define being Black as derogatory. Because I didn't find anything derogatory about my existence, I concluded that the world didn't know me. If they did, they would see that I am gifted with blessed positivity. I am also willing to share it with all who will listen and take the time to get to know me.

Back to equality for a moment— human nature makes us comfortable with those who look like us, talk like us, and share the same interests. There is no growth in our comfort zones. Stepping out of our comfort zone means we must trust the process and believe there is something to gain from learning to interact with and love those who don't look like us. If nothing else, the world would be a much better place. One profound conversation with my great-grandmother shaped my courage and bravery to step outside of my comfort zone. She taught me to believe I could do that, and eventually that belief became my reality. Like me, you will learn to become comfortable with the growing pains that this humanist shift will bring. Another purpose of this book is to share the guiding principles of my life: unity, forgiveness, and equality, amid all my struggles and differences.

I would be remiss if I didn't stress one of my true mantras related to equality. We must understand that Caucasians measure African Americans based on the values developed from their *White* experiences. It is a tall order to ask them to understand the *Black* experience, but we need to keep the doors open and invite them in for candid conversations.

The mantra or guiding beacons of my pursuit for equality and for my life are simple. I live using these guiding principles in all my endeavors and with everyone I meet.

"Give a man a fish and you feed him for a day. Teach him to fish and you feed him for a lifetime." — Lao Tzu.

I also believe in the serenity prayer:

"God grant me the serenity to accept the things I cannot change, the courage to change the things I can, and the wisdom to know the difference." — Reinhold Niebuhr.

CONCLUSION

As you have discovered and hopefully enjoyed, this book tells the story of my life through the Mississippi flowers that became the natural beauties from the conception of my life and traveled with me from place to place. I hope that each flower, representing a chapter, came together to let you envision the blossoming tapestry of my life thus far. I have so much more road to travel as I joyfully continue down the road of curiosity, crafting a beautiful bouquet that speaks of my spirited life.

My life has also been filled with many "pinch me" moments. I no longer have to share my fireplaces with snakes, my front yard with cows, or merge the inside of my home with the outside elements, such as extreme heat and cold. Yet, I remain very humble. The only fact I take great joy and satisfaction in is that my home is bigger than the home of the plantation owner (Mr. Randle) where I grew up. Yes, I have a few moments of vanity. I wasn't privileged to see the inside of his "big, white house." But I bet my right arm that it was no match for my five bedroom and four bathroom, very warm and comfortable home. This is a long way from a bedroom/living room and one outhouse with newspaper on a good day. I earned a yearly six-figure salary during my career—the career I loved because I served veterans who loved me back. That is a hell of a lot more than those seventy-seven cents I made from the first and *only* sack of cotton I picked at the age of eight. I have stopped living to go to work. Now, I am working on enjoying a life that includes traveling around the world at my leisure.

I keep a vase of open cotton bolts in my dining room to remind me and never let me forget where I came from. An appreciation for elegance came much later in my life. I had to acquire some of the finer things of life before I could truly appreciate them. Once discovering finer things, I still didn't think of myself as remarkable or extra special, but rather blessed by God to have come such a long way in life. The measure of how far you go has a lot to do with where you came from and how many struggles you have overcome.

Now, I call my two cars (Lexus) my modern "Tom" and "Jerry" (once my feet, my main transportation). These cars will take me around the world in great comfort. I have owned several houses and not a single one of them were shacks with holes, cracks or snakes in them. Yet, I do not forget that there are other stories similar to mine; I don't own the market on coming from humble beginnings. I am not the only person who has survived such a challenging life and thrived. This book is my platform to validate that we *all* can rise from the ashes, especially women, who find themselves in a situation where the odds are stacked against them. We just need to stop keeping the struggles of our journey to ourselves. We must empower each other to share and celebrate our joys as well as our pains. Growing pains always remind us that we are emotionally alive and more powerful as we become stronger and stronger.

I am glad for my backwoods country experiences, but I am not sure I would like to repeat them or wish them upon another human being. The hardest part about my life was the deep heartbreaks and the most wonderful part was discovering and understanding I had to learn to love myself first. This was the gateway to loving someone else and letting them love me. This means that after all the heartbreaks, I will always have someone to keep loving me—*me!*

Sometimes we confuse this concept with selfishness. I am a firm believer that you can't freely give or receive love until you learn to love yourself. I also learned to scream at the top of my lungs and cry my eyes out as I put all the broken bits and pieces of my heart back together again. This is the formula for becoming the woman I am today. Laughing out loud, even if I am the only one within listening range, is music that I want to hear these days.

As I look forward to the last chapters of my life, it is very clear that I made many mistakes. I am guilty of gifting people with a second, third, and fourth chance. These many chances have subjected me to both joy and thorns within both my romantic love relationships and career journeys. I heavily lean in with the fact that I stand on the shoulder of those that came before me. This keeps me traveling the path God and my great-grandmother paved for me. With both on my side, how could I miss the many gifts that are mine to claim? The road to accomplish my goals has been winding, rough, and heartbreaking. But the joy and happiness these chapters of my life have brought me along the way has been absolutely PRICELESS.

I learned to save money, despite not having a budget since 1989. I remember my great-grandmother always saving for a rainy day. I still pick up pennies with the mentality that one million dollars started with one penny. I might not be Madam C.J. Walker, but I *am* the first millionaire in the Henderson family. I know that is not a lot of money. You better believe I am working hard to spend *every* dime of it before I close my eyes for the last time. There will be no reason for family and friends to come looking for it when death paves the way to heaven for me.

I stand tall and proud each day as I sway toward the sun in the sky like the sunflowers that remind me of the interconnection of the beginning of my life and life as I live it today. I also believe there is strength in the fact that I can always go back to my roots. There will always be someone there waiting to welcome me back. Sometimes the someone might just be the spirit of those who never left because they never had the opportunity to do so. I am obligated to see the world on their behalf. So, watch as this forever-free spirit soars and lands on as many continents of the world as my pennies will allow. I will travel the world only to return to a place I can roam freely—home sweet home.

In hindsight, it looked like my family was planted and buried in darkness, but being the blessed children that we are, we never stopped forging to the daylight. We were committed to bending deeply, but we never became broken. We have learned to enjoy the view all the way from the bottom to the top, and we remember that the top is not always where you find the most sustainable view.

I imagine some of you might find my life a little foolish and crazy. You want to know what took me so long to learn life's most important lessons. Perhaps this book didn't touch your soul the way that I hoped. That is okay. I thank you for hanging in there to the end. If your soul was touched, even a little bit, perhaps you identify with the fact that naivety can cause us to move at a slower pace. We want to take all the necessary time to be true to ourselves. Like me, it might have taken you a bit longer to get to your place of maturity. I want you to know one thing: when I got there, there was no turning back. I have discovered the mighty strength and roaring courage to keep myself going forward.

I answered the question long ago about whether I felt the blooms of the magnolia tree would be as beautiful if the blooms were black instead of white. Like the true symbolism of the color white, the true symbolism of the color black also includes equal beauty, purity, sophistication, timelessness, optimism, hope, and another way of contemplating a different perspective—it is certainly *not* a superior or inferior perspective. Hopefully, I have prompted you to stop and consider this same thought-provoking question.

The magnolia tree is one of the first flowering trees to bloom each year. This tree has buds, blossoms, flowers, and forever greenery all at the same. To me, this is a divine sign that God is watching over us ALL—all the time, in every season. The blooms are for spring and summer, and the evergreen leaves represent fall and winter. The openness of the blooms of the magnolia tree is symbolic of being watchful, wakeful, vigilant, and experiencing an awakening.

This book is only going to go where GOD takes it. You are not reading it by accident or coincidence. Either God meant for you to read it, or you are one of my friends who wants to get *all* the *tea*. Whatever the case, I hope I didn't disappoint you. Either way, enjoy the book, because it is the combination of life's fragments... chapters... flowers... that will eventually make us whole.

Our life bouquets are all beautiful.

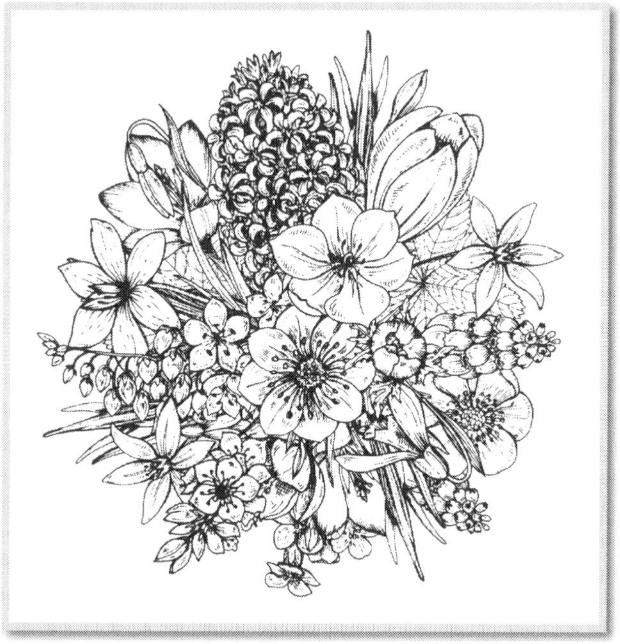

REFERENCES

"15 Flowers That Mean Love to Add to Your Bouquet | ProFlowers." 2021. ProFlowers Blog. August 3, 2021. https://www.proflowers.com/blog/which-flowers-mean-love.

"About the After Silence Rape and Sexual Abuse Survivor Message Board, Support Group, and Chat Room." n.d. https://www.aftersilence.org/inspiration.php.

Adam. "Sunflower Meaning and Symbolism." Flower Glossary, November 25, 2021.

> http://www.flowerglossary.com/sunflower-meaning-and-symbolism.

"All About King Protea." Web log. Maui Floral (blog), May 7, 2020.

> https://www.mauifloral.com/blogs/news/blog-post-3.

Christy.Kessler. "What Is a Eulogy?" Funeral Basics, September 24, 2018.

> https://www.funeralbasics.org/eulogy-remembrance

Christy.Kessler. 2017. "7 Popular Sympathy Flowers and Their Meanings." Funeral Basics. August 4, 2017. https://www.funeralbasics.org/7-popular-sympathy-flowers-meanings

Cruz, Julianne Robyn Dela. "Petunia Flower Meaning, Symbolism, and Uses You Should Know." GrowingVale, July 9, 2021.

>https://growingvale.com/meaning-symbolism/petunia-flower

"Daffodil" n.d. The Petal Factory.

>https://www.petalfactory.com.au/pages/the-meaning-of-flowers.

"Fire Lily." n.d. Kew. https://www.kew.org/plants/fire-lily.

Forbes, Maddie. "Verbena Flower: Meaning, Symbolism, and Colors." Pansy Maiden, September 25, 2022. https://www.pansymaiden.com/flowers/meaning/verbena

"How Do They Find Their Way Back?" Journey North Hummingbirds. Accessed January 22, 2023. https://www.journeynorth.org/tm/humm/Navigation.html.

info@terjemahansunda.com. n.d. "Terjemahan Bahasa Inggris › Indonesia: A study that tested several men's and women's fragrances" terjemahansunda.com. https://inggris-indonesia.terjemahansunda.com/terjemahan7/1040534-a-study-that-tested-several-men-s-and-women-s-fragrances.

Larson, Abigail. 2017. "Luxury Rose Delivery: The True Meaning of Rose Colors." Venus et Fleur. September 13, 2017.

https://www.venusetfleur.com/blogs/news/the-true-meaning-of-rose-colors

"Logo, Mission and Vision." n.d. Beacon of Hope Crisis Center. https://www.beaconofhopeindy.org/logo-mission-and-vision.html.

P., Rebekah. 2021. "Gladiolus Flower Meaning and Symbolism." Florgeous. July 19, 2021.

https://www.florgeous.com/gladiolus-flower-meaning

Petal Republic Team. "Candytuft Flower Meaning in the Language of Flowers." Petal Republic, July 31, 2022. https://www.petalrepublic.com/candytuft-flower-meaning

"Snapdragon Flower Meaning and Symbolism." WhenYouGarden.com. September 5, 2022. https://www.whenyougarden.com/snapdragon-flower-meaning-and-symbolism/snapdragon.

Stanton, Kristen M. "Orchid Meanings, Symbolism & Mythology + Orchid Uses." UniGuide®, December 13, 2022.

https://www.uniguide.com/orchid-meaning-symbolism

Stephens, Siva. "Flowers That Symbolize Change." Garden Guides. September 3, 2020.

https://www.gardenguides.com/13426233-flowers-that-symbolize-change.html

Swanson, Jacob. "How Do Hummingbirds Mate? Enter the Mating Dance." Wild Bird Scoop, August 12, 2022. https://www.wildbirdscoop.com/hummingbird-mating.html

"Sweat Smells like Ammonia: Causes and Treatment." Medical News Today. MediLexicon International. May 27, 2021.

https://www.medicalnewstoday.com/articles/sweat-smells-like-ammonia#causes-of-odor-in-sweat

"The Black Rose: History, Meaning, and Symbolism." www.Venusetfleur.Com. August 31, 2020. https://www.venusetfleur.com/blogs/news/the-black-rose-history-meaning

"Thistle Meaning and Symbolism."

https://www.buildingbeautifulsouls.com/?s=thistle

ABOUT THE AUTHOR

Sherry D. Henderson, author of *Black Magnolia: An Unequivocal Southern Belle* was born and raised on a modern-day plantation (cotton-cultivated land) in the backwoods of Mississippi, fifteen miles southeast of Clarksdale, Mississippi (Route 1, Box 204). Her great-grandmother was a sharecropper who raised her five grandchildren, and Sherry, her first great-grandchild. She and Sherry were inseparable until her death, when Sherry was eleven and a half years old.

Sherry resides in Aurora, Colorado, where she recently retired from a career as an Adult Nurse Practitioner. Her nursing career spans over thirty-eight years of service to others. She served the veteran population at the Department of Veteran Affairs Medical Center in Denver, Colorado, for thirty-six years. She spent the first two years of her career at the Mississippi Baptist Medical Center in Jackson, Mississippi.

Having grown up in the racially charged state of Mississippi, it was of utmost importance that she stayed committed to the unmovable values of her great-grandmother. Contrary to the values of the Deep South, she taught Sherry that Caucasian beauty was not superior to African American beauty. The real *kicker* was that she made

Sherry face the mantra of her life-long path, that *her* beauty was not superior to Caucasians. This value became the guiding post that lights her daily path and keeps her embracing and practicing the simple fact that we are equal in the eyes of God. Because she seared her great-grandmother's beliefs into her heart, she was able to face racially tinged and sometimes outright racially painted situations, deal with them head on, learn from them, and use the greatest bonding weapon in the world—LOVE. With love, Sherry learned not only to survive but to adapt and thrive in all type of environments and situations.

Sherry faithfully serves her community as a member of the Federal Employed Women (FEW), the Chi Eta Phi nursing sorority, and the National Black Nurses Association. As a member of FEW, she proudly served as the Rocky Mountain Regional Manager, Assistant Rocky Mountain Regional Manager, and Treasurer of the High Plains Chapter. In these FEW roles, she received Outstanding Member and Lifetime Achievement Awards. The FEW Rocky Mountain Region received several outstanding awards under her leadership.

Sherry received her Bachelor of Science in Nursing from the University of Mississippi (Ole Miss), a Master of Arts in Business and Personnel Management from Webster University, a Master of Science in Nursing from the University of Colorado, Colorado Springs (UCCS), and

Adult Nurse Practitioner Certification from UCCS. She was selected to be part of Sigma Theta Tau International Honor Society of Nursing. During her career, she was nominated several times for the prestigious Nursing Nightingale Awards. She was an outstanding trailblazer and pioneered many First Leadership endeavors at the Department of Veterans Affairs. She is also the former owner of Precious Moments Healthcare Agency, LLC.

Sherry is most passionate and forever-spirited about serving and advocating for the world's most honored veteran population. Her teaching and role model mantra stems from the Serenity Prayer and the quote, "Give a man a fish and you feed him for a day. Teach him to fish and you feed him for a lifetime." —Lao Tzu.

She has been a sports fanatic for as long as she can remember. She is also an avid traveler and reader. Sherry loves to explore autobiographies and historical documentaries of all of mankind. She has always been an advocate for humanity, but especially champions women to stand up and embrace their power as they strive to become self-sufficient, without losing their ability to love and let others love them. She first had to make many mistakes before she learned these pearls of wisdom and landed in a comfortable place of peace in her life. Sherry's willingness to bear all is a result of her commitment to help others, especially women, step into their truth and own their story.

Sherry's debut book is a portrait of her life: a memoir of humble beginnings to a place of celebrating her golden years in modern, emotional, financial, and physical bliss. Sherry is the sister of two brothers who would travel through fire and brimstone to protect her from all evils of hell and high water. She is loved and respected by her small, loved-filled family. She is a risk taker and sees failure as another opportunity to get up, dust herself off, and reach for higher dreams.

If this book inspires at least one person to be proactive, seek out healthy life goals, and learn to see subtle danger a long way off, Sherry believes it will be worth the joy and pain of sharing her story. She advises, "If unable to avoid unhealthy 'pies in the sky,' at least be able to assess the situation as soon and possible, develop a plan, and parachute to a sound and safe landing."

Made in the USA
Middletown, DE
07 March 2023